PUBLIC LAW
POLITICAL T

Public Law and Political Theory

MARTIN LOUGHLIN

CLARENDON PRESS · OXFORD
1992

Oxford University Press, Walton Street, Oxford OX2 6DP
Oxford New York Toronto
Delhi Bombay Calcutta Madras Karachi
Petaling Jaya Singapore Hong Kong Tokyo
Nairobi Dar es Salaam Cape Town
Melbourne Auckland
and associated companies in
Berlin Ibadan

Oxford is a trade mark of Oxford University Press

Published in the United States
by Oxford University Press, New York

© Oxford University Press 1992

British Library Cataloguing in Publication Data
Data available

Library of Congress Cataloging in Publication Data
Loughlin, Martin.
Public law and political theory / Martin Loughlin.
Includes bibliographical references and index.
1. Public law. 2. Political science. I. Title.
K3150.L68   1992   342—dc20   [342.2]   92–5647
ISBN 0–19–876267–4
ISBN 0–19–876268–2 (pbk.)

Typeset by Hope Services (Abingdon) Ltd.
Printed in Great Britain by
Bookcraft Ltd.
Midsomer Norton, Avon

Preface

THIS book originated in a rather different exercise. In 1986 I wrote a book called *Local Government in the Modern State*. There I developed a framework, loosely drawn from political science, to help me to make sense of the legal developments that were influencing the role of local government within our system of government. The framework was useful for that purpose but, by utilizing the perspectives of political science in order to try to understand developments in law, I was unable to reflect on the impact which these developments in turn had wrought on our traditions of public law. I therefore sought to remedy this deficiency by embarking on the task of writing another book, the objective of which was to address the recent experience of central–local government relations with the aim of raising issues concerning the nature of our system of public law.

After some years of working on this subject I had reached an impasse. It was not just the sheer volume of material with which I was required to deal, although that was difficult enough. The main problem was that I needed to construct some sort of framework by which to make sense of public law. I had tried to deal with this in the new book with an opening chapter addressing traditions of public law thought which could then provide a gauge for reflecting concerns about the specific material of the study. However, this chapter grew to unwieldy proportions. Eventually I decided to bite the bullet and write a book specifically on this subject. This is that book.

Despite its title the book should not be viewed as one which seeks simply to explore connections between two disciplines. Rather, it is an attempt to use methods and insights drawn from work in political theory to address what for me are the basic questions of public law. What is it that is distinctive about the subject? How might we attempt to characterize public law? In asking questions of this nature, issues which have all too frequently been either ignored or assumed in public law texts must be critically addressed. For this reason I have written the book with students of public law in mind; it is designed to be read in conjunction with, and in certain respects as an antidote to, the standard textbooks. Students of government might also find it of interest, along with those studying jurisprudence who, like me, feel that theory should not be divorced from practice.

In writing this book I have incurred many debts. I am very grateful to those public lawyers to whom I have paid particular attention in the text. The lucidity of their writing has facilitated my efforts to identify the hallmarks of their style and to examine the patterns of thought which have shaped their views. And I am especially grateful to the political theorists and intellectual historians whose work I have shamelessly plundered and harnessed to my own peculiar framework. I can only hope that they will see my ham-fisted efforts at translation as being in the service of a worthwhile cause.

On a more personal note, I have been more fortunate than I deserve in respect of both institutions and colleagues. The roots of the approach which is presented in this book were established in the innovative environment of Warwick Law School, where I taught until the early 1980s. On moving to the London School of Economics I reconnected with a particularly rich tradition of public law thought which is strongly associated with the School and which had greatly influenced me as an undergraduate. It was here I started the detailed work. The peculiarities of our dominant tradition in public law did not become entirely apparent, however, until I moved to Glasgow in 1988. Here it was a privilege to hold the John Millar Chair, someone whose pioneering work on public law had been unjustly eclipsed in the nineteenth century and whose methods have provided an inspiration for this book. On moving to Manchester in 1991 I have been surrounded by an unusually stimulating group of colleagues who have been particularly supportive in helping me to complete this project.

I am greatly indebted to Tim Murphy from LSE and to Michael Ford, Tom Gibbons, and Anthony Ogus from Manchester for reading drafts and providing incisive critical comments. Neil Duxbury, a colleague of mine at LSE and again at Manchester, had the misfortune of being on study leave during the final throes of the writing, a situation I have brazenly exploited. He has read versions of virtually all the chapters, made numerous comments and there is no doubt that the book is much better than it might have been as a result of his labours. I should also like especially to thank John Griffith, whose comments on an early draft made me realize that these thoughts, if worth sharing, required a book-length project.

Richard Hart at OUP has been a model of courtesy, efficiency, and understanding.

Finally, and most importantly, I am indebted to Chris, Beth, and Frances Foley. They have not encouraged me with this project. Nor should they have, since they have borne most of its negative consequences. Gratitude, I suspect, will not be enough.

MARTIN LOUGHLIN

Dobcross
January 1992

Contents

Contents

1

Public Law and the Scientific Quest

AT present, the study of public law is in a curiously unsatisfactory condition. Insofar as we can lay claim to a tradition of public law thought in this country, it is founded on the idea that we lack a distinctive system of public law. This tradition is based on the idea that legality is a singular and universal concept and the state and its officers are subject to the ordinary processes of law in much the same manner as all other persons are governed by law. Public authorities, therefore, hold no special status in the legal ordering of our society and there is nothing peculiar in the application of legal method to disputes involving public bodies. Our constitution is a product of the ordinary law of the land and the position of the state and its emanations is determined by general principles of private law.

This denial of the existence of a distinctive system of public law has cast a long and dark shadow over the subject throughout this century. As we enter its last decade the ideas on which this tradition is founded seem to hold little plausibility. The courts now make a conceptual distinction between matters of public law and private law and a special procedure—the application for judicial review— is used to process disputes concerning public law issues. Furthermore, much of European Community law, which is exerting a growing influence on our system of government, is based on the recognition of this distinction between public and private law. Today few who teach and write on the subject would, I suspect, support the traditional claim. But no-one, to my knowledge, has sought to explain precisely the sense in which public law might be considered to be a distinctive subject. We have rested for too long in the shadow of this traditional belief.

Unless those who work in the field are able to explain the distinctive nature of the study of public law, there seems little hope of attracting and maintaining a student's interest. But this issue is not simply an esoteric matter of academic concern. Public law deals with the legal arrangements which establish the institutions of the state and regulate the exercise of political power. It concerns some of our most basic and fundamental laws. Is it possible that there exists a link between the rigour and vitality of that subject and the soundness of the practical arrangements with which it is concerned? While I would counsel against any unreflective assumption that there is a necessary or important relationship between the vitality of scholarly considerations and the efficacy of practical concerns of attending to the business of government, we nevertheless should recognize that the growing dissatisfaction over our traditional beliefs about public law in Britain seems to have advanced hand-in-hand with an accelerating loss of confidence in the model status of the British constitution.

My aim in this book is to examine some of the questions which are raised when an inquiry is undertaken into the nature of public law. There is little doubt that the questions which present themselves are both exacting and perplexing. Furthermore, I have no doubt that others will hold different views, not only on the answers to the issues raised but, perhaps more importantly, on the nature of the questions that need to be addressed. My primary objective, then, is to provoke discussion and reflection on a range of issues which I believe are central to the study of public law but which, because of the volume of factual exposition in most courses, seem constantly to be neglected. At best, these issues are relegated to the background and to the lists of 'further reading'; at worst, they are considered as being unsuitable for student attention. What I hope to show is that such an inquiry is not an esoteric venture which will divert attention from the important issues and serve only to confuse the student but, to the contrary, that it is the only way of obtaining an adequate understanding of the nature of the subject.

THE DISTINCTIVENESS OF PUBLIC LAW

What is it, then, that is distinctive about public law? Is public law a discipline? If so, wherein does its distinctiveness lie? Is this specificity to be found in its scope, its rubric, its method?

For some, it is sufficient to identify a particular set of institutional arrangements which may be treated as forming a discrete object of analysis. This seems to be the approach adopted by Professor Birks when he suggests that 'few lawyers would deny that administrative law has a unity and an internal anatomy of its own, made explicit now by many textbooks'.[1] What is being suggested here, however, is simply that public law may be identified anatomically as a separate branch of legal study. While, as a result, particular concepts such as *ultra vires* or natural justice may have been developed, there is nothing in this argument which necessarily challenges the idea of the unity of law.

Others, however, have gone further and have intimated that public law can be placed on an acceptable footing only by laying bare the skeleton of principle that provides it with a conceptual unity.[2] This constitutes a more radical claim, since it implies that the subject possesses distinctive juristic foundations. Claims of this nature are sometimes made in conjunction with the argument, referred to above, that the tradition of ordinary law has cast a long shadow over the study of public law. This contention then takes the form of a lament; that public law is still secreted within the interstices of private law and has yet to develop its own philosophy and methodology. The implication here is that public law can and should articulate its distinctive juridical foundations.[3] These more radical claims are rooted in the belief that public law owes much of its dictinctiveness to its particular subject-matter. The fundamentally political nature of the relationships which public law regulates necessitates legal methodologies which are quite distinct from those of private law. It requires those called upon to exercize legal judgment in this field to understand the broader framework within which decision-making takes place.

In embarking on an inquiry into the nature of public law, then, we might proceed by examining the claim that somehow, because of the subject-matter and the demands which that imposes on method, public law is categorically different from private law. This, however, is not the method I propose to adopt. The difficulty with adopting that approach is that it begins with the implicit assumption that law in general is a discrete discipline. And only

[1] P. Birks, *An Introduction to the Law of Restitution* (Oxford, 1985), 3.

[2] See, e.g., T. R. S. Allan, 'Legislative Supremacy and the Rule of Law: Democracy and Constitutionalism' (1985) 44 *Camb. LJ* 111.

[3] See, e.g., J. D. B. Mitchell, 'The causes and effects of the absence of a system of public law in the United Kingdom' 1965 *Public Law* 95.

then does it proceed to examine the case for the distinctiveness of public law.

There is, I believe, a more interesting premiss from which to commence this inquiry. This is to start from the assumption that public law is simply a sophisticated form of political discourse; that controversies within the subject are simply extended political disputes. Since many argue that public law is rooted in its social, political, economic, and historical context this approach should ensure that our inquiry is embedded in the realities of the times. The adoption of this method of inquiry, in addition, will force us to try to articulate what, if anything, is special about law's claims. Furthermore, though to many people this method of inquiry may seem both novel and radical, this is not in fact the case. There is a long history of seeking to express and articulate the issues of public law in the context of the development of society.

THE SCIENCE OF LEGISLATION

During the eighteenth century, and under the influence of the Enlightenment movement, there emerged a 'science' that 'no longer appears on modern maps of knowledge'.[4] It concerned a project within the sphere of social, political, and legal thought, the objective of which was to draw connections between such facets of social character as property, opinion, manners, and justice and to derive general conclusions. This was the 'science of legislation'.[5] It was not a science in the modern sense entailing a striving for value neutrality. The objective was to formulate criteria for evaluating the laws and institutions of society and which could then be used to guide government on the use of the legislative power. It sought, in effect, to restore politics to the Aristotelian position as the 'master-science'.

The foundations of this science were laid by such European writers as Machiavelli, who used history to teach would-be rulers the principles of prudence, and Montesquieu, who in 1748 in *De l'Esprit des Lois* made an important breakthrough in tying his

[4] S. Collini, D. Winch, and J. Burrow, *That Noble Science of Politics. A Study in Nineteenth Century Intellectual History* (Cambridge, 1983), 1.
[5] See K. Haakonssen, *The Science of a Legislator: The Natural Jurisprudence of David Hume and Adam Smith* (Cambridge, 1981); id., 'John Millar and the Science of a Legislator' (1985) 30 (NS) *Juridical Review* 41; D. Lieberman, *The Province of Legislation Determined* (Cambridge, 1989).

consideration of constitutional forms to a comparative survey of manners and morals. According to Hume, Montesquieu's work established that: 'The laws have, or ought to have, a constant reference to the constitution of governments, the climate, the religion, the commerce, the situation of each society.'[6] Montesquieu's work directly influenced the thinkers of the Scottish Enlightenment movement. Of this group, Adam Smith was the pre-eminent figure.

Smith felt that, while Montesquieu had pointed us in the right direction, something was missing. That missing ingredient, which Smith supplied, was the idea of progress. The idea of progress furnished the key organizational principle which enabled Smith to convert Montesquieu's sociological approach from a static to a dynamic one. Through this framework, Smith embarked on a scheme for constructing a complete social philosophy, of which his *Theory of Moral Sentiments* (1759) and *Wealth of Nations* (1776) were only parts. It was a project which Smith was never to complete before his death. In particular, the feature of this project which is most directly relevant to the science of legislation, an account of the general principles of law and government, was never finished. Aspects of the scheme can, nevertheless, be seen in his *Lectures on Jurisprudence*.[7]

Montesquieu had demonstrated that any understanding of laws and constitutional practices had to be rooted in the general state of society. Smith and his fellow Scottish Enlightenment writers, through the idea of progress, transformed this insight into an elaborate sequence of stages in the historical development of civil society. This became known as the 'four stages' thesis; that is, there are four types of economic organization—hunting, pasture, agriculture, and commerce—through which societies pass and in respect of each there will arise certain distinctive forms of social and political superstructure.[8] These stages led from *rudeness* to *refinement* and, in accounting for this process, a new word was invented; *viz*, civil-ization.[9] These economic forms, it was felt, must be productive of correspondent habits, dispositions and ways of

[6] Hume, *Enquiries Concerning Human Understanding*; quoted in Collini, Winch, and Burrow, *That Noble Science of Politics*, 17.

[7] See A. Smith, *Lectures on Jurisprudence* (R. L. Meek, D. D. Raphael, and P. G. Stein (eds.)) (Oxford, 1978). See also Smith, *The Wealth of Nations* (W. B. Todd (ed.)) (Oxford, 1976), Book V.

[8] See Meek, *Social Science and the Ignoble Savage* (Cambridge, 1976), chap. 1.   [9] See Collini, Winch, and Burrow, *That Noble Science of Politics*, 18.

thinking. And with this process comes the gradual progress of jurisprudence with consequential improvements in law and government.

Smith's scheme was filled out in relation to law and government by John Millar, his former pupil, who was Regius Professor of Law at Glasgow University from 1761 until his death in 1801. Millar's study of constitutional development is laid down in *An Historical View of the English Government* (1787),[10] one of the earliest treatises of the emerging genre of English constitutional history. Millar arranged the constitutional history of England into three main periods: the period to 1066 which he termed the period of feudal aristocracy; 1066–1603, the period of feudal monarchy; and the period from 1603, the era of the commercial government. For Millar, English constitutional development is to be explained essentially in terms of the material progress of society. To appreciate the significance of his approach we might contrast Millar's views with those of Blackstone, his English contemporary.

Blackstone viewed English constitutional history in terms of 'a gradual restoration of that ancient constitution whereof our Saxon forefathers had been unjustly deprived, partly by the policy and partly by the force, of the Norman'.[11] It was precisely against this sort of vulgar Whiggism that Millar directed his criticism. 'In delineating the progress of the English government', he wrote, 'I have endeavoured to avoid those fond prepossessions which Englishmen are apt to entertain upon the subject.'[12] Millar argued that the early period of English government was rude and imperfect and often arbitrary; that is, exactly as one would expect in the infancy of every political system. The ancient English constitution, Millar commented, 'seems in fact to be that sort of political system which is likely to be established in all rude and extensive countries'.[13] Furthermore, in Millar's view, Magna Carta is not the great liberating document portrayed by vulgar Whigs:[14]

---

[10] The original version was a constitutional history from Saxon times to the Stuarts. When Millar died his executors found a version of the *Historical View*, which was almost ready for press, bringing it down to 1688. They attached to this certain other papers taking the history to contemporary times and published this in four volumes in 1803. It is this version which is used in this text.

[11] Blackstone, *Commentaries on the Laws of England* (1765–9) London, 15th edn., 1809), vol. IV, p. 413.

[12] J. Millar, *Historical View* (1803), vol. I, pp. iii–iv.

[13] Ibid. 252–3.   [14] Ibid., vol. II, pp. 80–1.

The parties concerned . . . were not actuated by the most liberal principles; and . . . it was not so much their intention to secure the liberties of the people at large, as to establish the privileges of a few individuals. A great tyrant on one side, and a set of petty tyrants on the other, seem to have divided the kingdom, and the great body of the people, disregarded and oppressed on all hands, were beholden for any privileges bestowed on them, to the jealousy of their masters.

Millar's general point is that the ancient constitution did not secure the liberty and natural rights of mankind. While he recognizes that the sovereign did not possess absolute power and the 'supreme authority in the state was originally possessed by a numerous body of landed proprietors', he reminds us that 'the rest of the community were either slaves, or tenants at will of their master'.[15] Millar argues that the 'low ranks' secured their liberty not by appeals to a romantic idea of the ancient constitution and not by pieces of paper. They achieved it by industry and material progress. The origin of liberty in Britain is modern, not ancient; it was a seventeenth-century endeavour culminating in 1688.

Those seventeenth-century struggles between the king and people, Millar felt, were unavoidable. The growth of manufacturing at the same time made the lower classes of people richer and more independent. But it also introduced mercenary armies, which increased the power of the Crown. Tension was bound to result. A further example of Millar's view that constitutional development was the product of the interplay of social forces is seen in the account he provides of the emergence of the idea of judicial independence. Millar suggests that the separation of judicial power from the king's prerogative 'was neither introduced from any foresight of its beneficial consequences, nor extorted from the monarch by any party that were jealous of his power; but was merely the suggestion of indolence; and was adopted by the king, in common with other feudal superiors, to relieve them from a degree of labour and attention which they did not chuse to bestow. It was, in reality, a consequence of the general progress of society' and the increasing division of labour.[16]

Millar's objective in *Historical View* was to chart relationships between economy, society, and polity and to explain these in respect of an evolutionary dynamic. While never unhistorical, its

[15] Ibid., vol. 1, pp. 374–6.   [16] Ibid., vol. 1, pp. 339–40.

objective was not to provide a detailed account of events but rather to discern general trends of institutional development. His target of attack was the romantic or vulgar Whig idea that the Anglo-Saxon possessed some genetic preference for liberty, embodied in an ancient constitution and refecting the genius of a people, and which momentarily had been suppressed as a result of the Norman invasion.[17] Nevertheless, Millar was also a Whig. He believed that 1688 was the crowning event in English history: 'Of all the great revolutions recorded in the history of ancient or modern times, that which happened in England, in the year 1688, appears to have been conducted in a manner the most rational and consistent with the leading principles of civil society.'[18] What distinguishes Millar from Blackstone, however, is that Millar rooted his views in an empirical, rationalist framework. His approach was part of an attempt to devise a science of legislation. If Blackstone is to be viewed as a vulgar Whig, Millar's approach was that of the scientific Whig.[19]

What, then, does Millar's work on a science of legislation reveal about the nature of the British constitution? Constitutional writing of Millar's period was replete with the imagery of machinery and the idea of checks and balances. These theories of mixed government fostered an idea of constitutionalism, in the sense that there existed within the polity some sort of balancing mechanism between royal integrity, aristocratic wisdom, and popular sentiment.[20] Millar did not jettison this language. He suggested that the British constitution was fortunate in possessing the advantages of both a monarchy and a republic since it united the dignity and authority of a hereditary monarchy with the joint deliberations of several chief executive officers. Here we find early recognition of the importance of the cabinet within the constitution.[21] Millar talks of Ministers as 'composing a select, or cabinet council, by whose concurrence and

---

[17] On the idea of the ancient constitution see below, Chap. 3 at pp. 42–6.

[18] Millar, *Historical View*, vol. III, p. 438.

[19] See D. Forbes, 'Scientific Whiggism: Adam Smith and John Millar' (1953–4) 7 *Camb. J.* 643; D. Forbes, 'Sceptical whiggism, commerce and liberty' in A. S. Skinner and T. Wilson (eds.), *Essays on Adam Smith* (Oxford, 1976).

[20] See M. J. C. Vile, *Constitutionalism and the Separation of Powers* (Oxford, 1967), chap. III.

[21] Cf. Bagehot's revelation that the Cabinet provided the 'efficient secret' of the constitution. See W. Bagehot, *The English Constitution* (1867) (R. H. S. Crossman (ed.)) (London and Glasgow, 1963), chap. 1.

direction the administration was visibly conducted'.[22] Dignity and efficiency, or authority and utility, are here conjoined. Monarchy provided a symbol of permanence and stability and guarded against disorder while the cabinet guarded against a single person assuming executive power.[23]

Although Millar retains the imagery of checks and balances within his discussion of the constitution, there is a significant difference between his views and traditional versions of the theory of mixed government. Millar's notion is not that of a balance between the different estates within the mechanisms of the constitution; it is simply a balance within the executive government. This is important. Millar's shift in the location of the balancing mechanism has the effect of destroying the old theories of political balance within the historic constitution. If the several elements of the polity do not provide a balanced constitution, where is the counter-balance to executive power to be found? For Millar, this is not located elsewhere in our constitutional mechanisms. Neither can it be found in some metaphysical conception of law. Millar rejects the view that law is determined by higher norms of divine origin and also refutes social contract theories: contract is not based in historical fact; the idea of tacit consent is contradictory; and, anyway, the idea of consent implies a degree of rationalization of social life of which mankind is on the whole incapable.[24]

The answer, it seems, is that it must be found outside politics and in society in general. As we have seen Millar, as a Whig, was a firm believer in the idea of freedom under law and he was greatly concerned about the enlargement of governmental power in the period after 1688. In *Historical View*, after considering the growth in the Crown's power, Millar asks: 'Has there occurred nothing on the other side to counterbalance the effect of this growing patronage and its correspondent influence? . . . Can we discover no circumstances of an opposite nature tending to preserve the former equilibrium, by supporting the popular part of our constitution?'[25] Millar's answer is that the development of a commercial society would, through the increase and spread of wealth, foster a feeling of independence and liberty through the great body of the people and, with the advance of science and literature, 'the narrow

[22] Millar, *Historical View*, vol. IV, p. 74.   [23] Ibid. 76.
[24] Ibid., Essay VII, 'The progress of science relative to law and government'.
[25] Ibid., 99–100.

political prejudices which had prevailed' would be dissipated and 'principles . . . much more favourable to the equal rights of mankind' would be introduced.[26] Millar therefore felt that the best way for government to promote these changes (and also to combat revolutionary doctrines) was to extend the suffrage to the educated middle class, thereby rallying the 'great body of the nation' round the constitution.[27]

Millar's views on law, government and the constitution have been presented in some detail for a number of reasons. The first reason is simply to highlight the existence of a distinguished strand of academic legal writing which recognized the need to locate the study of law and the constitution within a perspective which encompasses an examination of social and political developments. Our own project of seeking an understanding of the nature of public law by rooting it in an examination of political discourse should not therefore be considered as unprecedented or unusual. There are, however, other, more specific, reasons for examining this eighteenth century movement.

All too often, the study of public law begins with the examination of texts from the latter half of the nineteenth century. This, I believe, has major drawbacks. Most importantly, as we will see in the following section, by the late nineteenth century a much more limited conception of the boundaries of the subject had been erected, and this more restrictive sense of the subject has remained with us until the present day. But it seems also the case that we cannot fully appreciate the significance of the language, concerns, and methods of nineteenth-century writers without acquiring some familiarity with the work of their immediate predecessors. Millar's work, for example, helps us to see more clearly how our liberties are dependent on the circumstantial silence of the law and are protected, not by constitutional mechanisms, but by the vigilance of public opinion. The role of public opinion in influencing constitutional development, together with the ambivalence towards demo-

---

[26] Millar, *Historical View*, vol. IV, p. 100. See also A. O. Hirschmann, *The Passions and the Interests. Political Arguments for Capitalism before its Triumph* (Princeton, 1977), 87–93.
[27] Millar's views on the question of the extension of the franchise, however, seemed to become more radical in the later stages of his life: see, M. Ignatieff, 'John Millar and Individualism' in I. Hont and M. Ignatieff (eds.), *Wealth and Virtue: The Shaping of Political Economy in the Scottish Enlightenment* (Cambridge, 1983), 317 at pp. 327–32.

cracy and education, is, for example, a theme of particular importance in the work of Dicey.[28]

We may also see the influence of Millar's analytical framework on the work of Bagehot, that shrewd nineteenth-century analyst of the realities of the constitution. Millar maintained that the *Historical View* demonstrated that the main principles of government are authority and utility. He further argued that, while in the early ages, the rights of government rested on authority, with the progress of civilization it comes to rest on utility. To the extent that the principle of authority persists in government, Millar suggested that it serves essentially to bolster respect for power through symbols and traditions.[29] While this analysis is not unique (and is almost certainly derived from Adam Smith)[30] it is from this framework that we may identify the language that was popularized in the latter half of the nineteenth century by Walter Bagehot.[31] I refer to the distinction, so central to Bagehot's analysis, between the dignified and efficient functions of government. Bagehot suggested that in order to understand the British constitution, one had to appreciate the distinction between the dignified parts, 'which excite and preserve the reverence of the population' and the efficient parts, 'those by which it, in fact rules'.[32] The dignified parts are those through which the Government acquires and maintains authority and the efficient parts are those which employ the power of government. Of this, Richard Crossman concluded:[33]

By his distinction between the dignified and efficient parts of the Constitution, and his assumption that the former are preserved in order to conceal and win allegiance to the latter, Bagehot had provided himself with just that precision-instrument of political analysis which Bentham and the Mills had lacked.

Bentham and the Mills may have missed this, but Millar certainly had not. Again Crossman praises Bagehot for identifying the Cabinet as 'the efficient secret of the English constitution';[34] an

---

[28] A. V. Dicey, *Lectures on the Relation between Law and Public Opinion in England during the Nineteenth Century* (London, 1905).

[29] Millar, *Historical View*, vol. IV, Essay VII.

[30] See Smith, *Lectures on Jurisprudence* (Meek, Raphael, and Stein (eds.)) (Oxford, 1978). These lectures, produced from reports from the 1760s, deal with Authority and Utility under the head of 'Original Principles of Government'.

[31] Bagehot, *The English Constitution* (1867) (R. H. S. Crossman (ed.)) (London & Glasgow, 1963).

[32] Ibid. 61.   [33] Ibid. 16.   [34] Ibid. 65.

institution which Mill 'completely failed to see'.[35] Mill might have missed it but Millar had not.[36] In short, the simple and elegant framework which has contributed so much to the establishment of Bagehot as the classic introductory text to the constitution, seems clearly to have been pre-figured by Millar. What is different, and more ambitious, about Millar's work, however, is that, unlike Bagehot and other later nineteenth century commentators, he seeks to root an understanding of the constitution in a theory of society.

We should reflect, then, on this project of constructing a science of legislation. The project constituted a highly ambitious attempt to furnish prudential guidelines to those charged with the business of governing society. In adopting a scientific approach it became clear that a study focusing on the classification of constitutional forms would not be sufficient. Neither could political constitutions be framed from ideal models. Constitutions, it was discovered, arise from the slow progress of human experience. Once this was recognized, attention came to focus on the development of society and its institutions and in particular on the connection between commerce and liberty. The effect of this, however, was to deflect the study away from legal and constitutional concerns. 'The key move', according to Michael Ignatieff, 'was to treat "civil polity", not as a juridical nexus of rights and duties, but as a set of social and economic relations directed in the first instance to the production of subsistence and the reproduction of life. Law and rights were then interpreted as deriving from these relations.'[37] Ignatieff concludes that the project, which was initially created to solve certain problems in jurisprudence, somewhat ironically 'ended up by displacing law as a constitutive element of social order, and relegating it to a dependent position as an artefact of social relations'.[38] There could be no discrete theory of constitutions or public law.

In effect, Millar's work signals the disintegration of theories of the balanced constitution. Thereafter there could be no distinct science of government. Any theory of government and law must be rooted in a theory of society. This is, of course, an exceedingly

---

[35] Bagehot, *The English Constitution* (1867) (R. H. S. Crossman (ed.)) (London & Glasgow, 1963), 9.
[36] Millar, *Historical View*, vol. IV, p. 74.
[37] Ignatieff, 'John Millar and Individualism', 320–1.
[38] Ibid. at p. 321.

complex undertaking.[39] Millar was, like the rest of us, a product of his times and seemed, in particular, to go wrong in assuming that the increasing wealth generated by a commercial society would lead citizens to a heightened sense of their rights. In this respect, we may, with the benefit of hindsight, acknowledge that he did not adequately appreciate that new forms of capital created by the commercial society might not simply liberate but could also oppress. But as an academic lawyer seeking an understanding of the subject he was charged to profess, his general conception of the inquiry remains of profound importance to us today.

THE ANALYTICAL METHOD IN PUBLIC LAW

With the disintegration of the scientific Whig project, the self-congratulatory vulgar Whig voice reasserted itself in the early nineteenth century. The tone of this period is well reflected in the work of Hallam who, writing in 1818, suggested:[40]

No unbiased observer who derives pleasure from the welfare of his species, can fail to consider the long and uninterruptedly increasing prosperity of England as the most beautiful phaenomenon in the history of mankind. Climates more propitious may impart more largely the mere enjoyments of existence; but in no other region have the benefits that political institutions can confer been diffused over so extended a population; nor have any people so well reconciled the discordant elements of wealth, order, and liberty. These advantages are surely not owing to the soil of this island, nor to the latitude in which it is placed; but to the spirit of its laws, from which, through various means, the characteristic independence and industriousness of our nation have been derived. The constitution, therefore, of England must be to inquisitive men of all countries, far more to ourselves, an object of superior interest; distinguished, especially, as it is from all free governments of powerful nations, which history has recorded, by its manifesting, after the lapse of several centuries, not merely no symptom of irretrievable decay, but a more expansive energy.

The failure of the revolutions in France in 1830 and 1848 seemed to underwrite this propensity to treat respect for tradition and adaptation by gradual accretions as the key to successful constitutional development. Collini, Winch, and Burrow suggest that,

---

[39] Those interested in pursuing this issue might start with G. Hawthorn, *Enlightenment and Despair. A History of Social Theory* (Cambridge, 2nd edn., 1987).
[40] H. Hallam, *Middle Ages* (London, 12th edn., 1818), vol. 2, p. 267.

during this period, a 'distinctively nineteenth-century Romantic distrust of mere constitutional machinery and political rationalism generally . . . was added to the older English Whig veneration of precedent and the indigenous ancestral constitution'.[41]

By the latter half of the century, however, a rather different method of legal writing on the constitution had emerged. Writing in 1885 A. V. Dicey used Hallam's work specifically to illustrate the necessity of adopting a less self-complacent approach to the study of the constitution and a more precise and restrictive object of legal study. After reproducing the quotation from Hallam, Dicey comments:[42]

At the present day students of the constitution wish neither to criticise, nor to venerate, but to understand; and a professor whose duty it is to lecture on constitutional law must feel that he is called upon to perform the part neither of a critic nor of an apologist, nor of an eulogist, but simply of an expounder; his duty is neither to attack nor to defend the constitution, but simply to explain its laws.

As Dicey readily concedes, this explanatory approach is not without its pitfalls and that 'unless he can obtain a clue to guide his steps' the lawyer will find 'that the whole province of so-called "constitutional law" is a sort of maze in which the wanderer is perplexed by unreality, by antiquarianism, and by conventionalism'.[43] These three bogies—unreality, antiquarianism, and conventionalism—are the provenance of the lawyer, the historian and the political theorist respectively. Dicey considers each in turn.

The problem with the traditional legal approach to constitutional issues, Dicey suggests, is that its characteristic formalism leads to error. He supplies by way of example Blackstone's passage on the King's prerogative powers in relation to executive government in which Blackstone states that: 'This [power] is wisely placed in a single hand by the British constitution, for the sake of unanimity, strength and dispatch.'[44] 'The language of this passage', Dicey concedes, 'is impressive.' There is but one fault: 'the statements it contains are the direct opposite of the truth. The executive of

---

[41] Collini, Winch, and Burrow, *That Noble Science of Politics*, 20.

[42] Dicey, *Introduction to the Study of the Law of the Constitution* (London, 1885), 3. (Page references are taken from the 8th edn.—Dicey's last—which was published in 1915.)

[43] Ibid. 7.

[44] Blackstone, *Commentaries*, vol. 1, p. 250.

England [sic] is in fact placed in the hands of a committee called the Cabinet.'[45]

The constitutional historians do not, however, fare any better. The historian, Dicey suggests, is primarily concerned with ascertaining the steps by which a constitution has grown to be what it is and is only indirectly concerned with determining the present rules of the constitution. But their concern with origins and ancient forms is of little use to the constitutional lawyer:[46]

It boots nothing to . . . understand, if it be understandable, the constitution of the Witenagemoót. All this is for a lawyer's purposes simple antiquarianism. It throws as much light on the constitution of the United States as upon the constitution of England; that is, it throws from a legal point of view no light upon either the one or the other.

Dicey's irritation with the historian's inordinate devotion to the germs of our institutions is here evident. This is in all probability provoked by the views of certain historians who adhered to the idea of the ancient constitution and maintained a belief that 'the cunning of lawyers has by the invention of legal fictions corrupted the fair simplicity of our original constitution'.[47] Dicey heeds us to guard against the illusion that modern constitutional freedom has been established by what he calls 'an astounding method of retrogressive progress'; that 'every step towards civilisation has been a step backwards towards the simple wisdom of our uncultured ancestors'.[48]

Dicey finally considers the political theorists, who 'deal mainly with political understandings or conventions and not with rules of law'.[49] While paying tribute to their craft, he nevertheless identifies one difficulty in their method. While political theorists 'explain the conventional character of the understandings which make up a great part of the constitution, [they] leave unexplained the one matter which needs explanation. They give no satisfactory answer to the inquiry how it happens that the understandings of politics are sometimes at least obeyed as rigorously as the commands of law'.[50] It will scarcely come as a surprise that Dicey believes that lawyers may be able to solve this 'really curious problem'.[51]

Having considered the limitations of the various disciplinary perspectives on the study of the constitution, Dicey raises the question of whether there is a true law of the constitution to study:

[45] Dicey, *Law of the Constitution*, 8.   [46] Ibid. 14.   [47] Ibid. at p. 17.
[48] Ibid.   [49] Ibid. 20.   [50] Ibid. 21.   [51] Ibid.

'Is it possible that so-called "constitutional law" is in reality a cross between history and custom which does not properly deserve the name of law at all . . . ?' In an intrepid manner Dicey, albeit from a slightly different perspective, here formulates the key issue which this book seeks to address. The question, however, is raised by Dicey in a purely rhetorical manner. After a contrived protestation ('lawyers would gladly surrender a domain to which they can establish no valid title')[52] Dicey quickly provides us with a skilful and concise definition of constitutional law:[53]

Constitutional law . . . appears to include all rules which directly or indirectly affect the distribution or the exercise of the sovereign power of the state. Hence it includes (among other things) all rules which define the members of the sovereign power, all rules which regulate the relation of such members to each other, or which determine the mode in which the sovereign power, or the membership thereof exercise their authority. Its rules prescribe the order of succession to the throne, regulate the prerogatives of the chief magistrate, determine the form of the legislature and its mode of election. These rules also deal with Ministers, with their responsibility, with their spheres of action, define the territory over which the sovereignty of the state extends and settles who are to be deemed subjects and citizens.

He deliberately uses the term 'rules' and not 'laws' because these rules comprise two sets: laws in the strictest sense which are enforced by the courts; and conventions, understandings, habits, and practices which are not so enforced but which regulate the conduct of members of the sovereign power. Dicey then makes a startling claim: 'Once grasp the ambiguity latent in the expression "constitutional law", and everything connected with the subject falls so competely into its right place that a lawyer, called upon to teach or to study constitutional law as a branch of the law of England, can hardly fail to see clearly the character and scope of his subject.'[54] With conventions the lawyer has no direct concern, although Dicey does go on to argue the dependence in the last resort of conventions on the law of the constitution. The nature of the subject having been so clearly identified, Dicey is finally able to define the appropriate method of study:[55]

---

[52] Dicey, *Law of the Constitution*, at p. 22.
[53] Ibid. at pp. 22–3.   [54] Ibid. at pp. 29–30.   [55] Ibid. at p. 31.

The duty . . . of an English professor of law is to state what are the laws which form part of the constitution, to arrange them in their order, to explain their meaning, and to exhibit where possible their logical connection.

Here we see the method by which Dicey authoritatively (re)defined the scope and method of the study of public law which has had such a profound influence ever since. The scope is formalistically determined; and quite how we adopt this approach without falling into the Blackstonian trap of unreality Dicey fails to explain.[56] The method is mechanistic. Law is viewed as a datum to be analysed and classified and a descriptive account provided of how its various divisions fit together to provide an ordered whole. For Dicey an 'understanding' of constitutional law is achieved through this scientific method of observation and description.

We will reserve until later the examination of Dicey's theory of the constitution.[57] Here we are mainly interested in his approach in defining the scope and method of public law. What happened to ensure the entrenchment of this narrow analytical approach to the subject?

THE RISE OF FORMALISM

The Scottish Enlightenment movement of the latter half of the eighteenth century was above all a secularizing movement, which focused attention on humanistic concerns, asserted the autonomy of the human personality, and sought to explain the world rationally; that is, by reference to natural rather than supernatural phenomena. Theology gave way to social philosophy, theories of divine right were replaced by utilitarian theories of government, and natural law theories were challenged by an emerging positivist outlook. Writing in 1776, Jeremy Bentham called it 'a busy age, in which knowledge is rapidly advancing to perfection. In the natural world, in particular, everything teems with discovery and with improvement'. Great strides had been made in the natural sciences during this period. 'Correspondent to *discovery* and *improvement*

---

[56] Although Dicey does not make this explicit, he in all probability assumes that unreality is avoided by appreciating the relationship between law and convention, together perhaps with an understanding of the key legal principles of the constitution.

[57] See Chap. 7 below.

in the natural world', continued Bentham, 'is *reformation* in the moral.'[58] In fact, the period was marked not just by reformation in the moral and political sphere but also by revolution. It would, I think, be difficult to exaggerate the impact which the American and French revolutions of 1776 and 1789 had on the social and political consciousness of the times.

Within this milieu, the drive to establish a science of legislation may be viewed as an attempt to apply the experimental methods of the natural sciences to moral and political questions. The idea of science, however, retained a broad connotation amongst the Scottish thinkers and was still more or less interchangeable with the idea of philosophy. The eighteenth-century quest 'did not entail anxiety to achieve what a late nineteenth-century generation of social scientists would call "value-neutrality"'.[59] The more precise conception of science which gained ascendancy in the nineteenth century, and which focused on causal laws and quantitative methods, was a major contributor to the disintegration of the project.

During the nineteenth century, we see the fragmentation of Adam Smith's project and the emergence as separate disciplines of political economy, history, philosophy, and law within more technically precise boundaries. As a result of this process, much energy was spent within each of these subjects seeking to codify both its scope and its method. This is precisely what we see Dicey striving to achieve in the opening chapter to his *Law of the Constitution*, where he is at pains to distinguish the historian's and the political theorist's approach to the study of the constitution from that of the lawyer.

Dicey's formal analytical method is, however, almost the polar opposite of Millar's historical, sociological, and explanatory approach. The dramatic shift in approach may be understood largely in terms of the necessity, in constructing a distinct science of law, to move positive law from a peripheral to a central focus of study; and this could be achieved only by a change in method. Whereas Millar was concerned to establish connections, Dicey's objective is to sever links and to establish an autonomous subject. This reorientation in the focus of the subject is reflected even in the

[58] J. Bentham, *A Fragment on Government and An Introduction to the Principles of Morals and Legislation* (W. Harrison (ed.)) (Oxford, 1948), 3.
[59] Collini, Winch, and Burrow, *That Noble Science of Politics*, 14.

form of language which is used. Since analysis is often a function of the type of language we employ, it should not surprise us to see that, while Millar mainly uses biological metaphors and the language of evolutionism, Dicey's are almost exclusively mechanical. Since law may be viewed as an attempt to devise a precise and technical language, this point is perhaps of particular importance.[60]

The main influences in bringing about this shift in focus were the emergence of utilitarianism and legal positivism. The key figure in both movements was Jeremy Bentham. Bentham, like the Scottish thinkers, also talked about the need to construct a science of legislation. However, while Smith and Millar had sought an explanatory theory through an examination of the historical development of the forms of law and government, Bentham displayed much less interest in the historical method. Bentham was less concerned about exploring the past in order to explain the present than in examining the problems of present in order to devise reforms for the future.

Bentham's science of legislation or 'censorial jurisprudence' was critical rather than explanatory; it was directed to 'what the Legislator *ought* to do *in future*'[61] His utilitarian science of legislation was built on a classificatory system of pleasures and pains; all human action is caused by a desire for pleasure and an aversion to pain. Bentham believed that pleasure and pain could be measured in a 'felicific calculus' and that this utilitarian science thus provided the key to the science of legislation. The end of government was the achievement of the greatest happiness of the greatest number.[62] What is particularly interesting about utilitarianism for our purposes is that it is concerned almost exclusively with ends rather than means, with substance rather than form. In fact, the utilitarians abandoned almost entirely the Whig interest in constitutional forms. Bentham, for example, was scathing about any consideration of the British constitution in the language of balance and the like: 'Talk of *balance*, never will it do: leave that to Mother Goose and Mother Blackstone.'[63]

---

[60] On this subject see M. Landau, *Political Theory and Political Science. Studies in the Methodology of Political Inquiry* (New Jersey, 1972), chap. 3.

[61] Original emphasis. Bentham, *A Fragment on Government*, para. 13.

[62] Bentham, *An Introduction to the Principles of Morals and Legislation*, 113.

[63] Bentham, *The Works of Jeremy Bentham* (J. Bowring (ed.), 1843), vol. III, p. 450 (quoted in Collini, Winch, and Burrow, *That Noble Science of Politics*, 94).

As we have seen, Dicey seems to have acquired both Bentham's disinterest in the relevance of history for legal method and his penchant for classification. Dicey does not, however, retain a critical or normative aspect in his conception of legal science. To appreciate why, we must turn to the second intellectual movement shaped by Bentham, that of legal positivism. Legal positivism emerged from the growing recognition that there existed two distinct realms of human inquiry: the world of 'is' which dealt with facts, and the world of 'ought' which concerned standards of conduct. The realm of factual inquiry, it was felt, dealt with propositions which were either true or false, whereas the normative world did not. Since science was engaged with the former realm of inquiry a science of law would, it was assumed, need to be erected on a foundation of fact. This objective became the quest of legal positivism, which was pioneered by Bentham and refined by John Austin.

John Austin's work was greatly influenced by Bentham; it is also constructed on the principle of utility. Nevertheless, Austin's influence on nineteenth-century legal thought has been much greater than Bentham's. The reason for this is that, whereas Bentham was motivated by the desire to develop a censorial jurisprudence Austin's primary objective was simply to produce an expository jurisprudence. Bentham's thrust was utilitarian; he used the principle of utility as an instrument of law reform. Austin's approach was essentially positivist; he sought a method of defining law, systematically classifying its elements and developing the conceptual apparatus through which it could be 'scientifically' understood.

Austin, conscious of the is—ought distinction, tried to root his entire theory of law in fact. Law, he suggests, is a species of command. A command is 'distinguished from other significations of desire . . . by the power of the party commanding to inflict an evil or pain in case the desire be disregarded.'[64] Laws are a special type of command because they emanate from the sovereign of an independent political society and are issued to subjects. This sovereign power may be identified when the '*bulk* of a given society are in a *habit* of obedience or submission to a *determinate* or *common* superior'.[65] Although Austin uses normative language—

[64] J. Austin, *The Province of Jurisprudence Determined* ((1832); H. L. A. Hart edn., 1954), 14.   [65] Original emphasis. Ibid. 193.

rules, duty, authority of the sovereign—he seeks to explain their meaning entirely in descriptive language. Rules are commands of a general nature, duty simply means being liable to a sanction or the infliction of an evil, and the sovereign power is identified not by notions of authority but through observation of habitual patterns of submission.

We will return later to consider the significance in public law of Austin's empiricist conception of law.[66] It is sufficient at this stage to note that Austin, viewing the world of natural science as being founded on factual inquiry, sought to ensure the status of legal science by eliminating any normative dimension from the province of jurisprudence and sought similarly to place the roots of legal science on empirical observation. At this stage, however, it is important to be aware not only of the nature of Austin's legal science but also his method. In *The Province of Jurisprudence Determined* we see his formal classificatory approach clearly at work; the book, for example, commences with the painstaking exercise of defining and categorizing the subject of his study, positive law, from 'divine law' and 'positive morality'. Austin's objective was to place jurisprudence on as systematic and as scientific a basis as the growing neighbouring disciplines.

Austin's project struck a harmonious note with the academic lawyers who, during the latter half of the century, were just becoming established in the English universities. This group needed to be able to identify a role for themselves that would both establish their credibility as legal scientists and aid their quest for legitimacy in the eyes of both the universities and the legal profession. Austin's method, which served both to define an autonomous area of study and to restrict the province of the jurist to that of exposition, analysis, and ordering, met both requirements.

Dicey did more than most to elaborate this role. We have already seen how, in *The Law of the Constitution*, he followed Austin's classificatory approach to defining and categorizing his subject. In his Oxford inaugural lecture in 1883 he had also explicitly addressed the relationship between the profession and the academy:[67]

[The] . . . proper sphere of professorial activity is to supply all the defects which flow directly or indirectly from a one-sided system of practical

[66] See Chap. 8, pp. 197–201.
[67] Dicey, *Can English Law Be Taught At The Universities?* (1883); quoted in

training. It is for law professors to set forth the law as a coherent whole—
to analyse and define legal conceptions—to reduce the mass of legal rules
to an orderly series of principles and to aid, stimulate and guide the reform
and renovation of legal literature . . .

This again is precisely the nature of the task which Dicey set himself
in the *Law of the Constitution*.

The formal classificatory approach to public law, which is
derived from Austin's methods and is applied to public law by
Dicey, had achieved a pre-eminent status by the turn of the century.
It has remained the dominant method ever since. Austin's empiricist
theory has been largely superseded during this century by a
normative version of legal positivism which recognizes rules as
being the basic building blocks of a legal system and which then
invokes an ultimate rule ('the rule of recognition') which serves to
identify a legal system and to distinguish legal rules from moral or
political norms.[68] However, although Austinian positivism is no
longer the primary theory, Austin's *method* remains dominant.
This formalism is rooted in the view that law is a self-contained
body of rules which operates by means of a distinctive system of
conceptual thought. It is, for example, precisely this conception of
public law which Professor Birks seems to have had in mind in
suggesting that public law 'has a unity and internal anatomy of its
own',[69] a view strongly reinforced by his observation that this
anatomy is 'made explicit now by many textbooks'.[70]

There is a particularly important point to bear in mind when
considering the formal method. Many people, drawing the analogy
from the physical sciences, tend to assume that the idea of law as a
logical deductive system constitutes an important part of this
formalism. Nothing could be further from the intention of those
such as Dicey who shaped this method. That is, the 'distinctive
system of conceptual thought' I mentioned as a key part of
formalism is not a simple deductive system. In fact it incorporates
specific cultural pre-dispositions embodied in the common law

D. Sugarman, 'Legal Theory, the Common Law Mind and the Making of the
Textbook Tradition' in W. Twining (ed.), *Legal Theory and the Common Law*
(Oxford, 1986), 26 at p. 30.

[68] See Hart, *The Concept of Law* (Oxford, 1961).
[69] See, *An Introduction to the Law of Restitution*, 3.
[70] On the importance of textbooks to this conception of the subject see
Sugarman, 'Legal Theory, the Common Law Mind . . .'. On their importance in
public law see Chap. 3, pp. 47–8.

tradition. While this issue is examined in more detail later,[71] there is a related aspect of it which should be addressed immediately. This concerns the formalist's juristic attitude to legislation.

If the aim of formalism was to reduce areas of law to order and to reveal the coherence of law by laying bare its underlying principles, the idea of legislation posed a major difficulty. First, the increasing volume of new legislation threatened to produce a huge, unsurveyable heap of rules within the field and thereby to confound the exercise. Secondly, and perhaps more importantly, as much of the new legislation in the area of public law was antagonistic to existing common law principles, it posed a major problem for public lawyers who adopted this formal analytical approach. Since these lawyers apparently believed in the clearcut distinction between law as it is and law as it ought to be, a fundamental exercise in integration seemed to be required in the name of legal science. This, of course, did not happen. And the reason it did not was that ultimately this formalism existed to perform an ideological role. That is, the formal method established to promote the autonomy of law and the idea of legal science served essentially to ensure the academic lawyer's status in relation to the legal profession and, ultimately, to defend the common law tradition.

In conclusion we could say that formalism in public law is basically a formalism of form. Within the formalist approach there existed a specific ideological conception of legality. It is also important to register a point which is entirely neglected by those professors of public law who today take as the starting point the work of Dicey. It is this. That within the century which divides Millar from Dicey academic lawyers had shifted their focus from the attempt to devise a science of legislation to the search for a science of law *without* legislation.

Only Connect . . .

In recent years it has become fashionable for public lawyers to pay lip-service to the intrinsic and necessary connection between public law and politics. For some, this is the occasion for reflection on the jurisprudential basis of the subject; public law, they argue, must be rooted in political theory and thus in a particular moral

---

[71] See Chap. 3, pp. 42–50 and Chap. 7, pp. 146–53.

vision of the political community. For others, the event provides the opportunity for taking a sociological approach and emphasizing the necessity of connecting public law to the facts of political life. These cogitations—whether of a philosophical or a sociological nature—generally remain undeveloped; the importance of a reference to the connection is felt to be sufficient. Occasionally, such comments are little more than fairly unreflective assertions of writer's own political proclivities. In general, the precise nature of any such connection is rarely the subject of serious scrutiny.

These references are made not only by the avant-garde, but also by those who strictly adhere to the formalist approach. Back in 1960, for example, Stanley de Smith, the leading post-war scholar of the analytical method in public law, commented that:[72]

The lawyer's view of an approach to the Constitution cannot differ in essence from those of the political scientist. It is possible for the commercial lawyer and the economist, for the family lawyer and the sociologist, to regard one area of social activity from standpoints so far apart that contact becomes infrequent, indeed almost fortuitous . . . but in England the constitutional lawyer and the political scientist are for ever undivided.

Even more startling, however, were the comments of Sir William Wade, the most distinguished of our contemporary disciples of Dicey, in his Hamlyn Lectures in 1980. In introducing his theme Wade stated that:[73]

[B]ooks on constitutional law . . . are for the most part content to describe in dispassionate detail institutions whose merits may be highly debateable. Perhaps in this respect the attitude of constitutional lawyers is in a transitional phase. The Blackstone–Bagehot–Dicey era was the age of self-satisfaction. Their successors today adopt a stance of fairly strict neutrality. The next era, I hope, will be that of the critics . . . The danger before them is obvious: this path leads straight into politics. But if the price of preserving the purity of constitutional law is that one must ignore the political pros and cons of what are, after all, our most essential laws, then I would say that the price is too high and the lack of realism is excessive.

What are we to make of such comments from these quarters? Professor Wade's remarks are perhaps most instructive. His

---

[72] S. A. de Smith, *The Lawyers and the Constitution* (Inaugural Lecture, London School of Economics, 10 May 1960); quoted in V. Bogdanor, 'Constitutional Law and Politics' (1987) 7 *Oxford J. of Legal Studies* 454.
[73] H. W. R. Wade, *Constitutional Fundamentals* (London, 1980), 1–2.

references to 'the purity of constitutional law' and the 'strict neutrality' of Dicey's successors reveal his adherence to the formalist method. Even more significant as an indicator of his positivist outlook is the identification of politics as a danger zone. What Wade is signalling is the fact that, if lawyers consider political questions, they move from description to evaluation, from science to speculation, from an objective to a subjective realm. They cross the positivist divide between 'is' and 'ought'.

Before considering further the question of the necessity of division-crossing, we might consider briefly analogous developments in the field of political studies. During the latter half of the nineteenth-century politics struggled to achieve the status which first political economy and then law had achieved. The writing of the political journalist Walter Bagehot, for example, could be viewed as an attempt to rescue the study of politics from the grip of the constitutional lawyers. This was important since, notwithstanding the limiting categorization of legal science, lawyers continued to exert an influence over the language through which major political issues were discussed. Bagehot's method, however, was unlikely to satisfy the positivist requirements of science. As we have seen, he pointed to the perennial tensions between: authority and utility; the dignified and the efficient; the necessity of stability and the engine of progress; the traditional and the rational. His method was essentially the utilization of paradox.

The academics, however, did not progress that much further than Bagehot. As Collini, Winch, and Burrow indicate, Cambridge provided a good barometer.[74] Sir John Seeley, Regius Professor of History, argued that the science of politics was formed by the residue of generalizations deposited by history when the literary and picturesque qualities of the latter had been put away with childish things, and narrative had given place to analysis and induction.[75] Henry Sidgwick, the Cambridge philosopher, argued in 1865 that 'history will have in the future less and less influence on Politics in the most advanced countries. Principles will soon be everything and tradition nothing: except as regards its influence on the form.'[76] But an indication of the difficulties is furnished by

---

[74] See Collini, Winch, and Burrow, *That Noble Science of Politics*, chap. XI.
[75] J. R. Seeley, *Introduction to Political Science* (London, 1896), p. 12. Quoted in Collini, Winch, and Burrow, p. 225.
[76] Quoted in Collini, Winch, and Burrow, p. 287.

Maitland's terse comment that political science was 'either history or humbug'.[77] The new century thus opened with Graham Wallas's famous statement that: 'The study of politics is just now in a curiously unsatisfactory condition.'[78] And Collini, Winch, and Burrow's conclusion to their masterly survey was that 'there was no more an achieved science in 1930 than there had been in 1830'.[79]

During the twentieth century the struggle continued. Despite resistance, the search for a scientific understanding of political phenomena continued. The objective of this political science was to establish itself as an empirical discipline based on an inductive methodology, which would permit the testing of hypotheses and thence the identification of regularities which would permit scientifically valid generalizations to be drawn. Certain advances have been made in the development of a political science in this form. This form of political science, however, is based on a study of political behaviour and with this switch to behaviour as the object of study, political scientists have largely ceased to be interested in constitutions. They may not, like Hallam, have gloried in the edifice but, by ignoring these structural dimensions may well have conveyed a sense that the constitution is a neutral medium through which the business of politics is conducted.

In recent years, however, the disenchantment with the construction of an empirical science of politics has caused some to return to the consideration of constitutional questions. During the 1970s, for example, Nevil Johnson produced a stimulating essay dealing with the malaise in government and the paucity of our constitutional thought.[80] More recently, and in similar vein, David Marquand, in *The Unprincipled Society*, presents a thesis as bold and ambitious as Hallam's. Just as Hallam linked Britain's wealth and liberty to the genius of the constitution so Marquand argues that Britain's economic decline in the twentieth century is directly connected to its failure to adapt its political institutions and establish a developmental state more suited to the social and ecomomic realities of twentieth-century life. In a reversal of Hallam, Marquand argues that our constitutional heritage and our legal tradition, have become major obstacles to successful social adjust-

[77] Quoted in ibid. 349.
[78] G. Wallas, *Human Nature in Politics* (London, 1908), 1.
[79] Collini, Winch, and Burrow, *That Noble Science of Politics*, 376.
[80] N. Johnson, *In Search of the Constitution* (London, 1977).

ment.[81] This is a controversial thesis and it is no part of our current
objective to begin to evaluate it. We might simply remark that the
reflective contributions to constitutional thought have come, not
from the public lawyers, but from certain political scientists adrift
from the mainstream of their discipline.

The fact that such critical contributions have not come from
public lawyers should come as no surprise. It provides a further
indication of the dominance of the positivist temperament in public
law entailing, as it does, a radical break between description and
evaluation and an analytical method which greatly inhibits any
broader conception of understanding. But if public law is to break
from the shackles of such restrictions, individual critiques such as
those provided by Johnson from a conservative perspective and
Marquand from a liberal perspective will not be sufficient. We must
learn more from the general message of the failure to construct an
objective political science.

One major difficulty has faced those who have tried to develop a
scientific conception of politics: can agreement be reached on what
constitutes the raw material of politics? Here, there has been
sustained criticism that it cannot. This school of criticism argues
that the language that is invoked—and not simply the language of
liberty, justice, and democracy but also our concept of the political
realm itself—is the language of 'essentially contested concepts'.[82]
When we encounter people who disagree about the meaning of
such concepts, so this argument goes, they are invariably engaging
in disputes which are not simply about the use of words but about
matters of substance. Further, these are matters of substance on
which there can be no demonstrable truth.

If this criticism is sound, however, it surely tells against the
attempt to construct a science of public law just as much as to the
construction of an empirical political science. That this is only just
coming to be realized is the reason that this chapter opened with an
adaptation (albeit to different effect) of Graham Wallas's statement
in 1906 to the effect that political science is in a curiously

[81] D. Marquand, *The Unprincipled Society. New Demands and Old Politics*
(London, 1988).
[82] See W. B. Gallie, 'Essentially Contested Concepts', vol. 56, *Proceedings of the
Aristotelian Society* 167 (1955–6); W. E. Connolly, *The Terms of Political
Discourse* (Oxford, 2nd edn., 1983).

unsatisfactory condition. Given the nature of this criticism and its apparent applicability to public law, we must examine recent developments in political theory to see what light they shed on our endeavour.

2

Public Law and Political Theory

THE DEATH AND REBIRTH OF POLITICAL THEORY

IN 1956 Peter Laslett, remarking on the fact that we no longer have philosophers applying 'the methods and the conclusions of contemporary thought to the evidence of the contemporary social and political situation', declared: 'For the moment, anyway, political philosophy is dead.'[1] Laslett suggested that this break with a 300 year old Anglo-Saxon tradition stretching from Hobbes to Bosanquet was the result of the rise of positivism, the effect of which was to signify that there was no such rational discipline capable of yielding genuine knowledge. The rise of political science based on the model of the natural sciences and focusing on the rigorous collection of data, the discovery of correlations, and the formulation of testable hypotheses, had signalled the end of that subject. To the extent that there was a role for philosophy in the field of political studies, it was to analyse the language employed in political discourse and to eliminate verbal confusions which may inhibit advances in political science.[2]

Laslett's assessment did not, however, go unchallenged. In a direct response, Isaiah Berlin argued that the attempt to press political studies into a natural scientific framework had distorted and obscured many of the issues which were indispensable to the understanding of political life.[3] In particular, Berlin stressed that human beings were self-interpreting creatures: 'men's beliefs in the sphere of conduct are part of their conception of themselves and others as human beings; and this conception in its turn, whether

---

[1] P. Laslett (ed.), *Philosophy, Politics and Society* (Oxford, 1956), Introduction, p. vii.
[2] See, e.g., T. D. Weldon, *The Vocabulary of Politics* (Harmondsworth, 1953).
[3] I. Berlin, 'Does political theory still exist?' in P. Laslett and W. G. Runciman (eds.), *Philosophy, Politics and Society (Second Series)* (Oxford, 1962), 1.

conscious or not, is intrinsic to their picture of the world'.[4] The
significance of this statement is that it suggests that the beliefs
which we hold cannot be treated simply as subjective states; they
are *constitutive* of our actions. If correct, this then cautions that
there can be no neat division between subjective and objective in
the field of social studies. Description and identification of human
action is 'shot through with evaluation'.[5]

Berlin's essay contained two primary thrusts. First, it indicated
that, while political theory may be suppressed by intellectual
fashion, the subject itself will not disappear. Secondly, that if a
positivist political science were in fact to become triumphant, the
achievement would not be a victory for objectivity and neutrality
but for a particular ideological belief.

Berlin's general point about intellectual fashion has been borne
out by subsequent history. Indeed, since Laslett's initial statement
in 1956, his commentaries can be viewed as a faithful barometer of
the state of political theory. In the volume in which Berlin's essay
appeared he suggested that, while there has been no resurrection
'the mood is very different and very much more favourable than it
was six years ago'.[6] In the third series of *Philosophy, Politics and
Society* the editors suggested that there was 'little purpose in
labouring the point that political philosophy in the English-
speaking world is alive again'.[7] Reservations were nevertheless
expressed in the fourth series, with the editors expressing 'considerable doubts about the prospect of any complete recovery'.[8] By the
end of the 1970s, however, it was felt that political theory
'obviously flourishes, all over the English-speaking world and
outside it too'.[9]

The reasons for this apparent rejuvenation are obviously many
and various. During the 1950s, for example, several eminent
political scientists, especially in the United States, had proclaimed

---

[4] I. Berlin, 'Does political theory still exist?' in P. Laslett and W. G. Runciman
(eds.), *Philosophy, Politics and Society (Second Series)* (Oxford, 1962), at 13.
[5] Ibid. 17.
[6] Ibid. at p. vii.
[7] Laslett and Runciman, *Philosophy, Politics and Society (Third Series)* (Oxford,
1969), 3.
[8] P. Laslett, W. G. Runciman, and Q. Skinner (eds.), *Philosophy, Politics and
Society (Fourth Series)* (Oxford, 1972), 1.
[9] P. Laslett and J. Fishkin (eds.), *Philosophy, Politics and Society (Fifth Series)*
(Oxford, 1979), 1.

the end of ideology.[10] This proclamation was founded on the belief
that the achievements of advanced industrial societies were such
that the days of ideological tumult were over. The following
decade, however, was marked by such major social forces as the
emergence of civil rights movements, the rise of the 'new left', and
the 'rediscovery of poverty', all of which served to confound that
prognosis. Another factor worth noting concerns developments,
not in the field of politics, but in the natural sciences. What is here
particularly noteworthy is the publication in 1962 of Thomas
Kuhn's highly influential *The Structure of Scientific Revolutions*.

Kuhn argues that, although in the history of the natural sciences
there is often a period in which several schools of thought exist in
relation to the explanation of any particular phenomenon, occasionally a qualitative change occurs and a 'paradigm' is established.
Paradigms, Kuhn informs us, are 'universally recognized scientific
achievements that for a time provide model problems and solutions
to a community of practitioners'.[11] He provides as examples
Ptolemaic (or Copernican) astronomy and Aristotelian (or Newtonian)
dynamics. Such achievements share two essential characteristics.
First, it is 'sufficiently unprecedented to attract an enduring group
of adherents away from competing modes of scientific activity'.[12]
Secondly, it was also 'sufficiently open-ended to leave all sorts of
problems for the redefined group of practitioners to resolve'.[13] The
importance of paradigms, then, is that they give rise to 'normal
science'. The scientific community imposes the paradigm through
the standard textbooks and through education which Kuhn refers
to as a 'process of professional initiation'.[14] Scientific discovery
then comes about with the awareness of an anomaly; 'the
recognition that nature has somehow violated the paradigm-
induced expectations that govern normal science'.[15] This is met by
attempts at assimilation or by marginalization or suppression. If
this fails, the transition to crisis or 'extraordinary science' begins
and at this stage a 'proliferation of competing articulations, the
willingness to try anything, the expression of explicit discontent,
the recourse of philosophy and to debate over fundamentals'

[10] See, e.g., D. Bell, *The End of Ideology* (New York, 1961).
[11] T. S. Kuhn, *The Structure of Scientific Revolutions* (Chicago, 2nd edn., 1970),
p. viii.
[12] Ibid. 10.
[13] Ibid.   [14] Ibid. 47.   [15] Ibid. at 52.

occurs.[16] Through this process a revolution occurs with the eventual establishment of a new paradigm.

Kuhn's work is particularly interesting because it presents development in the natural sciences in a rather different light to many who hold it up as a model for other fields to emulate. The scientific community does not appear as a group of researchers interested in the impartial search for truth but rather as a political community seeking to impose order. Furthermore, 'truth' itself is displaced from the pedestal on which it is placed by empiricists since it is itself shaped by the prevailing paradigm. Kuhn's theory has been highly influential and it provides an important plank in the general challenge to positivist thought on a number of fronts over recent decades. To the extent that it has done so, it has helped to shape a climate which has been conducive to the recent revival of political theory.

In the process of rebirth over the last two decades, the form which political theory takes has altered somewhat. It differs from political philosophy in a traditional sense because 'it is less formal and atomistic, less concerned to establish logical relationships between individual political concepts'.[17] Political theorists, in this less conceptualistic mode, 'would prefer to understand their role . . . as a goad—inducing people to reconsider beliefs previously taken for granted, to notice the fuller implications of their value commitments, or perhaps to recognize the incompatibility between different goals that they espouse'.[18]

THE REBIRTH OF POLITICAL THEORY AND THE STUDY OF PUBLIC LAW

Lawyers have been largely oblivious to these debates on the nature, status and relevance of political theory. But surely these discussions should have a direct impact on the ways in which we think about and construct the subject of public law. If Sir Isaiah Berlin's comments have force, that thrust must touch the human

---

[16] T. S. Kuhn, *The Structure of Scientific Revolutions* (Chicago, 2nd edn., 1970), at 91.

[17] D. Miller and L. Siedentop (eds.), *The Nature of Political Theory* (Oxford, 1983), 'Introduction', p. 1.

[18] Ibid.

sciences in general. His comments on the distortive effects of the imposition of a positivist framework and the lack of a clear distinction between description and evaluation in relation to human conduct have equal applicability to the way in which we view public law. If the institutionalization of a positivist outlook in political studies is essentially an ideological triumph, it should also be looked upon as being such in relation to public law.

During the late eighteenth century academic lawyers such as Millar conceived of their subject in terms of the 'principles of law and government'. The radical separation of the study of law from the study of government was a late nineteenth-century endeavour. As we have seen, the objective seems to have been to forge a conception of legal science that both identified an autonomous subject of study and established a place within a professional world-view. Above all, this was a positivist achievement. By the late twentieth century, however, this positivist construct, even in the eyes of its most eminent practitioners, is failing to respond to the felt necessities of the time. The time is ripe for a rethink of the foundations of the subject.

At this moment of crisis we might have much to learn from the lessons of political science. It is fanciful to believe that we can begin where Millar left off; in seeking to reconstruct principles of law and government. Just as political theory has recently re-emerged in a less atomistic and less conceptualistic guise from that of traditional political philosophy, so also we must realize that there is no going back to the agenda of an earlier century. Nevertheless, an exploration of the relationships between public law and political theory has the merit of challenging dogmatic objectivism in the field of public law and encouraging a healthy and sceptical spirit of inquiry.

Perhaps the most important message of post-empiricist political theory is that there is an intrinsic connection between fact and value built into the conceptual structures that we erect and that this insight applies also to the edifice of public law we have built. For some, however, this insight has been the occasion for moving from one extreme to the other; from dogmatic objectivism to radical subjectivism. This recent attachment to the cult of subjectivity has been much stronger in the United States, where they tend not to do things by halves. It has been a prominent strand in the self-styled Critical Legal Studies movement there where, through the method of 'trashing',[19] it forms a distinctive jurisprudence of drag.[20] It has, however, also occasionally entered the recent British discourse on public law.[21] While it may have a role to play in shocking us out of an unquestioning acceptance of the orthodoxy of formalism in public law, to accept it uncritically would, I think, be to deny the value of recent developments in political theory.

THE VALUE OF POLITICAL THEORY

While post-empiricist political theory may not be scientific if the model of science adopted is that of the 'value-freedom' often associated with the natural sciences, this does not mean that it cannot be of assistance in helping us to understand the political world. What this recent political theory in effect presents is a basic challenge to the categorial distinction between the subjective and the objective. In particular, it challenges 'objectivism'; the idea that phenomena can be categorized as 'out there' and consequently observable. This objectivism, then, is founded on the belief that there exists certain basic, uninterpreted facts which provide a foundation for all empirical knowledge. When we reject objectivism, however, we do not as a consequence reject the idea of objectivity. This point is explained rather well by Richard Bernstein:[22]

[B]y 'objectivity' we mean that in any domain of human inquiry . . . there are intersubjective standards of rationality or norms of inquiry by which

[19] M. Kelman, 'Trashing' (1984) 36 *Stan. L. Rev* 283; A. D. Freeman, 'Truth and Mystification in Legal Scholarship' (1981) 90 *Yale L.J.* 1229.

[20] I use this term because drag works on the principle that you must dress up for an occasion, but only so long as it is not the occasion to which you are actually going. This is rooted in the ethnomethodological method of 'throwing' someone; that is, acting on assumptions that are rather different to those which the other person takes for granted, as when a daughter acts likes a lodger. The connections between 'throwing' and 'trashing' are therefore rather similar; both are designed to shock people out of treating tacit assumptions as being self-evident. For a critique of this dimension of the Critical Legal Studies Movement (albeit written before the movement had been formed) see: E. Gellner, 'The Re-Enchantment Industry, or the Californian Way of Subjectivity' 5 *Philosophy of the Social Sciences* 173 (1975).

[21] A. Hutchinson, 'The Rise and Ruse of Administrative Law and Scholarship' in his *Dwelling on the Threshold. Critical Essays in Modern Legal Thought* (Toronto, 1988), chap. 4. The incoherence of Hutchinson's position is illuminated in N. Duxbury, 'Deconstruction, History and the Uses of Legal Theory' (1990) 41 *N. Ireland L.Q.* 167.

[22] R. Bernstein, *The Restructuring of Social and Political Theory* (Philadelphia, 1976), 111.

we attempt to distinguish personal bias, superstition, or false beliefs from objective claims. . . . This does not mean, however, that there is a simple or direct way of stating the norms of the appropriate inquiry, or that there cannot be significant disagreement about these norms and their application, or even whether what counts as objective in one domain of inquiry can do so in another. The attempt to specify a single univocal set of criteria as a basis for distinguishing what is genuinely objective from what is not, has been one of the most obsessive and futile preoccupations of modern thinkers since Descartes. But we are not therefore obliged—as it is often claimed—to retreat to skepticism, self-defeating relativism, or irrational subjectivism. The lesson to be learned, rather, is how difficult and complex it is to articulate standards of objectivity relevant to different domains of inquiry, and the ways these standards are themselves open to criticism. Furthermore—and this is perhaps the most important point—the very standards of objectivity and rationality themselves depend on the existence of communities of inquirers who are able, willing and committed to engage in argumentation.

The rejection of a positivist philosophy of social science, then, does not lead us to reject the value of social and political theory. Rather, it opens up a more complex, more challenging and more liberating view of theory. Although rejecting objectivism the idea of objectivity, understood as a striving for systematic inquiry, underpins the endeavour.

Since fact and value are built into our conceptual structures, we might say that the task of theory in relation to the social and political world is to render explicit our self-understandings. In order to achieve this objective we must go through a number of stages. As a starting point, we must develop explanatory frameworks which try to reveal the value of assumptions, the causal relations and the dominant features of our social practices. Through this process, however, a range of conceptual structures in relation to a particular practice may emerge. These various conceptual structures may give certain features of their schemes a different stress, they may provide differing accounts of causal relations between key features, and they will incorporate certain value positions. That is, they present rival explanatory accounts of practices.

The task of theory must then be to bring to consciousness the assumptions secreted within such structures. Once these assumptions have been presented systematically, the next task is to subject these structures and assumptions to scrutiny in accordance with such canons of rationality as consistency, coherence and contradiction. Finally, as much of the earlier discussion indicates, we must approach this exercise with a degree of historical sensitivity. The spirit in which this venture should be undertaken has been eloquently summarized by Sir Isaiah Berlin, who states that:[23]

The history of thought and culture is . . . a changing pattern of great liberating ideas which inevitably turn into suffocating straitjackets, and so stimulate their own destruction by new emancipating and, at the same time, enslaving conceptions. The first step to the understanding of men is the bringing to consciousness of the model or models that dominate and penetrate their thought and action. Like all attempts to make men aware of the categories in which they think, it is a difficult and sometimes painful activity, likely to produce deeply disquieting results. The second task is to analyse the model itself, and this commits the analyst to accepting or modifying or rejecting it, and, in the last case, to providing a more adequate one in its stead.

This agenda for post-empiricist political theory is precisely the agenda which I think needs to be set for the study of public law. We need to lay bare the conceptual structures through which we come to describe and explain the subject, and to understand the relations and features entailed in these structures and the assumptions on which they are founded. And we must subject the structures and assumptions which pervade public law thought to critical scrutiny.

A theoretical approach to public law must therefore be *interpretative*, *empirical*, *critical*, and *historical*. It must be interpretative because in the field of law fact and value cannot be kept categorially distinct. It must be empirical in the sense of being rooted in an understanding of the realities of government and the functions which law is expected to perform in relation to the political system. It must be critical both in subjecting various interpretations to rational scrutiny and to inquiry in respect of empirical understandings of the functions of government and law. Finally, it should be undertaken with a degree of historical sensitivity and with a sense of the changing needs of societies through time. These various facets of a theoretical approach obviously interact and mutually reinforce each other. Through such an approach we might come closer to a thorough understanding of the subject.

---

[23] Berlin, 'Does political theory still exist?' in Laslett and Runciman (eds.), *Philosophy, Politics and Society (Second Series)* (Oxford, 1962), 19.

THEORIES AS MAPS

We may explain this theoretical approach to the study of public law by invoking the metaphor of the map. The task of theory is to render explicit and systematic those conceptual structures that implicitly shape our views about the subject. As we have seen, however, this theoretical approach may reveal a variety of conceptual structures. Following Charles Taylor, we may view these various theories as constituting rival maps of the terrain. In Taylor's words 'the terrain of possible practices is being mapped in contour, and this purports to give the shape and slope of the heights of value'.[24] The value of a map, then, is revealed simply by seeing 'how well you can get around using it'.[25]

This idea of theories as maps has been elaborated upon by Alisdair MacIntyre, who suggests that theories, like maps, are essential guides even though they be less than complete or are inaccurate in certain respects. But there is no novelty in this fact:[26]

The adventurous seamen of the late Middle Ages and the early modern age must often have survived on the basis of a map (sometimes in the form of a diagram and sometimes in the form of a description) itself grossly inaccurate, but continuously emended or added to by *ad hoc* corrections in this or that port. What is important to observe here is that the emendations and additions were only able to afford the guidance that they did in fact afford by being ancillary to the original map. Lacking that map, there would have been no focus, no way of organizing, often indeed no way of characterizing the items in the list of emendations and additions. And, that is to say, a false map may under certain conditions provide the rational agent with what is a great deal superior to no map at all.

The message here is that we need maps to enable us to move around the legal landscape. Maps can guide even when they are grossly inaccurate, because without a map there would be no way of focusing or organizing one's journey. Maps may even possess the characteristics of being *both* false and illuminating. But better that we have incomplete or inaccurate maps than no map at all.[27]

---

[24] C. Taylor, 'Social Theory as Practice' in *Philosophical Papers 2. Philosophy and the Human Sciences* (Cambridge, 1985), 91 at p. 110.

[25] Ibid. at p. 111.

[26] A. MacIntyre, 'The indispensability of political theory' in Miller and Siedentop (eds.), *The Nature of Political Theory* (Oxford, 1983), 17 at p. 32.

[27] See also A. MacIntyre, *Whose Justice? Which Rationality?* (London, 1988). In

This approach to the study of public law is potentially very challenging since there are particularly rich lands to survey. We need to appreciate how certain practices acquire meaning, how particular meanings are related to concepts, and how a variety of concepts are linked together in structures as theoretical frameworks. This is an interpretative exercise. Having identified the main conceptual structures which infuse practices with meaning we must then assess how these theoretical frameworks relate to the political and social realities of the world in which we live. This is to some extent an empirical exercise. However, insofar as we should also assess the manner in which these realities have changed over time, it is also an historical exercise. Finally, we must examine the alternative maps of the conceptual terrain being surveyed and evaluate their rival claims. This constitutes an exercise in critical scrutiny.

THE JOURNEY

In this book my aim is to examine public law from the general theoretical approach outlined. The essay proceeds at three different levels of abstraction. At the lowest level I propose to analyse the views of the major writers in public law; those who have had a significant impact on the way we think about the subject. At the intermediate level my aim is to articulate the main conceptual structures or, more loosely, 'styles' of public law thought. At the highest level, I will examine the main political theories or ideologies which have shaped our thinking about matters of law and government. The general objective is to examine relationships between these three strands of thought: to view the main structures of public law thought through the grid of political ideology; to assess the shared patterns of thought between particular public lawyers; and to try to discern connections between the approaches of public lawyers and the thrust of political ideologies. By doing so I hope to be able to draw out some general points about the nature and distinctiveness of the subject.

I do not wish to underestimate the complexity of this exercise, nor to pretend to have all the answers. There is for example, and as

this book MacIntyre shows us how we can make progress even when two sets of 'maps' come into confrontation.

Hawthorn—following Heidegger—reminds us, no escape from translation in interpreting these texts.[28] Furthermore, the task of relating theory to practice, thought to life, is an exceedingly complex task, if only because there are so many layers of life in play at any one moment in time that they will not permit any straightforward explanation. This may engender a particular form of resistance on the part of lawyers, if only because one of the primary functions of law is to provide practical guidance. We are therefore reminded of the dilemma of modernity; 'everything which is complex is useless, everything which is simple is false'.[29] The most important aim of this book is to raise some fundamental questions and to outline some maps which, despite their deficiencies or inaccuracies, might provide useful guides. As has already been suggested, incomplete or inaccurate maps are better than none at all.

The aim of the book, therefore, is essentially therapeutic. It is an exercise in what Richard Rorty calls 'edification'.[30] It is a project of trying to find 'new, better, more interesting, more fruitful ways of speaking' about public law.[31] It commences on the assumption that in order to begin to understand public law we must first try to make it strange. Only then will we begin to understand the conceptual structures which exert influence in the field. It is only by becoming self-conscious of these discursive structures that we may then be in a position to assess the source of their power and their suitability to meet challenges of contemporary conditions.

Although the essay involves the three levels of abstraction previously mentioned, it does not proceed from the lowest to the highest. The intermediate level, in a sense, forms the critical part of my venture since it is at this level that we identify and seek to lay bare the conceptual structures which shape the way we think about the subject. The essay therefore proceeds first by identifying and sketching these structures (Chapter 4). Thereafter we explore the relationships between these styles of public law thought and the main ideologies which have shaped constitutional politics (Chapters 5 and 6). Having identified these styles and examined the extent to which their foundations lie in political ideology, we turn to the

---

[28] G. Hawthorn, *Enlightenment and Despair* (Cambridge, 2nd edn., 1987), p. ix.
[29] P. Valery, *History and Politics* (New York, 1962), 37.
[30] R. Rorty, *Philosophy and the Mirror of Nature* (Oxford, 1980), chap. VIII.
[31] Ibid. at p. 360.

work of those who have influenced the shape of public law. Our aim in so doing is primarily to assess the degree to which their work should best be seen as rooted in a particular style or theoretical framework (Chapters 7 and 8). Finally we draw some general reflections on the appropriateness of these styles to the challenges facing public law today (Chapters 9 and 10).

However, before we embark on that journey there is a preliminary matter to consider. We must focus our inquiry by providing the reader with an introduction to the intellectual traditions which pervade the teaching of public law in the law schools of the United Kingdom. By so doing we should be able to see more clearly what is entailed in adopting an interpretative or hermeneutical approach to the study of public law. In Chapter 3, then, we consider the relationship betwen practice and meaning by examining the importance of interpretation in the study of public law.

3

Interpretation in Public Law

MY task in this book is a theoretical one. This, however, should not be taken to suggest that it is concerned essentially with esoteric ideas. It is theoretical in the sense that it begins with the ordinary material of public law and tries to extend our understanding of that material by seeking to discover what is *implied* in it. It tries to make clear something which, although dimly apprehended, is obscure. That is, it is an exercise in trying to move from a position of knowing something indistinctly and confusedly to a position in which our knowledge is more explicit and systematic. In order to carry out this task we must challenge the impact which the scientific quest has had on public law thought. Just as the attempt to press political studies into a natural scientific framework has distorted and obscured many of the issues that are indispensable to an understanding of political life, so also this claim may be made for law. The conception of law which we obtain from the formalist approach and the adoption of the analytical method obscures more than it reveals.

This is scarcely a novel approach. As we have seen, the view of the natural sciences that is held up by formalists as a model to emulate has itself been subjected to major criticisms. Many now accept that science reflects human purposes as much as it reflects the world. We have also seen that developments in political theory have challenged the idea that, within the human sciences, fact and value can be left categorially distinct. Given the importance of the human factor in all forms of scientific progress we need to appreciate how knowledge is given shape and acquires meaning through the development of conceptual structures or interpretative frameworks. The road of progress on this theoretical journey thus seems to point in the direction of taking an interpretative approach. But this approach is likely to encounter resistance in the study of public law.

The Common Law Mind and the Order of Things

One initial difficulty we face in seeking to lay bare the most influential theoretical frameworks within public law arises from the fact that in Britain there is a deep-seated sense that the subject is concerned with the 'order of things'. Public law is viewed as a practical discipline involving description and analysis of the organizational rules of the political order. Dicey's approach has thus retained a powerful grip over teaching and thinking about the subject.

This view of public law as reflecting the 'order of things' is strongly reinforced by the peculiar nature of the British constitution. As a result of the absence of acute political crisis in recent times there has been no modern constitutional settlement. The legal forms of our constitution reflect a medieval order and, because of the lack of any permanent rupture, we have experienced an unusual degree of institutional continuity. To the extent that these forms and institutions have been adapted to reflect modern political changes the accommodation has generally been achieved through custom and practice. These customs and practices are, of course, what Dicey labelled 'the conventions of the constitution'.[1] But, to the extent to which there has been no formal break, the lines of continuity remain.

The continuity of these forms and institutions have, in conjunction with the dominant cultural conservatism of the legal profession, contributed to the retention of what is virtually a pre-modern cosmology within public law. The world is seen as embodying an underlying scheme which makes sense and which, in effect, constitutes a natural and immutable order.

It is, I believe, important to identify the pervasiveness of this view, even though its authority may have been on the wane in recent times. This belief reflects the dominance of what may be called 'the common law mind', which in public law is closely associated with the myth of the ancient constitution. The idea of 'the common law mind' reflects an essentially medieval idea of law as 'a thing ancient, immanent and unmade'.[2] The connection

---

[1] See Chap. 1 pp. 14–17. Dicey was apparently the first to use this expression although the term quickly caught on. See W. S. Holdsworth, 'The conventions of the eighteenth century constitution' (1932) 17 *Iowa Law Review* 161.

[2] J. G. A. Pocock, *The Ancient Constitution and the Feudal Law* (Cambridge, rev. edn., 1987), 16.

between the common law mind and the myth of the ancient constitution can readily be discerned. If the common law is in fact ancient custom which exists 'time out of mind of man'[3] this strengthens the idea of law as being something that is not simply a product of human will. In particular, if the common law is older than the king then it suggests that law cannot be viewed simply as the king's command. Furthermore, if common law rights were immemorial then it could even be argued that it was beyond the power of the king to repeal or amend these rights. Here we find the essence of the idea of the ancient constitution.

This appeal to the ancient constitution assumed a particular importance during the constitutional conflicts of the seventeenth century. These conflicts concerned not just the location of the sovereign power of the state—in the Crown or in Parliament?—but also the relationship between sovereignty and law. The common lawyers resisted claims that the idea of sovereignty formed part of constitutional thought. In doing so, they rejected any notion that William I was a conqueror; if it were conceded that William became king by conquest then, at that precise moment, the ultimate source of authority in the State would appear to vest in the king. William, they argued, was 'a claimant to the crown under ancient law who had vindicated his claim to the crown by trial of battle with Harold, a victory which brought him no title whatever to change the laws of England'.[4]

It is worth providing certain specific illustrations of the thoughts of the common lawyers during the seventeenth century. In 1612 Sir John Davies provided a remarkably explicit and elaborate explanation of the nature of the common law:[5]

For the *Common Law of England* is nothing else but the *Common Custome* of the Realm; and a Custome which hath obtained the force of a Law is always said to be *Jus non scriptum*: for it cannot be made or created either by Charter, or by Parliament, which are Acts reduced to writing, and are alwaies matter of Record; but being onely matter of fact, and consisting in use and practice, it can be recorded and registered no-where but in the memory of the people.

---

[3] Sir Edward Coke, Preface to *Third Reports* (T.F. vol. II), pp. ix. Quoted in Pocock, *The Ancient Constitution*, 38.

[4] Pocock, ibid. 53.

[5] Sir John Davies, Preface to *Irish Reports* (1612: London, 1674); quoted in Pocock, *The Ancient Constitution*, at p. 32.

For a Custome taketh beginning and groweth to perfection in this manner: When a reasonable act once done is found to be good and beneficiall to the people, and agreeable to their nature and disposition, then do they use it and practise it again and again, and so by often iteration and multiplication of the act it becometh a *Custome*; and being continued without interruption time out of mind, it obtaineth the force of a *Law*.

And this *Customary Law* is the most perfect and most excellent, and without comparison the best, to make and preserve a Commonwealth. For the *written Laws* which are made either by the Edicts of Princes, or by Councils of Estates, are imposed upon the Subject before any Triall or Probation made, whether the same be fit and agreeable to the nature and disposition of the people, or whether they will breed any incovenience or no. But a *Custome* doth never become a Law to bind the people, untill it hath been tried and approved time out of mind, during which time there did thereby arise no incovenience . . .

These views are given specific expression in relation to the issue of sovereignty by Sir Edward Coke CJ in his famous interview with James I in 1607:[6]

Then the king said, that he thought the law was founded upon reason, and that he and others had reason as well as the judges: to which it was answered by me, that true it was, that God had endowed his Majesty with excellent science, and great endowments of nature; but his Majesty was not learned in the laws of his realm of England, and causes which concern the life, or inheritance, or goods, or fortunes of his subjects are not to be decided by natural reason, but by the artificial reason and judgment of law, which law is an act which requires long study and experience before that a man can attain to the cognisance of it; and that the law was the golden metwand and measure to try the causes of the subjects; and which protected His Majesty in safety and peace: with which the King was greatly offended, and said, that then he should be under the law, which was treason to affirm, as he said: to which I said, that Bracton saith, *quod Rex non debet esse sub homine sed sub Deo et lege.*

These expressions of the idea of the ancient constitution by the common lawyers are important for a number of reasons. First, as J. G. A. Pocock suggests, this idea can be seen as part of an 'attempt to settle fundamental political questions, notably those involving law, right and sovereignty, by appeal not directly to abstract

[6] Coke, *Twelfth Reports, Prohibitions del Roy* (1607) 12 Co. Rep. 63. See R. F. V. Heuston, *Essays in Constitutional Law* (London, 1964), chap. 2. See also Coke, *Seventh Reports, Calvin's Case* (1608) 7 Co. Rep. 3b.

political concepts, but to the existing "municipal" laws of the country concerned and to the concepts of custom, prescription and authority that underlay them'.[7] Secondly, as Coke makes explicit, law is quite distinct from natural, speculative or theoretical reason. It is an 'artificial reason', the knowledge of which is acquired not by thinking but through experience of the decisions of judges. Law, in this conception, is not rational in the sense of being reducible to principles.[8]

Finally, we should note that these ideas continued to exercise an important influence on legal and political thought long after 1688. Many have argued that the events of this time constituted a triumph for the idea of the ancient constitution. But Coke's ideas referred to the entire corpus of English law, including the customs of the high court of Parliament, and it is difficult to see how the idea of the ancient constitution could be reconciled to the growing sense of parliamentary sovereignty. Much of the work of Thomas Hobbes can be seen as an attempt to refute Coke's views.[9] While Hobbes's views on these matters were directly challenged, and Coke's defended, by Sir Matthew Hale CJ in the 1670s,[10] it is difficult to see how they could survive into the eighteenth-century and beyond. Nevertheless, reflections of the idea of the ancient constitution can be seen in such prominent eighteenth-century legal and political thinkers as Blackstone and Burke.[11] Burke, for example, argued that both our political knowledge and our political institutions were products of experience and had therefore been shaped by the processes of trial and error and incremental and circumstantial adjustments. The authority of our constitution,

[7] Pocock, *The Ancient Constitution*, 17.
[8] For an examination of this issue see J. U. Lewis, 'Sir Edward Coke (1552–1633): His Theory of "Artificial Reason" as a Context for Modern Basic Legal Theory' (1968) 84 *L.Q.R.* 330. For an attempt to defend this approach today see C. Fried, 'The Artificial Reason of the Law or: What Lawyers Know' (1981) 60 *Texas L. Rev* 35.
[9] 'Students of [Hobbes's] thought have perhaps neglected to note how much space is devoted to refutation of such ideas as that law is law because it is immemorial custom: several paragraphs of *Leviathan*, the greater part of the *Dialogue of the Common Laws* and much of *Behemoth* are directed to this end . . .' Pocock, *The Ancient Constitution*, 162.
[10] See Holdsworth, *History of English Law* (A. C. Goodhart and H. S. Hanbury (ed.)) (London, 1956), vol. 5., Appx. III 'Sir Matthew Hale's Criticisms on Hobbes's Dialogue of the Common Laws'.
[11] See Pocock, 'Burke and the Ancient Constitution—A Problem in the History of Ideas' (1960) 3 *Historical Journal* 125.

argued Burke, lies in the fact that it is a 'prescriptive constitution', by which he meant that 'it is a constitution whose sole authority is that it has existed time out of mind'.[12] And, as Pocock comments, most of Burke's main points 'can be found in Hale rebuking Hobbes, in Coke rebuking James I, or in Davies rebuking the partisans of written law'.[13]

Pocock argues that during the eighteenth century the ideas of the ancient constitution came to be absorbed into the ideas of the mixed or the balanced constitution, ideas which we encountered when considering Millar's work.[14] But what specifically of the common law mind? Here, I believe, the habits of thought which constitute the idea of the common law mind have lived on in legal if not political thinking. If in political discourse the myth of the ancient constitution came to be absorbed with the idea of the balanced constitution in the eighteenth century, what happened in the nineteenth century was that in legal discourse the habits of thought of the common law mind were absorbed with the formalist, analytical method.

Before turning to the nineteenth-century absorption, we might recall the basic issue. The particular history and peculiar nature of our constitutional arrangements have strengthened the claims made for the idea of the ancient constitution. The habits of thought that make up the idea of the common law mind are so rooted in legal consciousness that they have become almost instinctual. As a result, there exists a deep seated feeling that law is concerned with 'the order of things'. Law is, of course, not a 'thing' and is not concerned with the 'order of things'. If our legal culture reflects certain traditional views and ways of doing things that culture should be seen as the carrier of certain values. Law is a phenomenon which is concerned not with the order of things but with the order of meanings. That is, the habits of thought which make up the idea of the common law mind are essentially those which assert the superiority of the common law and project a belief in the 'artificial reason' of the common law. These habits reflect particular beliefs about the political system and the role which law and judges play in relation to that system.

---

[12] Quoted in Pocock, 'Burke and the Ancient Constitution—A Problem in the History of Ideas' (1960) 3 *Historical Journal* at p. 140.

[13] Pocock, *The Ancient Constitution*, 243.

[14] See Chap. 1, pp. 8–13.

Public Law Teaching and the Common Law Mind

The absorption of the values of the common law mind with the analytical method was largely the work of the newly established academic lawyers who, as we have seen, emerged during the latter half of the nineteenth century.[15] Their objective was to present the law as a systematic and coherent structure founded on general principles. But how could the anti-rationalist common law method be reconciled with an ostensibly rationalist formalist exercise? The answer, it appears, was that 'although law may appear to be irrational, chaotic and particularistic, if one digs deep enough and knows what one is looking for, then it will soon become evident that the law is an internally coherent and unified body of rules'.[16] These methods could not, of course, be so smoothly reconciled and, as Sugarman suggests, the exercise was 'shot through with self-contradictions, omissions and absurdities'.[17] This tension was in fact overcome by a refusal to take the rationalistic exercise seriously. The primary technique by which these academic lawyers transmitted knowledge was through the textbook. Dicey's *The Law of the Constitution* may therefore be seen as part of a general movement in nineteenth-century legal education in which the textbook tradition was established. The primary objective of these textbooks seemed to be to initiate the reader into the beauty and intricacies of the 'artificial reason' of the common law. To some extent, the emergence of the textbook in the late nineteenth century can be viewed as an exercise in codification. But this was not a genuine codification. Codification is anathema to the common law mind for two main reasons. First, for reasons already examined, codification goes against the grain of the 'artificial reason' of the common law. Secondly, codification is in reality an assertion of sovereignty; if Parliament were to codify the law, including the common law, then it would mark the establishment of the superiority of statute law. The codifying dimension of the

---

[15] See Chap. 1, p. 21.

[16] D. Sugarman, 'Legal Theory, the Common Law Mind and the Making of the Textbook Tradition' in W. Twining (ed.) *Legal Theory and Common Law* (Oxford, 1986), chap. 3, at p. 26. This is a very valuable essay but Sugarman seems to adopt a more general idea of 'the common law mind' with the result that, rather than viewing it as being absorbed into formalism he actually equates it with formalism. The two methods should, however, be kept analytically distinct.

[17] Ibid. at p. 27.

nineteenth-century legal textbooks was an exercise in constructing the subject in the image of the common law mind.[18] These textbooks asserted the superiority of the common law and instilled a perception of statute law as an alien incursion.

During the twentieth century this textbook tradition has flourished in public law, mainly through the work of Dicey, Anson, E. C. S. Wade, de Smith and H. W. R. Wade.[19] Although it may have been challenged within the last two decades or so, the values of this tradition, a blend of the analytical method and the common law approach, still dominate thinking about the study and practice of public law. Furthermore, this expository approach still seems to prevail, despite the apparent concerns of such leading figures within this textbook tradition as de Smith and H. W. R. Wade.[20] While the evaluative element in courses on public law may have increased in recent years, the overall effect seems to have been to create confusion and uncertainty of expectation.

Consider, to take a pedagogical example, the examination papers which are set in relation to courses on public law. The standard examination question routinely asks examinees not only to describe but also to interpret and evaluate. But what is our expectation of students who are asked (perhaps implicitly) to examine the reasons for the disintegration of the conventions of ministerial responsibility, or assess the fairness of our electoral arrangements, or are required to evaluate whether or not we need a Bill of Rights or a decentralized system of government? Is there something within the subject which enables them to deal with such normative matters? If not, whence do we expect students to acquire their understanding: common sense, life experience, what they have digested through the mass media?

My point is that, although an evaluative element has permeated the syllabus, public law courses are rarely structured in a form to enable students to reflect systematically on normative issues.

---

[18] This view is elaborated in relation to Dicey in Chap. 7, pp. 141–6.

[19] A. V. Dicey, *The Law of the Constitution* (London, 1885; 10th edn., 1959 with intro. by E. C. S. Wade); W. R. Anson, *The Law and Custom of the Constitution* (Oxford, 1886; 4th edn., 1909); E. C. S. Wade and G. G. Phillips, *Constitutional and Adminstrative Law* (London, 1931; 10th edn., 1985 by A. W. Bradley); S. A. de Smith, *Constitutional and Adminstrative Law* (Harmondsworth, 1971; 6th edn., 1989 by R. Brazier); Wade, *Administrative Law* (Oxford 1961; 6th edn., 1988).

[20] See Chap. 1 above at pp. 24–5.

Consequently, when facing such examination questions, they are afloat in a sea of social meaning without maps, instruments, or training. What value should we ascribe to their opinions on these matters? By what standards do we evaluate their essays? When we ask for explanation we are inviting the student to make sense of the issue by reference to some general ideas about the world; we are asking the student to theorize. 'Common sense', 'experience', 'media presentation' may be quite inadequate sources of explanation since theorization could lead us to conclusions which are in certain respects counter-intuitive and contrary to our immediate experience of the world.

Reflections of this nature concerning the law school easily lend themselves to a radical interpretation. Examinations—and courses—are structured in this way precisely because what is in fact taking place in law schools is not the search for knowledge or understanding. Rather it is instruction in a particular way of thinking. On this view, the examination example provides a simple but illuminating illustration. The evaluative element in the question tends to be both an essential and marginal component. And the effect of this combination is to instil the feeling that there is nothing too seriously wrong that a few institutional reforms would not cure. Indeed, from this traditional perspective, to advocate institutional change is to adopt the role of the 'radical'.[21]

The fact is that such confusion exists largely because, although academic lawyers feel the need to make connections and open up the subject for evaluation, our construction of the subject is still rooted in a clear distinction between description and evaluation. The primary objective in the teaching of public law is to convey 'facts' about the legal framework of government. Consequently, to return to the examination illustration, having presented the 'facts' relevant to the issue under consideration, the student is at liberty to round off the answer with a 'balanced' appraisal of the broader issues. What underpins this approach is the assumption that the law provides a neutral medium through which to examine these issues. While we may disagree about values, the law can at least provide us

---

[21] A good example of what I have in mind is: J. Jowell and D. Oliver (eds.) *The Changing Constitution* (Oxford, 2nd edn., 1989). Even texts written by lawyers who appear to take a more self-consciously radical approach tend to be drawn into an institutional perspective: see, e.g., I. Harden and N. Lewis, *The Noble Lie. The British Constitution and the Rule of Law* (London, 1986).

50   *Interpretation in Public Law*

with an objective grammar and vocabulary within which those disagreements may be contested.

THE FACT–VALUE DISTINCTION

Can description and evaluation be so neatly divided? Can we discern and arrange 'facts' about the British constitution without adopting value positions? To my mind, knowledge in the subject must be related to human purposes and with the meanings we impart to situations. This denotes, first, that knowledge must be sought in meaning. Secondly, it suggests that knowledge is relational. These points indicate that we cannot determine truth or falsity outside the social context of human purposes. The points highlight the centrality of interpretation, of relating text to context, and of achieving understanding by relating the parts to the whole. However, while this may be a necessary exercise, it is also a rather problematic undertaking.

This approach obviously entails a rejection of a clear fact-value distinction. It rejects the idea that there can be knowledge which is both precise and final. The best we can achieve through interpretation is to try to understand more clearly, through peeling away layers of misconception and ambiguity, that which we already understand obscurely and indistinctly. From this it follows that there can be no value-free facts about the British constitution. All is not hopelessly relative. But to the extent that there is agreement about the nature and meaning of the constitution it is essentially because certain understandings are accepted from a broad range of interpretative positions. This type of agreement exists, however, only if we stick within what Charles Taylor calls 'narrow-gauge discoveries'; that is, statements which 'just because they are, taken alone, compatible with a great number of political frameworks, can bathe in an atmosphere of value neutrality'.[22]

Take, for example, our understanding of the prerogative powers of the Crown. In considering the constitutional position, we may all agree that the Queen cannot unilaterally exercise the prerogative power to declare war on a foreign power. This consensus arises, I suggest, because the statement accords with virtually all theories of the role of the monarchy under the British constitution. When we

[22] C. Taylor, *Philosophical Papers 2. Philosophy and the Human Sciences* (Cambridge, 1985), 90.

consider the Queen's powers in relation to the appointment and dismissal of Ministers or the dissolution of Parliament, however, the issue becomes a matter of some controversy. Does the Queen simply perform a 'dignified' constitutional role, suggesting that she must exercise her powers solely in accordance with the wishes of her Ministers? Or does the Queen have a residual 'efficient' role to resolve critical constitutional periods and actively exercise the power of a Head of State? In examining this issue, we are not concerned with constitutional fact. The problem is not fundamentally one of presenting evidence within an established constitutional order. The issue is controversial precisely because different theories of the constitution accord different roles to the monarch.

Far from being unusual, this example illustrates the sorts of issue which commonly arise in public law. It suggests that any serious study of the subject must be interpretative and must seek an understanding of practices by examining their meaning from a variety of perspectives provided by a range of explanatory frameworks. Indeed, it might be argued that such an approach is especially important in relation to the British constitution, precisely because of the factors which have led to the traditional dominance of the 'common law mind'. That is, it is because of the remarkable degree of continuity in British governmental structures that we have been required to make incremental adaptation of constitutional arrangements in accordance with changes in social and political conditions. These adaptations, to an unusual degree, have not been made by formal processes resulting in changes in the rules but through the modification, adjustment and elaboration of custom and practice. Evolutionary changes of this nature can only be understood by taking an interpretative approach.

These sorts of ideas are not in themselves novel. It is, I take it, precisely the point which Sir Ian Gilmour had in mind in suggesting that in Britain the 'idea of the constitution' is more important than the constitution itself.[23] But, just like the comments made on the connections between public law and politics, such statements tend to be made without any systematic consideration being given to their implications. One reason for failing to carry through the implications of such insights is that it leads quite rapidly to an opening of Pandora's Box.

---

[23] I. Gilmour, *Inside Right: A Study of Conservatism* (London, 1977), 70; quoted in C. Turpin, *British Government and the Constitution* (London, 1985), 17.

THEORY AND PRACTICE

One major difficulty with this theoretical approach to the study of public law is that it does not accord a privileged status to professional understandings or to the traditional grid of interpretation. If theorization means that we genuinely seek to understand the institutions and practices of public law, then any characterization of the meanings underlying these practices is open to question by someone offering an alternative explanation. The criterion of objectivity—or, perhaps more accurately, inter-subjectivity—is simply that interpretation which renders an account of the practice in the most illuminating light or which clarifies the meaning that otherwise was obscure or fragmentary. Problems arise from taking this approach as a result of both the range and potential complexity of the competing explanations. We are immediately faced with the need to confront such basic questions as the nature of order in society, the foundations of authority in government and the character of democracy. In turn, this feeds in to second order—but no less perplexing—questions about the meaning of such concepts as sovereignty, responsibility, rights, representation, and the rule of law.

With this approach we might begin with a consideration of the practices of government. We are immediately confronted with an interpretative question of how we should characterize behaviour in government. How we describe events, ascribe causality between events, impute motive or intention, discern meaning, and apply norms as standards of evaluation are all interpretative matters. Furthermore, the primacy of the normative realm, which is the characteristic of traditional constitutional analysis, should not be assumed. To view governmental practice from the perspective of constitutional norms may result in misinterpretation. If, for example, we seek an interpretation of practice from the perspective that 'Ministers should do X in circumstances Y' this could lead us to an uncritical and unwarranted ascription of behaviour to the authority of a constitutional standard.

It was as a result of perceived distortions flowing from such an approach that many political scientists were led to reject the orthodox normative interpretation. They switched instead to behavioural analysis. Consequently, rather than adopting a normative perspective they commenced with an investigation of the behaviour of Ministers. Through a systematic study of behaviour they then sought to derive general conclusions. As a result, they tried to assess the variables at play in the practice of Ministerial resignation. The results, as S. E. Finer's classic analysis on this subject shows, are interesting.[24] For ministerial resignation to occur, Finer argues that three variables have to come into alignment: the Minister must be compliant, the Prime Minister firm, and the party clamorous. Finer suggests that this conjunction is rare—and is quite fortuitous. Furthermore, from a normative (or constitutionalist) viewpoint, it is also indiscriminate in the sense that which Ministers escape and which are caught has very little to do with the gravity of the offence.

What Finer's analysis shows is that the focus on government practices from the perspective of traditional constitutional analysis is misleading. It leads too easily to a false ascription of meaning to events and, by trying to generalize from the exceptional cases and ignoring the common case (in which resignation does not occur), has a distortive effect. The behavioural focus therefore seems to provide an important corrective to traditional constitutional analysis. However, in excluding the normative in the exercise of determining 'scientific' laws of ministerial resignation, it may go too far. That is, the beliefs of actors involved in the processes of government, however partial or misguided, must surely form part of any explanatory theory. Consequently, while the purely normative approach of traditional constitutional analysis can be distortive, so too may a purely descriptive account. The general point here is that an exercise in interpretation constitutes a fusion of description and evaluation; there may be a perennial tension between the empirical and the normative but this must be recognized and neither element may be ignored in seeking an explanatory theory which is rooted in practice.

Some may suggest that this conclusion is scarcely surprising in relation to those governmental practices influenced by constitutional conventions. Conventions, after all, are the product of a combination of the descriptive and the normative since the existence, meaning and weight of the convention depend on historical practice. If sound, however, my argument must apply across the field of public law. Let us examine, then, the role of the courts in public law. By

[24] S. E. Finer, 'The Individual Responsibility of Ministers' 34 *Public Admin.* 377 (1956).

way of illustration, consider the case of *R* v. *Secretary of State for the Home Department, ex parte Swati.*[25]

In the *Swati* case the Court of Appeal denied Swati leave to obtain judicial review of an immigration officer's decision to refuse him entry to the country as a visitor for one week. Under the Immigration Rules Swati, since he did not have an entry clearance certificate, was obliged to satisfy the immigration officer that he was 'genuinely seeking entry for the period of the visit as stated by him'. After interview, Swati was denied entry since the immigration officer was not satisfied that he was seeking entry for the limited period of one week. While in detention pending removal, Swati applied for judicial review of the officer's decision. Applicants for judicial review must, however, obtain the leave of the court and in this case it was refused on the grounds that there was no evidence of procedural irregularity or irrationality and that the court had to take account of alternative remedies available to the applicant. The latter point referred to the existence of a statutory right of appeal against the decision; the drawback of this remedy from the applicant's viewpoint was that it was exercisable only after he had left the country.

How are we to interpret this decision? Generally lawyers would analyse the Court of Appeal's decision by reference to the existing normative legal material to assess whether it accords with the weight of authority. The immigration officer was, for example, under a duty to give reasons for her decision. Was the bald statement that she was not satisfied sufficient? Here it might be argued that existing authority requires that reasons should not simply be intelligible but also probative.[26] On the other hand, to impose that requirement might be to require 'not the reasons for the refusal, but the reasons for the reasons for refusal'.[27] A second issue for consideration is that, even if one accepts the view that where an alternative remedy exists judicial review should be permitted only in exceptional circumstances, it may be argued that these circumstances actually existed in this case. Since the effectiveness and convenience of these alternative remedies are relevant factors, it might on this point be argued that the opportunity to appeal only

[25] [1986] 1 W.L.R. 477.
[26] See, e.g., *Re Poyser & Mills Arbitration* [1964] 2 Q.B. 467.
[27] [1986] 1 W.L.R. 477 at 490 (per Parker LJ).

after being returned to Pakistan was scarcely an effective remedy in this case and, on that ground, leave should have been granted. Such arguments form part of conventional legal analysis. We might note that there is an element in the analysis which concerns not just the strength of previous authority but also how we conceive of the process of legal analysis. The thrust of our arguments in respect of this case might, for example, be affected by our conception of the judicial process and whether we regard rules or principles as being the basic building blocks of our legal order.[28] Consequently, the issue of whether or not the Court of Appeal reached the correct decision in the *Swati* case requires that we subject their justifications to critical scrutiny in order to assess whether, as a matter of logic, they are convincing. It also requires us to consider whether their interpretation of the law provides us the most convincing elaboration of that theory which provides the best account of the nature of British administrative law.

Arguments of this nature are complex enough. However, it should be noted that such arguments commence from the premise that the normative material of law is authoritative. But, just as constitutional analysis may distort explanation, so also with conventional legal analysis. What, for example, of sociological explanations? Might not the behaviour of judges be examined to assess whether or not the weight placed on injustice to the 'immigrant' is equal to the weight placed on a similar degree of injustice to a policeman?[29] Alternatively, we might examine the trends of judicial review in the 1980s and assess the burden which this has placed on the High Court. What we would find is that civil applications for judicial review more than doubled between 1981 and 1985 and that on average immigration cases constituted around 40 per cent of these applications, and in 1986 constituted nearly 60 per cent.[30] Given the strain of this caseload on the courts, might not the *Swati* decision, effectively removing the remedy of judicial review in the largest category of immigration cases, best be

[28] I refer here to the debate within jurisprudence on the nature of adjudication: see, H. L. A. Hart, *The Concept of Law* (Oxford, 1961), chap. 7; R. Dworkin, *Taking Rights Seriously* (Cambridge, Mass., 1977), chaps. 2–4; id., *A Matter of Principle* (Cambridge, Mass., 1985), Pt. II; id., *Law's Empire* (London, 1986).

[29] Cf. *R. v. Chief Constable of the Merseyside Police, ex parte Calveley* [1986] 2 W.L.R. 144.

[30] See M. Sunkin, 'What is happening to applications for judicial review?' (1987) 50 *M.L.R.* 432.

56   *Interpretation in Public Law*

viewed as an administrative or managerial response by the High Court to this situation?

We can therefore look to a broad range of analyses in our effort to understand the decision in *Swati*. And again, a clear division between normative and behavioural explanations runs through these various analyses. The challenge of interpretative theory, however, is to break down that distinction and to seek some sort of synthesis. One cannot assume a priori the primacy of the normative realm. Neither can one simply ascribe causes from effects. The issues involved concern the interpenetration of the normative and the empirical. Both dimensions need to be examined carefully in providing explanatory theories in public law.[31]

This could be an illuminating exercise, but the scale of the challenge should not be underestimated. In particular we must be particularly conscious of the problems which could arise both in the ascription of causal effectiveness to intentions and also with regard to the temporal question.[32] The former problem arises from the fact that an action may be informed by a number of intentions and it is therefore only by ranking intentions that we can begin to ascribe in terms of causal effectiveness. In attempting to explain a Ministerial resignation, for example, we need not only assess the range of possible intentions but must also weigh their influence on conduct. Did the Minister resign: (*a*) because his actions infringed the constitutional conventions on ministerial responsibility and impelled resignation?; (*b*) because of his failure to maintain the confidence of the Prime Minister or Cabinet colleagues?; (*c*) because of his failure to maintain support of the Parliamentary party?; (*d*) in order to assist his party by deflecting and deflating a challenge to the competence of the Government?; (*e*) in an attempt to weaken the Government, assume the moral high-ground and launch a challenge for the party leadership? The problem with many accounts, even more sophisticated accounts,[33] is that no serious attempt is made to

[31] For a similar argument see: S. Lukes, *Essays in Social Theory* (London, 1977), chap. 1.

[32] See A. MacIntyre, 'The indispensability of political theory' in D. Miller and L. Siedentop (eds.), *The Nature of Political Theory* (Oxford, 1983), 17 at pp. 25–32.

[33] See G. Marshall, *Constitutional Conventions. The Rules and Forms of Political Accountability* (Oxford, 1984); Brazier, *Constitutional Practice* (Oxford, 1988). For a similar analysis in relation to Brazier's work see T. C. Daintith, 'Political Programmes and the Content of the Constitution' in W. Finnie,

rank intentions: would the Minister still have resigned had the Prime Minister been protective? the parliamentary party supportive? the Government strong? the Prime Minister's position impregnable?

The temporal problem concerns the period of time within which we interpret action. That is, effective understanding involves understanding 'how far the short-term intentions of an agent are dependent for their existence and character upon his or her longer-term intentions'.[34] Intentions may carry different weights in assessing behaviour depending on the timescale of the analysis.

From the above, we can see that any attempt to derive theories which are sensitive to practice is anything but straightforward. The project provides a challenging agenda. But can we justify such a major re-orientation of the subject?

THE INTERPRETATIVE APPROACH

The interpretative approach which I have advocated rejects any approach which incorporates an implicit predisposition in favour of a particular type of interpretation which is compatible with a professionally prescribed view of the subject. It opens up a range of important issues for examination and encourages us to render explicit, systematic and rigorous what in legal writing and legal practice is often implicit and based on intuition or 'common sense'. The implications of adopting this theoretical approach to public law is that all matters of interpretation are rooted in explanatory theories; that a broad range of theories can be constructed; that none can claim a privileged status; and that all must be equally subject to critical scrutiny. In this sense all knowledge in public law is theoretical. This does not mean that facts are irrelevant; rather that they must be ordered in some way before they acquire significance. And this can be achieved only by constructing a 'map' of the subject.

C. Himsworth, and N. Walker (eds.), *Edinburgh Essays in Public Law* (Edinburgh, 1991), 41 at pp. 44–5.

[34] MacIntyre, 'The indispensability of political theory', at p. 27.

4

The Structures of Public Law Thought

ONE basic objective of this book is to indicate that there has been little genuine debate within the subject of public law. Confusion reigns, since any disputes which do arise seem to be conducted on the assumption that the issue of controversy is that of the true weight of the evidence whereas in fact such disputes tend to concern the more fundamental issue of what constitutes evidence. Consequently, I suggest that there is little consensus amongst public lawyers about the basic contours of their discipline. Consensus exists only amongst those who share the same theoretical framework. If this analysis seems convincing our most important task in seeking to understand the subject must be to examine the conceptual structures which dominate public law thought. It is only by analysing the languages and traditions that shape these contrasting maps of the landscape, by charting their transformations, and by comparing and evaluating them in the light of our horizons that we will be able to achieve some progress in the subject.

STYLES OF PUBLIC LAW THOUGHT

The next stage in this project must therefore be to try to identify the basic conceptual structures that dominate the public law landscape. My argument here is that there exist two basic 'styles' of thinking about public law matters. My use of the term 'style' in this context is deliberate. What I have in mind is a spirit, culture or set of values that may be manifest in particular writings even though it is not made explicit. The idea of style suggests something that is neither fixed nor finished. There is no changeless core which can be precisely defined or which can be identified by reference to an authoritative text. The process of identifying adherence to these styles is not a matter of logical deduction or of necessary connection. Incorporated within these styles are a variety of beliefs, many of which may be pulling in different directions or competing with one another. Nevertheless, although this idea of style is rather fluid that attribute should not be taken to suggest that the idea of style lacks distinctiveness. Styles have identity; but that identity will be of a complex nature.

Styles are amalgams of a number of forces, are constantly being developed and are likely to exhibit internal tensions. Nevertheless, they constitute identifiable wholes. How then do we identify these styles? As a starting point we might borrow Weber's notion of 'ideal types'.[1] Weber argued that since reality is infinitely various it cannot be classified and conceptualized in a definitive manner. One way in which we might obtain an understanding of society is by constructing ideal types of social action. These ideal types are not constructed by seeking to generalize from experience but are deliberately constructed on certain assumptions about conduct. In this manner Weber is able to develop models for understanding certain social phenomena, such as the economy or law, without denying the variety of activity encompassed within these practices. As a starting point, then, the ideal types of these two dominant style of public thought will be sketched.

THE IDEAL TYPES OF NORMATIVISM AND FUNCTIONALISM

The two basic styles which dominate public law thought I call 'normativism' and 'functionalism'. I shall argue that between the ideal-typical representatives of each of these contrasting styles there is an almost complete lack of consensus over the fundamental issues of public law. The disagreements between representatives of these two styles are not explicable in terms of the weight of the evidence within a neutral framework definitive of the subject. These disagreements are rooted in different conceptions of the nature of the subject. These differences must be understood in terms of the culture and values which underpin their styles of thought; and ultimately these differences are founded on differences concerning fundamental questions about the nature of human beings, their

---

[1] M. Weber, *Economy and Society* (G. Roth and C. Wittich (eds.)) (New York, 1968), 19–22.

societies and their government. In order to expose these fundamental differences and to justify these claims I will first try to
present the basic characteristics of the normativist and functionalist
styles in their ideal-typical forms.

The normativist style in public law is rooted in a belief in the
ideal of the separation of powers and in the need to subordinate
government to law. This style highlights law's adjudicative and
control functions and therefore its rule orientation and its
conceptual nature. Normativism essentially reflects an ideal of the
autonomy of law. The functionalist style in public law, by contrast,
views law as part of the apparatus of government. Its focus is upon
law's regulatory and facilitative functions and therefore is orientated
to aims and objectives and adopts an instrumentalist social policy
approach. Functionalism reflects an ideal of progressive evolutionary
change.

When presented in this form the idea that there exist fundamental
disagreements between those who adopt these different styles is
scarcely surprising. Because what is evident when the styles are
presented in this form is that there is not even agreement about the
concept of law. For the normativist, law precedes legislation
whereas for the functionalist legislation, as an embodiment of the
democratic will, is the highest form of law. Differences of a similar
nature may be seen with respect to such ideas as rights and
representation. The normativist believes that rights precede the
state whereas for the functionalist rights emanate from the state.
Within the functionalist style democratic representation is the
foundation of legitimacy whereas within normativism the status of
democratic representation is treated in a more ambivalent manner.
Within the functionalist style, democracy reflects the idea of ethics
in politics; for many who adopt a normativist style it is associated
with uniformity and mediocrity. In surveying these general differences we may say that the functionalist style can be seen as trying to
break down the dichotomies that have been erected by the
normativists between (on the one hand) government/discretion/
policy and (on the other) law/rules/rights.

Behind these different conceptions of law, legislation, rights, and
representation lie perhaps even more fundamental disagreements.
Normativism and functionalism, for example, adopt fundamentally
different conceptions of liberty, order, and the state. The normativist views liberty as the absence of external constraint while the

functionalist views freedom as an actual capacity for doing or enjoying something. For the normativist liberty might be identified with an absence of legal controls, whereas for the functionalist greater legal controls might mean more liberty. Significant differences may also exist with the conception of order in society. Many normativists adopt an atomistic view of the relationship between individual and the state while functionalism rends to be built on an organic conception of that relationship. Finally, the positive state is generally characterized by the normativist as 'the servile state' while the functionalist views it as an expression of the growing moralization of society.

In presenting these sketches of the styles I have sought to construct models which accentuate the differences. I have done so in order to provide an insight into these two dominant conceptual structures of public law thought. These sketches are, however, simply starting points. I do not suggest that there are two distinct schools and that adherents of each of these schools adopt a uniform approach to the subject. As I have already mentioned, these styles are amalgams of a number of forces and are being constantly developed, often in response to internal tensions. But what should now be clear is that these differences between normativism and functionalism are not simply differences of emphasis; they fundamentally reflect differences of principle. In short, public law consciousness in Britain is a polarized consciousness and it is in the styles of normativism and functionalism that we may identify the essential polarities.

STAGES IN UNDERSTANDING PUBLIC LAW THOUGHT

This sketch of the dominant styles provides us with a focus for considering the nature of public law thought. But in order to assess the importance of these styles in understanding the nature of public law we must engage in two forms of exercise. First, we must seek to understand the sets of values that inform these styles. In order to undertake this task we need to examine the extent to which these styles acquire their character and their shape from certain political ideologies. Our first task, which is undertaken in the following two chapters, is to examine the extent to which these styles are rooted in the major political ideologies which the nineteenth century bequeathed to the twentieth.

Secondly, in order to understand the importance of these styles to the practice of public law, we must examine the extent to which these styles are identifiable in public law discourse. It is, I hope, obvious that in studying work within public law I am not suggesting that all writers on the subject can neatly be fitted into particular styles in catalogue fashion. That would imply a degree of reflection and coherence in the work of most writers which it is part of my thesis to suggest does not exist. And the reason why this degree of self-reflection does not exist is precisely because we have failed to think through the foundations of the subject and nature of the exercise of public law. Nevertheless, it is evident in the thesis I am presenting that, in relation to most contributions to the subject, the characteristics of either the normativist or functionalist style should be apparent.

Finally, after having examined the intellectual foundations of these styles and assessed their importance in understanding the practice of public law, we should be in a position to reflect on the current state of the subject. By virtue of the claims which are being made it is clear that in evaluating the clash between these styles the answer to the question of which is best suited to the needs of the day cannot be the subject of deduction or demonstration. But this should not deter us from engaging in the critical exercise of seeking to root thought in life.

5

Foundations of Normativism

THE foundations of the normativist style in public law are to be found in the political ideologies of conservatism and liberalism. These are strange bedfellows. Conservativism as a form of thought is traditionalist, is primarily concerned with the issue of authority and views the individual organically, as part of a social order. Liberalism is a rationalistic theory which has little regard for the past, is primarily concerned with liberty and is constructed on the assumption of the autonomy of the individual. Despite such important differences, these two political ideologies nevertheless share certain affinities with respect to their visions of law and government. It is this common core of shared understanding about law and government that provides us with an insight into the normativist style in public law. In order to reveal these foundations we must therefore examine the main tenets of conservative and liberal political thought.

Since there is no strict school nor formula of belief that we may label conservatism or liberalism, an insight into the character of these political ideologies is sought through an examination of particular theorists. This approach presents us with a particular problem since we must ensure that the representative chosen provides us with a good insight into that political theory. However, this method also has certain advantages. By choosing to study one representative, for example, we might obtain a more acute insight into the attempt to present the theory as a coherent whole; that is, we may be able to re-create in a more sympathetic fashion the sense of what connects with what. By studying one thinker who has contributed much to the development of a certain type of political thought we might, as a result, avoid the problem of simply re-creating mythologies. The representatives—Michael Oakeshott on conservatism and F. A. Hayek on liberalism—are chosen because they seem to be the most insightful of the modern theorists on the issues which are central to our concerns.

THE CONSERVATIVE DIMENSION

Oakeshott and political thought

Although existing mainly in the form of essays, Michael Oakeshott's work nevertheless constitutes a systematic theory of human conduct and politics. Some would argue that his voice is unique and denies easy classification; he is 'a traditionalist with few traditional beliefs, an "idealist" who is more sceptical than many positivists, a lover of liberty who repudiates liberalism, an individualist who prefers Hegel to Locke'.[1] Nevertheless, although shedding much of the metaphysical or religious foundations of traditional conservative thought, Oakeshott's work can be seen as an attempt to portray a systematic and authentic account of conservative political thought in the contemporary world.

Oakeshott's first book, *Experience and its Modes*,[2] was an exploration of the idea of philosophy. While a formal study of the nature and tasks of philosophy, this book is particularly interesting because it projects a theory of knowledge which subsequently provided the foundation for his studies of politics. Many of these essays on politics are collected together in *Rationalism and Politics* (1962). It is only much later, in *On Human Conduct* (1975), that Oakeshott provided us with a comprehensive account of his views on government and law. Nevertheless, despite this work spanning almost half a century, it can be understood as forming a coherent and systematic theory. His work, therefore, is especially valuable for our purpose. While Oakeshott addresses basic questions concerning politics, government, and law, these are rooted in a particular theory of knowledge and human conduct. It is perhaps because of Oakeshott's philosophical approach to his subject that we are able, through the study of his thought, more clearly to discern both the roots of conservative political thought and its links with a particular approach to the issues of public law.

Epistemological foundations of political thought

Much of Oakeshott's writing on politics takes the form of a critique of Rationalism in post-Renaissance political thought. Rationalist politics, argues Oakeshott, is the enemy of the

---

[1] M. Cranston, 'Michael Oakeshott's Politics' (1967) 28 *Encounter* 82.
[2] (Cambridge, 1933).

traditional, the customary and the habitual. The Rationalist views the mind as a finely tempered, neutral instrument and never doubts the authority and power of reason. Political activity consists in bringing 'the social, political, legal and institutional inheritance of his society before the tribunal of his intellect; the rest is rational administration'.[3] Politics thus becomes a matter of solving problems in the manner of an engineer by the application of the appropriate technique; it is the 'politics of felt need', the 'politics of perfection', and the 'politics of uniformity'.[4]

In order to understand the basis of Oakeshott's critique of Rationalism in politics we must appreciate its epistemological roots. Oakeshott's analysis has its source in an Hegelian epistemo- logy which enters English philosophy through the work of F. H. Bradley and Bernard Bosanquet. This Hegelian approach rejects a strict separation between the universal and the particular and it therefore challenges the Cartesian opposition between knowledge and belief. The Hegelian method postulates the idea of the 'concrete universal'. This concrete universal unites universality and particularity and asserts the primacy of experience. Experience is the only reality. Working within this Hegelian framework Oakeshott also suggests that experience may be viewed from limited standpoints or 'modes'. These epistemological questions are examined in his first book.

Oakeshott's objective in *Experience and its Modes* is to clarify the nature of philosophy. His method is to distinguish philosophy, which he equates with experience, from the various modes of experience. According to Oakeshott, the criterion of experience is the achievement of an absolutely coherent world of experience. Coherence rather than correspondence is, therefore, the criterion of truth and reality. And whenever experience is pursued without hindrance it is called philosophy.

While we seek the achievement of a coherent world of experience, we might, nevertheless, at any given moment construct a 'mode'. These modes are abstractions; they amount to the organization of the whole of experience from a partial and defective point of view. Oakeshott examines the most important modes of experience, which he identifies as science, history, and practice,[5] in order to

[3] M. Oakeshott, *Rationalism in Politics* (London, 1962), 4.
[4] Ibid. 5–6.
[5] In a subsequent essay, Oakeshott adds to these the contemplative, or poetic,

show how their methods are partial and defective and therefore do not take us nearer the overall coherence of the world of experience which it is the objective of philosophy to pursue.

Oakeshott suggests that each mode of experience constitutes a self-contradiction since the aim it pursues contradicts the criterion of coherence it implicitly acknowledges. Philosophy, by contrast, does not elaborate a mode of experience but rather requires its surrender. In *Experience and its Modes* Oakeshott seeks to demonstrate this by examining history, science, and practice. In relation to history, for example, he argues that history is a world of thought or ideas and not a world of fact since nothing is simply 'given'. It is constructed rather than discovered by the historian. The only history we have is that which is made by historians. There is no history independent of experience; the course of events as such is past and is incapable of entering present experience. Historical experience is partial because of the essential arbitrariness involved in distinguishing one historical event from another. This defect, which history cannot ever overcome, ultimately renders it defective.

When considering science, Oakeshott's aim is slightly different. The idea that science is a product of thought, a world of experience rather than pure fact, is not really controversial. The key issue which Oakeshott addresses in relation to science is the belief that science *is* experience; that is, the belief that the methods of science are fitted to a reality which exists outside scientific thought. His target of attack here is positivism, which we can understand as the identification of natural science with knowledge itself. Oakeshott argues that the positivist fails to identify the essentially abstract character of science as a mode of experience. He argues that science moves within a world of ideas. It is the world conceived in terms of quantity. We do not in scientific experience move from an external world of things to an abstract world of ideas; we always move within a single world of quantitative ideas. It is the world conceived from an abstract and limited standpoint; the world conceived in terms of measurement. Science ultimately is self-contradictory precisely because, although it begins with a supposal about reality,

---

mode: see 'The voice of poetry in the conversation of mankind' in *Rationalism in Politics*, 197. We might note here that the language adopted by Oakeshott ('the conversation of mankind') is that of Bagehot. See W. Bagehot, *The English Constitution* (R. H. S. Crossman (ed.)) (London, 1963), 274.

it also depends upon a concrete reality; and once scientists admit the necessarily hypothetical character of that knowledge, they cease to be scientists. Science, then, is not the whole of experience but only an abstract mode of experience.

Oakeshott finally considers the world of practical experience. He considers the practical, the orientation to action, to be our most familiar mood. Here he challenges the notion that practice is activity and not thought. His argument is not simply that action is preceded by thought. Action is a form of thought. This does not mean that action is reflective or self-conscious. But nothing is simply given and immediate. Everything we do belongs to a world of meaning. Nothing escapes the criterion of experience. Practice implies a world of fact and is concerned with the alteration of 'what is' to make it conform with an unrealized idea, a 'to be'. It is important to recognize, however, that this world of fact is presupposed. Furthermore, because practice, like any other mode of experience, pursues coherence the 'to be' is more coherent than 'what is'. Coherence, however, must be understood in terms of value, of 'what ought to be'. But this discrepancy between 'is' and 'ought' can never be resolved. Every practical success is partial since a new problem always emerges demanding a new resolution. If the discrepancy between 'is' and 'ought' were ever finally resolved in effect the world of practical experience would be destroyed. Practice, like all other abstract modes of experience, is ultimately self-contradictory.

As mentioned, Oakeshott's objective here is to identify the nature of philosophy. In Oakeshott's conception philosophy is a radical undertaking; it requires the renunciation of anything less than an absolutely coherent world of experience. It is an activity that must be distinguished from the various abstract modes of experience. Philosophy can make no relevant criticism of these modes; philosophy is, for example, an escape from practical living, a refuge from life.

At this stage the reader may be left wondering about the relevance of all this. It should be emphasized that this rather high-flown detour from our primary thrust in this book has not been made in order to identify the nature of philosophy. Its main objective is to understand Oakeshott's idea of the modes of experience. The idea of modes, for example, helps us to appreciate the limitations of a scientific approach to the practical matters of law and politics.[6] In particular, Oakeshott's conception provides us with an insightful critique of Dicey's method in *Law of the Constitution*.[7] Oakeshott, for example, indicates that the only relevant criticism within a mode is by the methods of that mode. By invoking the idea of modes, then, we obtain a much sharper distinction between the purposes of the historian and the lawyer than Dicey outlines. And if the only relevant criticism of the practical experience of law is that of life then we can clearly identify the limitations of seeking to evaluate through the prism of science. Practical truth is the truth we can live by and act upon.

There is, however, also a more specific reason for considering Oakeshott's modes of experience. Without understanding this philosophical background it is difficult to appreciate the distinctiveness of Oakeshott's critique of rationalism. According to Oakeshott the 'hidden spring' of rationalism is a doctrine about human knowledge. In order to clarify this Oakeshott distinguishes between two sorts of knowledge, which he calls technical and practical knowledge. Technical (or scientific) knowledge is susceptible of precise formulation. It is the sort of knowledge that may be laid down in rules and can be learned from books. The technique of cookery is contained in cookery books and the technique of discovery in natural science may be found in the rules of research, observation and verification. Practical (or traditional) knowledge, however, is not susceptible of formulation of this kind. It is 'know how' which is often expressed in the customary or traditional way of doing things. No one, for example, supposes that the knowledge that belongs to a good cook is confined to what is or may be written down in the cookery book. This type of knowledge can neither be taught nor learned. It exists only in use and may be imparted and acquired through apprenticeship and practice.

Oakeshott argues that these two sorts of knowledge, distinguishable but inseparable, are the twin components of knowledge involved in every concrete human activity. The error of Rationalism lies in its attempt to reduce the complexity of experience to rules, to technical knowledge. 'The cookery book' Oakeshott writes, 'is not an independently generated beginning from which cooking can spring; it is nothing more than an abstract of somebody's knowledge of how to cook: it is the stepchild, not the parent of the

---

[6] See Chap. 1, pp. 17–23.   [7] See Chap. 1, pp. 14–17.

activity.'[8] The rules are internal to the practices. We need something else—some notion of judgment which emerges from practical experience—in order to understand how and when to apply (and modify) the technical rules.

Rationalism in politics

Having considered the various modes of experience (including science and practice) and the different sorts of knowledge involved in concrete human activity, we may now address Oakeshott's argument about the emergence of Rationalism in politics. His argument is essentially that Rationalist politics developed as a result of the disintegration of traditional polities. The new rulers and the newly formed political societies of the post-Renaissance period lacked political experience. This was fertile ground for inculcating the view of politics as technique. Government comes to be seen as a matter of *administration* rather than *rule* and the ideologies of Machiavelli, Locke, Bentham, and Marx provide us with the modern cribs to politics; a political training in default of a political education.[9] Initially, these cribs were designed to instruct new rulers or new ruling classes. With the founding of new societies such as the United States, however, the entire political society is founded on a Rationalist politics of abstract principle. Rationalism, then, is born of political inexperience. The consequence is expressed by Oakeshott thus:[10]

Like a foreigner or a man out of his social class, he [the Rationalist] is bewildered by a tradition and habit of behaviour of which he knows only the surface; a butler or an observant house-maid has the advantage of him. And he conceives a contempt for what he does not understand; habit and custom appear bad in themselves, a kind of nescience of behaviour. And by some strange self-deception, he attributes to tradition (which, of course, is pre-eminently fluid) the rigidity and fixity of character which in fact belongs to ideological politics. Consequently, the Rationalist is a dangerous and expensive character to have in control of affairs, and he does most damage, not when he fails to master the situation (his politics, of course, are always in terms of mastering situations and surmounting crises), but when he appears to be successful; for the price we pay for each of his apparent successes is a firmer hold of the intellectual fashion of Rationalism upon the whole life of society.

[8] *Rationalism in Politics*, 119.
[9] Ibid. 23–7.   [10] Ibid. 31.

Rationalism, then, has its roots, not in the rise of science or the application of scientific methods to non-scientific phenomena, but with a misunderstanding of reason and the mistaken identification of knowledge with technique.

Rationality, as distinguished from Rationalism, is considered by Oakeshott as 'faithfulness to the knowledge we have of how to conduct the specific activity we are engaged in'.[11] This faithfulness does not, however, suggest that there is nothing more to be achieved in activity. Our knowledge is never fixed and finished but is fluid and our objective in activity is to enhance its coherence. But what is the activity of politics?

For Oakeshott, politics is 'the activity of attending to the arrangements of a set of people whom chance or choice have brought together'. The activity 'springs neither from instant desires, nor from general principles, but from the existing behaviour themselves'. A political ideology, then, should be viewed as an abridgement of a particular tradition. In itself there is no harm in an abridgement; it is possible 'that the distorting mirror of an ideology will reveal important hidden passages in the tradition, as a caricature reveals the potentialites of a face'. But it is dangerous insofar as the ideology may become a substitute for the tradition—the servant become the master—because politics involves 'the pursuit, not of a dream, or of a general principle, but of an intimation'.[12]

The emphasis here is on politics as a tradition of behaviour. Such a tradition of behaviour 'is neither fixed nor finished; it has no changeless centre to which understanding can anchor itself; there is no sovereign purpose to be perceived or invariable direction to be detected; there is no model to be copied, idea to be realised, or rule to be followed'.[13] 'In political activity', writes Oakeshott, 'men sail a boundless and bottomless sea; there is neither harbour for shelter nor floor for anchorage, neither starting-place nor appointed destination. The enterprise is to keep afloat on an even keel.'[14] But this does not mean that the tradition of behaviour is arbitrary and without identity. The idea that provides it with cohesion is a 'principle of *continuity*: authority is diffused between past, present and future; between the old, the new and what is to come. It is

---

[11] *Rationalism in Politics*, 99–100.
[12] Ibid. 123–5. On politics as 'the pursuit of intimations' see ibid. 133–6.
[13] Ibid. 128.   [14] Ibid.

steady because, though it moves, it is never wholly in motion; and though it is tranquil, it is never wholly at rest. . . . Everything is temporary, but nothing is arbitrary.'[15]

Government and law

Oakeshott's analysis in his essays collected in *Rationalism in Politics* provides us with an insight into a conservative approach to modern politics. The implications for our understanding of the nature of government and law are not presented in a systematic fashion until *On Human Conduct*. In order to situate those views we must begin with Oakeshott's account of the nature of human conduct. Oakeshott suggests that human conduct, which should be understood as reflective consciousness, is structured in terms of 'practices'. A practice is 'a set of considerations, manners, uses, observances, customs, standards, canons, maxims, principles, rules, and offices specifying useful procedures or denoting obligations or duties which relate to human actions and utterances'.[16] Oakeshott identifies two sorts of practices. Practices, he says, may be classified as either 'prudential' or 'moral'. A prudential practice is instrumental in nature, being designed to achieve a specific substantive purpose. A moral practice, on the other hand, is not instrumental to the achievement of any substantive purpose; it is a practice without extrinsic purpose. A railway timetable provides a good and simple example of a prudential practice. Speakers of a common language, by contrast, are bound together by a moral practice. A moral practice, Oakeshott suggests, is like a language 'in being an instrument of understanding and a medium of intercourse, in having a vocabulary and syntax of its own, and in being spoken well or ill'.[17]

Human associations, then, can be viewed as being structured in terms of either prudential or moral practices. Oakeshott calls an association formed of prudential practices an enterprise or transactional association. This may be contrasted with a moral or rule-based association which is not held together by a common purpose but merely by the authority of common practices. Members of an enterprise association are joined in seeking a common substantive satisfaction, whether it be profit maximization as in the case of a

---

[15] Ibid. (original emphasis).
[16] M. Oakeshott, *On Human Conduct* (Oxford, 1975), 55.
[17] Ibid. 62.

company or a change in human behaviour as in the case of the Anti-
Bloodsports League. Enterprise associations may have constitutions,
officers, meetings to determine policy, and so on. But such rules and
practices are merely 'the prudential disposition of the available
resources, instrumental to the pursuit of the common purpose and
desirable in terms of their utility, which in itself lies in their
uninterrupted functionality'.[18] The character of this mode of
association is encapsulated in the notions of purpose, plan, policy,
and power. By way of contrast members of a moral or rule-based
association share nothing other than their recognition of the
authority of those practices; sharers of a common language, for
example, may say what they like so long as they comply with the
canons of that language. Moral association is a human relationship
based on 'the mutual recognition of certain conditions which not
only specify right and wrong in conduct, but are prescriptions of
obligations'.[19]

The significance of this analysis lies in the fact that Oakeshott
believes that 'civil association' is a form of moral association. Civil
association must be viewed essentially in terms of law and of the
constitutional offices of legislative, executive, and adjudicative rule.
For Oakeshott the two most basic activities of civil association are
law-making and ruling. The office of the legislature is sovereign and
is not bound by the sanction of any superior authority, any
constitutive purpose, or the approval of subjects. The 'apparatus of
rule' consists of adjudication and administering and enforcing the
law. Citizens have an obligation to obey law by virtue of the fact
that it is made in accordance with established procedures. This
system of conditions Oakeshott calls *respublica*.[20]

Respublica does not define or describe a common substantive
purpose. It corresponds to Hobbes's idea of *civitas*[21] insofar as it
entails a sovereign right to make law, an obligation on citizens to
obey law, and views civil liberty as based essentially on the subject
having the rights both to have the laws enforced and to act without
restraint in situations governed by the 'circumstantial silence of the
law'.[22] Oakeshott does not, however, adopt the Hobbesian idiom

---

[18] Oakeshott, *On History* (Oxford, 1983), 124.
[19] Ibid. 132.   [20] *On Human Conduct*, 147.
[21] T. Hobbes, *Leviathan* (1651) (C. B. Macpherson (ed.)) (Harmondsworth,
1968), Pt. II.
[22] *On History*, 158.

of social contract. *Respublica* derives its authority from the continuous acknowledgement of citizens and this lies in the recognition of their general obligation to obey law rather than in their response to specific precepts. To recognize a rule as a rule is not to recognize it in terms of approval or disapproval. We recognize it in terms of its *authority* and we recognize subscription to it as an obligation. The authority of *respublica* is the product of history. It has nothing to do with the utility, justice or rationality of the conditions of *respublica*.

But what of law within *respublica*? According to Hobbes, law is a command, the expression of the will of the sovereign. No law can be unjust within his scheme since it is only with the establishment of law that one can distingush between right and wrong. Oakeshott's view of law has certain similarities, but he does not adopt the command theory of law. In order to appreciate Oakeshott's position we must draw a distinction between *lex*, a rule understood in terms of its authenticity, and *jus*, a rule recognized by the rightness of what it prescribes. Oakeshott argues that legal validity is a matter of authenticity rather than justice, whether justice is viewed in terms of intrinsic rationality, utility, or conformity to some fundamental law. The basic requirements of the rule of law, therefore, are merely that a system of law, understood as *lex*, exists as a result of the establishment of legislative, executive and judicial offices.[23] Law is obligatory because it is authoritative.

Oakeshott, however, also contends that these offices are subject to the morality inherent in the rule of law; what may be termed the *jus* of *lex*. These are the conditions which distinguish a legal order: 'rules not secret or retrospective, no obligations save those imposed by law, all associates equally and without exception subject to the obligations imposed by law.'[24] These conditions also entail an independent judiciary which performs a particular type of deliberative role which Oakeshott calls 'an exercise in retrospective casuistry'.[25] That is, adjudication is deliberative rather than deductive; it is concerned with the *meaning* of *lex* in a contingent situation and 'meanings are never deduced or found but are always attributed or given'. Nevertheless, adjudication must not be understood as the arbitrary exercise of the subjective will of the

[23] Ibid. 140–8.
[24] Ibid. 140. See also *On Human Conduct*, 153 n. 1.
[25] *On History*, 145.

judge, nor a resolution in terms of social policy nor 'the common purpose or interest' of civil association. In adjudicating, a meaning is attributed to a rule of law which cannot be said to be correct or incorrect. The conditions to be satisfied are simply that the meaning 'must be one which *lex* will tolerate and one which dispels the uncertainty in such a manner as to settle the dispute without immediately provoking further controversy'.[26] And the *jus* of *lex* may be understood in terms of faithfulness to the formal principles inherent in the character of *lex*.

In Oakeshott's account of the ideal character of civil association, his views on the nature of law and government are rendered explicit. The civil condition is a moral or non-instrumental practice which is not concerned with substantive considerations. In these passages we may, in particular, discern Oakeshott's views on the relationship between freedom and authority. We see, for example, his debt to Hobbes, who placed great emphasis on the idea of authority and sought to detach it from the idea of consent. We can understand what Oakeshott meant when he stated that 'Hobbes is not an absolutist precisely because he is an authoritarian'.[27] Finally, we can see that Oakeshott, while rejecting natural law as a criterion by which to determine the justice of law nevertheless does not accept a purely formal positivist account of law. Oakeshott recognizes a morality inherent in the rule of law and suggests that to deliberate the *jus* of *lex* involves not deduction but a particular kind of moral consideration; that the prescriptions of law 'should not conflict with a prevailing educated moral sensibility' of a people.[28]

The State

According to Oakeshott, civil association must be understood as a form of moral association. Civil association is comprehensive, compulsory, and exclusive since citizens are subject to one sovereign who has authority over all within that jurisdiction and whose laws are obligatory. It is a rule-articulated association which leaves its citizens free to pursue their own interests; civil association is not constituted for any common purpose. The key to civil association as a moral association is to be found in the office of rule and the

[26] *On Human Conduct*, 134.
[27] Oakeshott, 'Introduction' in T. Hobbes, *Leviathan* (Oxford, 1946), p. lvii.
[28] *On History*, 160.

nature of the rule of law. Civil association, however, is not sustained by a universal moral reason. But neither is it a form of enterprise association. If it were, it would not be an association of equal citizens but of members with differing status; subjects would not be free to pursue their own purposes but would be required to perform particular roles; government would be a matter of management rather than rule; and government would also be provisional rather than unconditional and non-retractable. The authority of civil association is an endowment which is not traceable to any particular source and which lies only in 'continuous acknowledgement' based not on acts of obedience 'but in the continuous recognition of the obligation to subscribe to its prescriptions because it has a certain shape'.[29]

Oakeshott here is identifying the ideal character of civil association. In the final essay in *On Human Conduct*, however, he turns his attention to the question of the place which this ideal character occupies as a practical engagement in history. That is, he addresses the question of the state.

Oakeshott traces the emergence of the modern state from the transformation of feudal relations into an association defined by law; in other words, through the transformation of a 'lordly proprietor of a domain' into a single, inalienable sovereign ruler occupying an office of authority.[30] He argues that our views on the nature of the modern state have been polarized between two modes of identification. First, there is the conception of the state as *societas*. The idea of the state as *societas* corresponds to civil association in that it provides a vision of the state as a non-purposive, rule-based institution. This conception of the state underpins the work of Machiavelli, Hobbes, Locke, and Montesquieu. Secondly, some theorists—including Bacon, Fourier, Marx, and the Webbs—have formed a view of the state as *universitas*. *Universitas* may be identified with enterprise association since it embodies the idea of a managerial state constituted in the pursuit of a set of purposes.

Oakeshott suggests that the state 'may perhaps be understood as an unresolved tension·between the two irreconcilable dispositions

---

[29] Oakeshott, 'The Vocabulary of a Modern European State' (1975) XXIII *Political Studies* 319, 328.

[30] Id., *On Human Conduct*, Part III ('On the Character of a Modern European State').

represented by the words *societas* and *universitas*'. This tension, he continues, 'has imposed a particular ambivalence upon all the institutions of a modern state and a specific ambiguity upon its vocabulary of discourse: the muddle in which we now live where "law", "ruling", "politics", etc., each have two discrepant meanings'. Oakeshott believes that this tension 'is central to the understanding of a modern European state and office of its government'.[31] Thus, the issue is not whether the state is an association defined in terms of law, but whether this law is instrumental or non-instrumental. The issue is not whether or not a government is sovereign but whether that government is the custodian of a system of non-instrumental rules or is concerned with the management of a common purpose.

Oakeshott argues that in modern times the conception of the state as *universitas* has taken hold, primarily as a result of the extension of the executive apparatus of civil rule. He suggests that this conception of the state, together with the emergence of Rationalism in politics, has subverted the moral integrity of civil association. In modern times, this has culminated in the emergence of the 'Servile State' in which the state is viewed as a corporate productive enterprise, Parliament has been reduced to a market in which private interests clamour for awards, and civil law has been displaced by the administration of instrumental rules and orders.

Oakeshott and conservatism

Where does Oakeshott stand in relation to conservative thought? Consideration of this question requires us first to examine what is generally understood by conservatism. Following Samuel Huntington, we can begin to assess this question by identifying three broad and conflicting conceptions of conservatism.[32] First, there is the *aristocratic* theory which defines conservatism as 'the ideology of a specific and unique historical movement: the reaction of the feudal–aristocratic–agrarian classes to the French Revolution, liberalism, and to the rise of the bourgeoisie at the end of the eighteenth century and during the first half of the nineteenth century'.[33] This conception views conservatism as a historically

---

[31] *On Human Conduct*, 200–1.
[32] These are taken from Samuel P. Huntington, 'Conservatism as an Ideology' (1957) 51 *American Political Science Review* 454.
[33] Ibid.

specific movement associated with feudalism and the landed interest and opposed to industrialism, democracy, and individualism. Secondly, there is a *situational* conception of conservatism. This conception arises out of a 'distinct but recurring type of historical situation in which a fundamental challenge is directed at established institutions and in which the supporters of those institutions employ conservative ideology in their defense'. The essence of this conception is the 'passionate affirmation of the value of existing institutions'.[34] Thirdly, there is an *autonomous* definition of conservatism in which conservatism is not necessarily connected to any economic group and is not rooted in a particular historical configuration. Under this conception conservatism is an autonomous system of ideas defined in terms of universal values such as justice, order, balance, and moderation.

Huntington argues that, despite the different focus adopted by these three conceptions, they all basically agree as to the content of conservatism as an ideology. That common content, Huntington argues, is found in the basic elements of Edmund Burke's thought. These basic elements are as follows:[35]

1. Human beings are religious creatures and religion is the foundation of civil society.
2. Society is the natural, organic product of slow historical growth.
3. Humans are creatures of instinct and emotion as well as reason. Prudence, prejudice, experience, and habit are better guides than logic, abstractions, and metaphysics. Truth exists not in universal propositions but in concrete experience.
4. The community is superior to the individual. Rights derive from duties.
5. Social organization is complex and always includes a variety of classes, orders and groups. Individuals, except in an ultimate moral sense, are unequal.
6. A presumption exists in favour of any settled scheme of government against any untried project.

Huntington's argument is that the theory of conservatism to be preferred is that which most adequately and completely explains Burke's ideology. He goes on to argue that the situational theory,

[34] Ibid. 455.
[35] Ibid. at p. 456. On Burke see also Chap. 3 above pp. 45–6.

the defence of established institutions, most closely meets these criteria. While Huntington has identified much of what is generally understood as conservative thought there is one aspect, which is of particular importance for our task, which he seems to under-emphasize. This aspect is brought out by Robert Eccleshall who suggests that 'the function of conservative ideology is to obscure the nature of power relationships by presenting them as permanent and desirable features of human life'.[36] Eccleshall points to the fact that Burke traced the horrors of revolutionary France to an unveiling of illusions:[37]

> But the age of chivalry is gone. That of sophisters, economists, and calculators, has succeeded . . . All the pleasing illusions, which made power gentle and obedience liberal, which harmonised the different shades of life . . . are to be dissolved by this new conquering empire of light and reason. All the decent drapery of life is to be rudely torn off.

This theme of the mystification of power is a distinctive hallmark of conservatism. We can see the importance of the theme in Bagehot's analysis of the constitution where he distinguishes between the 'dignified' and the 'efficient' functions of the constitution.[38] And we see it also in the myth of the ancient constitution founded on the immemorial, artificial reason of the common law.[39] This mystifying theme is particularly important in distinguishing conservatism from liberalism.

Some aspects of the mainstream conservative themes can be seen reflected in Oakeshott's work. Oakeshott's distinction between technical and practical knowledge, for example, in certain respects parallels Burke's distinction between speculative reason and practical reason. Many have thus latched on to Oakeshott's use of tradition to identify him as a Burkean conservative. When, however, one examines Oakeshott's political writing in the context of his philosophical work it is clear that his notion of tradition is different from that of Burke. In Paul Franco's words:[40]

---

[36] R. Eccleshall, 'English Conservatism as Ideology' (1977) XXV *Political Studies* 62, p. 67.

[37] E. Burke, *Reflections on the Revolution in France* in *Works* (Bohn edn., 1897), II pp. 348–9; ibid. at p. 66.

[38] See Chap. 1, p. 11.

[39] See Chap. 3, pp. 45–6.

[40] P. Franco, *The Political Philosophy of Michael Oakeshott* (New Haven, 1990), 7.

Oakeshott's notion of tradition arises out of a genuinely philosophical analysis of human activity and in no way presupposes (as I think Burke's appeal to tradition does) a belief in the wisdom or rationality of history. . . . Oakeshott's conservatism does not appeal to any sort of metaphysical or religious beliefs for sanction or support; nor does it hark back to a more integrated and traditional form of society.

While we have examined Oakeshott as a conservative thinker therefore we must be careful to distinguish him from the religious conservatism of Burke and from the mainstream forms of conservatism which Huntington identified in the aristocratic and situational theories as ideological defences of the *ancien régime* or of established institutions. In Huntington's scheme Oakeshott's theory is an attempt to develop an autonomous or philosophical theory of conservatism. This may be particularly important when we come to assess the relationships between the normativist style in public law and the political theory of conservatism.

The value of Oakeshott's political theory

In Chapter 2 I suggested that the approach to be adopted in this book was interpretative, empirical, critical, and historical. Oakeshott's political theory is both hermeneutical and historical and, on that basis, is likely to provide much of value to our exercise. Oakeshott's theory in fact draws on both Hegel and Hobbes to provide an analysis of politics, law, and the state. From Hegel he derives his basic manner of thinking, asserting the primacy of experience. From Hobbes, whose *Leviathan* he describes as 'the greatest . . . masterpiece of political philosophy written in the English language',[41] he inherits the authoritarian aspects of his theory, the outlines of his distinction between state and society,[42] and the rejection of the view that civil association must derive its authority from the inherent justice of some 'higher' law or a set of fundamental values.

We see the importance of Hobbes for Oakeshott when we appreciate Hobbes's achievement in effectively rejecting rationalism with his replacement of reason by will as the foundation of political authority. For Hobbes, legitimate authority derived only from an act of will by the person under an obligation. Although individual

[41] Introduction to Hobbes, *Leviathan* (Oxford, 1946), p. viii.
[42] Cf. Oakeshott, 'The Authority of the State' XIX *The Modern Churchman* 313 (1929–30), an early essay which portrays a more Hegelian conception of the State.

consent was of central importance to Hobbes, he did not believe that the authority of law rested on the fact that it promoted a desirable objective or that it reflected a profound truth. Rather, the authority of law rested solely on the fact that it was promulgated by the authorized ruler. And for Hobbes the idea of the sovereignty of the ruler was paramount. Oakeshott rejects the view that the Hobbesian conception of sovereignty entails absolutism or despotism; it is simply a logical necessity. For Oakeshott, modern collectivism is not to be traced to Hobbesian authoritarianism. It is rather to be traced to the survival of feudal notions of lordship.

Of particular importance for our purposes is Oakeshott's attempt to reconcile Hobbesian principles, which are closely associated with utilitarianism and legal positivism, with his conception of law. Oakeshott's political theory may in fact be viewed as an ambitious attempt to provide a framework in which H. L. A. Hart's normative version of legal positivism[43] may be synthesized with Lon Fuller's analysis of the internal morality of law.[44] This attempt may be seen primarily in Oakeshott's account of how the apparatus of rule acquires authority and in his view that the relationship between state and society is shaped by the intrinsic moral character of law.

Oakeshott does not agree with Hart's views either about the need for a 'minimum content of natural law' or that there can be a single ultimate rule of recognition in the sense of an unconditional and unquestionable norm from which all others derive their authority.[45] For Oakeshott the authority of *respublica* does not arise from the mere existence of a rule of recognition. But neither does it depend on some higher authority or a social contract. Its authority is subscribed to in conduct. It is in this way that Oakeshott shows that governmental authority is distinguishable from the mere possession of superior power by the State.

This insightful analysis is, nevertheless, not without its difficulties. Oakeshott's rejection of any attempts to found civil association on

---

[43] H. L. A. Hart, *The Concept of Law* (Oxford, 1961).

[44] L. L. Fuller, *The Morality of Law* (New Haven, 2nd edn., 1969). The apparently conflicting nature of their accounts is highlighted by the famous Hart–Fuller debate. See: Hart, 'Positivism and the Separation of Law and Morals' (1958) 71 *Harv. L. Rev* 593; Fuller, 'Positivism and Fidelity to Law—A Reply to Professor Hart' (1958) 71 *Harv. L. Rev.* 630.

[45] See Hart, *The Concept of Law* (Oxford, 1961), chaps. IX and VI respectively; Oakeshott, *On Human Conduct*, Part II.

a legitimizing principle is a critical aspect of his theory. It is essential not only to the establishment of unconditional authority but also because the lack of any foundational purpose lies at the heart of his distinction between civil and enterprise association. But, having constituted a sovereign office of legislature, he does not follow Hobbes in holding that the authority of law rests solely on authorization. The authority of law is, as we have seen, provided by what Oakeshott called the *jus* of *lex*. It is, however, unclear how the rule of law qualification is established. Oakeshott recognizes that the 'most difficult feature of the civil condition to identify and get into place has been the law'.[46] His attempt to achieve this by incorporating an intrinsic moral quality into the concept of *lex*, however, is not entirely convincing. He states:[47]

What this mode of association requires for determining the *jus* of a law is not a set of abstract criteria but an appropriately argumentative form of discourse in which to deliberate the matter; that is, a form of moral discourse, not concerned generally with right and wrong in conduct, but focused narrowly upon the kind of conditional obligations a law may impose, undistracted by prudential and consequential considerations, and insulated from the spurious claims of conscientious objectors, of minorities for exceptional treatment and, so far as may be, from current moral idiocies.

Earlier in his essay on the rule of law Oakeshott had suggested that to deliberate the *jus* of *lex* is 'to invoke a particular kind of moral consideration: . . . the negative and limited consideration that the prescriptions of law should not conflict with a prevailing educated moral sensibility capable of distinguishing between the conditions of "virtue", the conditions of moral association ("good conduct"), and those which are of such a kind that they should be imposed by law ("justice")'.[48] What this requires in practice, however, remains ambiguous.

Ambiguity is also a feature of Oakeshott's discussion of the nature of civil association. Is there in fact such a clear distinction to be maintained between civil association or *societas* and enterprise association or *universitas*? Oakeshott recognizes that these are ideal characters and that the character of the modern European state is essentially ambivalent. But he warns that the ideas of civil association and enterprise association cannot be understood as

[46] *On Human Conduct*, 181.   [47] *On History*, 160–1.   [48] Ibid. 160.

complementary characteristics; they each stand for an independent, self-sustaining mode of association. Critics, however, have argued that it is difficult to envisage any conception of a state which does not incorporate a purposive quality.[49] One prime responsibility of all states is the conduct of foreign policy. Yet this seems to be a purposive activity. If this argument is correct then the critical distinction between civil and enterprise association would appear not to be a qualitative distinction but merely one of degree. However, once this is conceded the basis of Oakeshott's theory is challenged since he views these two forms of association as categorially distinct moral conditions and as shaping two wholly different manners of government and two profoundly different characters of human identity.[50]

Some have gone even further to suggest that, since people are purposive beings, all practices, including moral practices, are purposive in nature: 'a practice without a point is an empty ritual'.[51] This seems to take the issue too far since Oakeshott clearly has in mind a sense of purpose which imposes a relatively specific objective on individuals. The rules of the road, for example, have a purpose since they are designed to prevent collisions. But they do not impose specific destinations on drivers. Rather they are considerations which should be taken into account by drivers in seeking to pursue their own destinations.[52] Nevertheless the distinction is not straightforward.

There is a further category of difficulty with Oakeshott's theory. This concerns the idea that politics is rooted in a tradition of behaviour. This idea of the centrality of tradition raises three issues. First, we need to ask: whose tradition? which society? Is it the collegiate world of the Oxbridge common room? Or the society constituted by the class that traditionally was born to rule? Perhaps it is English society in general? Or even the whole of Britain, including England, Wales, Scotland, and Northern Ireland? Even if

---

[49] See J. Shklar, 'Purposes and procedures', *Times Literary Supplement* (12 Sept. 1975), p. 1018; R. N. Berki, 'Oakeshott's concept of civil association: notes for a critical analysis' (1981) XXIX *Political Studies* 570.

[50] Oakeshott, 'The Masses in Representative Democracy' in A. Hunold (ed.), *Freedom and Serfdom: An Anthology of Western Thought* (Dordrecht, 1961), 151.

[51] See, B. Parekh, 'The Political Philosophy of Michael Oakeshott' (1979) 9 *Br. J. of Pol. Sc.* 481, pp. 503–4.

[52] See Franco, *The Political Philosophy of Michael Oakeshott* (New Haven, 1990), 225–6.

we can identify the relevant society, we also need to be able to identify the content of that political tradition.[53] Secondly, and bearing in mind the ambiguity of the distinction between the two forms of association, we must ask whether the political tradition of twentieth-century Britain is similarly deserving of respect. In modern Britain the State is generally acknowledged to have kept the peace and retained the allegiance of its citizens during a period of great social change. We might therefore ask whether, even within the framework of Oakeshott's thought, this should be considered an achievement of great importance—not simply prudentially but also morally. Finally, one major gap in Oakeshott's theory is that it says nothing about the fundamental issue of how *societas* may be reconstituted in the modern age. Without this, Oakeshott's views might be felt only to betray 'a tone of sentimental nostalgia for the pre-industrial age in which the ideals of *societas* were understood to have had social and political correlatives in some objective form of social life'.[54]

These criticisms of Oakeshott's conception of tradition should not be ignored. But it is important to recognize, as has been mentioned, that Oakeshott does not adopt the Burkean idea of tradition as providing stability and sees tradition as a contingent, fluid process. Within Oakeshott's philosophical notion of tradition there are ambiguities, conflicts, and choice. Furthermore, Oakeshott's notion of tradition does contain within it—in the idea of coherence—criteria of self-reflection. As Oakeshott puts it: 'A tradition of behaviour is not a groove within which we are destined to grind out our helpless and unsatisfying lives'.[55]

It is important to consider these ambiguities in Oakeshott's theory and the criticisms that are made of his theory. Such points, nevertheless, should not detract from the overall value of his political theory. Oakeshott's theory in general provides us with profound insights not only into the nature of government and law, but more especially in helping us to make sense of the British constitution.

[53] On this point see W. J. M. Mackenzie, 'Political Theory and Political Education' (1955–6) 9 *Universities Quarterly* 351, p. 361.
[54] C. Covell, *The Redefinition of Conservatism* (London, 1986), 140.
[55] *Rationalism in Politics*, 127. On this notion of tradition we might also consider the work of a recent defender of tradition: see H.-G. Gadamer, *Truth and Method* (New York, 1975); id., *Reason in the Age of Science* (Cambridge, Mass., 1981).

THE LIBERAL DIMENSION

The other major intellectual source of the normativist style in public law is liberalism. The values of classical liberalism assert the dignity of the individual, the primacy of individual freedom, the virtues of markets, and the requirement of limited government operating under the rule of law. While Oakeshott can be viewed as having embraced certain tenets of a liberal philosophy he is highly critical of the rationalistic and atomistic nature of liberal thought. In the work of F. A. Hayek, however, liberal values are articulated and defended within an intellectual framework which qualifies the rationalism and atomism of classical liberalism. This makes Hayek's work particularly useful for the purpose of laying bare the ideological foundations of the normativist style.

Hayek and political thought

Friedrich von Hayek's early career was devoted entirely to economic theory. Although born and educated in Vienna in 1931 he was appointed Tooke Professor of Economic Science in London University where he remained until accepting a Chair of Social and Moral Sciences at the University of Chicago in 1950. During the 1920s and 1930s Hayek's economic theory can be understood as an attempt to construct a theory of money, capital, prices, and production to rival that of Keynes.[56] By the time of the depression years of the mid-1930s, however, Keynesian theories were triumphant both politically and in the universities. Hayek nevertheless continued with these themes in the post-war period; in particular, a critique of socialist economic planning provided a major theme in his post-war work.

Through his technical economic theories Hayek gradually began to draw more general theoretical conclusions.[57] He explained his interest in moral, political, and legal issues as that of 'an economist who discovered that if he was to draw from his technical knowledge conclusions relevant to the public issues of our time, he had to make up his mind on many questions to which economics

---

[56] See J. R. Hicks, 'The Hayek Story', in *Critical Essays in Monetary Theory* (Oxford, 1967).

[57] See A. I. Ogus, 'Law and Spontaneous Order: Hayek's Contribution to Legal Theory' (1989) 16 *J. of Law & Society* 393, 394–6.

did not supply an answer'.[58] During the post-war period Hayek has drawn out some of the assumptions underpinning his economic theorizing and developed them into a general theory of society. The keystone of his work not only in economics but also in political and legal theory is the idea of 'spontaneous order'. This concept views human society as being equipped with an internal gyroscope which establishes a natural ordering mechanism in society. The notion of spontaneous order was first developed by Hayek in relation to markets. But he later applied this insight to the central issues of political and legal theory. These views, laid out primarily in *The Constitution of Liberty*[59] and his three-volume work, *Law, Legislation and Liberty*,[60] provide us with a powerful insight into the liberal theory of government and law.

Epistemological foundations of Hayek's thought

Hayek's epistemological views have certain similarities to those of Oakeshott. Hayek accepts the primacy of practice in the construction of human knowledge.[61] It is this epistemological belief which provides the foundation for his concept of 'spontaneous order'. Hayek formulated this concept essentially as a result of his inquiries into the nature of order in society. He distinguishes between two different types of order, which he calls *taxis* and *cosmos*. *Taxis* refers to the kind of order which is made and which is imposed from without; it is the order of an organization. The vision of social order which results from *taxis* rests on 'a relation of command and obedience, or a hierarchical structure of the whole of society in which the will of superiors, and ultimately of some single supreme authority, determines what each individual must do'.[62] *Cosmos* refers to the kind of order which is grown and which results from an equilibrium set up from within. *Cosmos* is spontaneous order. Social order from the perspective of *cosmos* is based on 'the discovery that there exist orderly structures which are

[58] F. A. Hayek, *Studies in Philosophy, Politics and Economics* (London, 1967), p. vii.
[59] (London, 1960).
[60] Vol. 1. *Rules and Order* (London, 1973); Vol. 2. *The Mirage of Social Justice* (London, 1976); Vol. 3. *The Political Order of a Free People* (London, 1979).
[61] See, e.g., Hayek, *The Sensory Order: An Inquiry into the Foundations of Theoretical Psychology* (London, 1952).
[62] Hayek, *Law, Legislation and Liberty. Vol. 1. Rules and Order* (London, 1973), 36.

the product of the action of many men but are not the result of human design'.[63]

Hayek argues that the belief that social order is based on *taxis* is the result of the growth of 'constructivist rationalism'.[64] Constructivist rationalism, which Hayek associates with the thought of Descartes, Hobbes, Rousseau, and Bentham, is founded on a belief that social institutions are, or ought to be, the product of deliberate design. The errors of constructivist rationalism stem from the belief that reason alone enables human beings to construct society anew. Hayek points to the fact that many social institutions which are essential to the successful pursuit of our aims are the result of customs, habits, and practices which are not the product of design or invention and which, although they govern thought and action, are often not brought to consciousness. Further, Hayek argues that constructivist rationalists are guilty of 'the synoptic delusion'; that is, the belief that all relevant social facts are capable of being known to some one mind, and that it is possible to construct from this knowledge of the particulars a desirable social order.[65]

Spontaneous social orders, by contrast, are evolutionary in nature and are not the product of rational design. Hayek gives as examples of spontaneous social orders the growth of language, morals, law, and markets. Since such orders are not the product of a directing intelligence they cannot be said to have a particular purpose. Furthermore, participants in such orders may utilize and develop a heritage of knowledge which they may never be capable of grasping as a whole. Take as an example the formation of market exchange relations. Hayek argues that these are self-generating structures which have a tendency to equilibrium. Markets are thus superior mechanisms to central planning systems because they have in-built discovery procedures through the ability of the pricing system to register preferences. Planning systems, by contrast, are defective precisely because they are based on the synoptic delusion. Hayek believes that all spontaneous social orders have these knowledge-bearing or information-carrying characteristics; that is, precisely the characteristics which Adam Smith had in mind when he referred to the 'invisible hand' of the market.[66]

---

[63] Hayek, *Law, Legislation and Liberty. Vol. 1. Rules and Order* (London, 1973), 37.

[64] Ibid. chap. 1.   [65] Ibid. 14.

[66] A. Smith, *An Inquiry into the Nature and Causes of the Wealth of Nations*

Finally, spontaneous orders are superior insofar as the Darwinian principle of natural selection applies to them. Since they are the products of continuous evolution, the practices which survive are those which enhance the reproductive fitness of those groups. We can see certain similarities between Hayek's approach and the conservative philosophy of Oakeshott. Oakeshott's attack on rationalism, which incidentally included an attack on the doctrinal nature of Hayek's *The Road to Serfdom*,[67] is transformed by Hayek—who utilizes Popper's distinction between a naïve and a critical rationalism[68]—into an attack on constructivist rationalism. By deflecting Oakeshott's arguments into a critique of constructivist rationalism Hayek seeks to maintain a rationalist approach which may avoid many of Oakeshott's criticisms. Hayek wishes to do so because he is not simply a traditionalist and is seeking to harness his insights to the task of providing a modern, rational reconstruction of liberalism.

Through his use of the concept of 'spontaneous order' Hayek avoids an extreme atomistic individualism, often associated with classical liberalism, since the concept of spontaneous order recognizes the existence of an order in society which is formed by the social matrix. Furthermore, Hayek's concept of 'spontaneous order' has much in common with Oakeshott's idea of 'moral association'. But there remain important differences. Hayek, for example, tends to trace the problems of constructivist rationalism to the rise in authority of the natural sciences and hence takes the form of a critique of 'scientism'.[69] Oakeshott, however, considers this conception of 'scientism' to be mistaken since, as we have seen, he does not take the view that science is a separate kind of experience. The error of rationalism, in Oakeshott's argument, does not arise from the application of scientific methods to non-scientific material, but rather results from a mistaken understanding of the nature of reason.[70] Perhaps more importantly, however, Hayek's concept of spontaneous order is inextricably linked to the

(W. B. Todd (ed.)) (Oxford, 1976) vol. 1, p. 456. On Adam Smith generally see Chap 1, pp. 4–6.

[67] (Chicago, 1944). See Oakeshott, *Rationalism in Politics*, 21.

[68] See *Rules and Order*, 29.

[69] Hayek, *The Counter-Revolution of Science* (Glencoe, Ill., 1952).

[70] See Oakeshott, 'Scientific Politics' (1947–8) 1 *The Cambridge Journal* 347; Franco, *The Political Philosophy of Michael Oakeshott* (New Haven, 1990), 114–15.

notion of personal liberty. This may be seen most clearly in his views on law and government.

Law and government

For Hayek, law consists of rules of just conduct; that is, of 'purpose-independent rules which govern the conduct of individuals towards each other, are intended to apply to an unknown number of further instances and, by defining a protected domain of each, enable an order of actions to form itself wherein the individuals can make feasible plans'.[71] Hayek suggests that law is coeval with society. It therefore precedes the emergence of the State and is certainly not the creation of a governing authority. Hayek argues that 'an order of the complexity of modern society can be designed neither as a whole, nor by shaping each part separately without regard to the rest, but only by consistently adhering to certain principles throughout a process of evolution'.[72] This form of law, called *nomos*, is the law of liberty. *Nomos* is essentially the product of spontaneous growth. It is perhaps most clearly reflected in the continuous, adaptive processes of the common law.

Although this idea of law as a general, abstract, and non-purposive body of rules may be equated with the idea of common law, Hayek does recognize that, even with a system compatible with the ideals of *nomos*, there is a role for legislation. While judges can continually work to improve the system, legislative intervention will occasionally be necessary, either to extricate the law from the dead ends to which gradual evolution may occasionally lead, or to deal with altogether new problems. Legislation, however, is a dangerous invention: 'It gave into the hands of men an instrument of great power which they needed to achieve some good, but which they have not yet learned so to control that it may not produce great evil'.[73] One of the errors attributable to constructivist rationalism has been to view law as a prescription posited by authority; that is, of equating law with legislation. This view of the nature of law Hayek calls *thesis*. With the emergence of *thesis* the idea of law, which in the sense of *nomos* was viewed as a constraint on power, is transformed into an instrument for the use of power.

Hayek views the growing dominance of the conception of law as *thesis* as posing a grave threat to liberty. This dominance in modern

---

[71] *Rules and Order*, 85–6.   [72] Ibid. 60.   [73] Ibid. 72.

times is attributed by Hayek to the success of the Philosophical Radicals of the nineteenth century in replacing the ideal of government under law with the ideal of a government controlled by a popular assembly and free to take any action of which that assembly approved.[74] As a result, 'governmental assemblies, whose chief activities were of the kind which ought to be limited by law, became able to command whatever they pleased simply by calling their commands "law"'.[75] This conception of law as *thesis* is therefore a product of constructivist rationalism: it is born of the belief that law is the result of human design; that order in society is founded on the conception of law as *taxis*; and that the political authority is capable of acquiring all the knowledge it needs in order to exercise its absolutist powers wisely.

Conservatism or liberalism?

There are clear parallels between Hayek the economist, concerned with the analysis of market and command economic systems, and Hayek the political theorist, attentive to the conditions of order and freedom in society. Just as markets, with their knowledge-gathering characteristics, are inherently superior to centralized planning systems so also is the common law, with its ability to respond to changing circumstances, more likely to maintain order and freedom than a central legislature responding to the concerns of transient majorities. We may also discern close similarities between Hayek and Oakeshott on law and government. The views of both theorists seem to be based on the distinction between a law-governed nomocratic social order and a purpose-governed teleocratic order. So wherein lies the difference between conservatism and liberalism?

Some insight may be gleaned by comparing Oakeshott's 'On being Conservative'[76] with Hayek's 'Why I am not a Conservative'.[77] In the former essay Oakeshott reiterates his belief that the business of government is simply to rule. This involves the specific and limited activity of establishing and enforcing general rules of conduct which enable people to pursue their activities with the minimum degree of frustration. Oakeshott recognizes that this

---

[74] For our purposes we can assume that, in referring to the Philosophical Radicals, Hayek has in mind Jeremy Bentham and John Austin. On their influence, under the banner of legal positivism, see Chap. 1, pp. 17–23.

[75] *Rules and Order*, 130.

[76] *Rationalism in Politics*, 168.

[77] *The Constitution of Liberty* (Chicago, 1960), 397–411.

sentiment may be shared by liberals. Liberals, however, quite unnecessarily seek to justify this sentiment by appealing to highfalutin metaphysical beliefs such as the belief that private property is a natural right or that freedom of choice is an absolute value. According to Oakeshott, something less pretentious will do; viz., 'that we are not children *in statu pupillari* but adults who do not consider themselves under any obligation to justify their preference for making their own choices'.[78] Oakeshott here is in effect emphasizing the conservative distrust of abstract ideas and theories; conservatism 'is not a creed or doctrine, but a disposition'.[79] It is on this specific point that we see the basis of disagreement.

Hayek argues that a consequence of their distrust of abstract theories is that conservatives are unable to offer any alternative to the direction in which social forces are moving; they look to the past rather than the future. Furthermore, because of this distrust of abstraction the conservative 'neither understands those spontaneous forces on which a policy of freedom relies nor possesses a basis for formulating principles of policy'.[80] Hayek, for example, believes that conservatives deceive themselves when they blame the evils of our time on democracy. Democracy and unlimited government may be connected. However, it is not democracy but unlimited government that is objectionable. 'It is not who governs,' contends Hayek, 'but what government is entitled to do that seems to me the essential problem.'[81]

It is on the basis of these distinctions that Hayek seeks to avoid certain criticisms that have been applied to Oakeshott. As we have seen, in taking the philosophical approach which he does, it is not clear precisely how, having established the existence of a sovereign office of legislature, Oakeshott seeks to establish the rule of law qualification on the exercise of this power. Similarly, having identified the ideal characters of *societas* and *universitas* and recognized the existence of both modes in the history of the European state, it is not clear precisely why Oakeshott comes down in favour of *societas*. By contrast, Hayek justifies the moral superiority of *societas* by taking a clear ideological line in which the idea of liberty is established as the predominant value in his philosophy.[82] Furthermore by taking an ideological rather than

---

[78] *Rationalism in Politics*, 187.   [79] Ibid. 168.
[80] *Constitution of Liberty*, 401.   [81] Ibid. 403.
[82] Hayek writes, for example, that 'freedom can be preserved only if it is treated

merely a dispositive approach he is able to lay down principles for the reconstruction of *societas* in the modern age. It is to this exercise that we now turn.

The liberal ideal of constitutionalism

In *The Constitution of Liberty* Hayek aims 'to picture an ideal, to show how it can be achieved, and to explain what its realization would mean in practice'.[83] As the title itself indicates, that ideal is liberty. Liberty for Hayek has a specific meaning. It means simply freedom from coercion by others and it is achieved when a sphere of private autonomy is created.[84] This idea of liberty is not a natural condition but is created and preserved by the 'rule of law'. At the core of the constitution of liberty, then, lies the concept of the rule of law. Hayek makes this plain when he states that 'freedom under the law . . . is the chief concern of this book'.[85]

In *The Road to Serfdom* Hayek wrote: 'Nothing distinguishes more clearly conditions in a free country from those in a country under arbitrary government than the observance in the former of the great principles known as the Rule of Law.'[86] Recognizing that that concept can carry a broad range of meanings Hayek, in *The Constitution of Liberty*, seeks to explicate these principles. For Hayek the rule of law is a meta-legal doctrine or a political ideal which serves to impose a limitation on all legislation. Formally it requires, first, that laws be general and abstract rules; that is, that they are addressed to all as contrasted to specific commands to specific persons. The chief safeguard for freedom here is that these rules apply to the governors as well as the governed. Secondly, this concept requires that laws be known and certain. Hayek argues that this requirement is particularly important for economic activity. He doubts 'whether the significance which the certainty of the law has for the smooth and efficient working of economic life can be exaggerated' and suggests that 'there is probably no single factor which has contributed to the greater prosperity of the Western world compared with the Orient than the relative certainty

as a supreme principle which must not be sacrificed for particular advantages', that a 'successful defence of freedom must . . . be dogmatic and make no concessions to expediency', and that freedom 'will prevail only if it is accepted as a general principle whose application to particular instances requires no justification.' See *Rules and Order*, 57, 61.

[83] *The Constitution of Liberty*, p. vii.   [84] Ibid. chap. 1.
[85] Ibid. 6.   [86] *The Road to Serfdom* (London, 1944), 54.

of the law which in the West had early been achieved'.[87] A third
requirement is that these general rules be complemented by the
equality of all before the law. This is liberalism's concession to
democracy: 'Equality of the general rules of law and conduct . . . is
the only kind of quality conducive to liberty and the only equality
which we can secure without destroying liberty'.[88] These requirements of generality, certainty, and equality of law are vital for the
protection of liberty.

But in addition to the political ideal of the rule of law Hayek also
recognizes the need for a set of principles of institutional design to
ensure that the power of the state could not be exercised in such a
way as to compromise individual liberty. He argues the need for: a
written constitution which is compatible with the rule of law; the
separation of legislative, executive, and judicial power so that a
system of checks and balances will be in place; a bicameral
legislature, to provide an additional check; a federal system of
government to protect against big, centralized government; a bill of
rights which will protect a sphere of private autonomy; judicial
review to ensure an effective mechanism of protection; and specific
limitations on legislative and administrative discretion.[89] In *Law,
Legislation and Liberty* Hayek went even further and suggested
that, since legislation proper 'should not be governed by interests
but by opinion', what is required 'is an assembly of men and
women elected at a relatively mature age for fairly long periods,
such as fifteen years'.[90]

Hayek is thus not content to leave the protection of liberty to the
nobility of spirit of rulers. His general objective in *The Constitution
of Liberty* was 'to restate . . . the traditional doctrine of liberal
constitutionalism'. As we have seen, the realization of this objective
requires that a broad variety of mechanisms are institutionalized so
as to ensure that the business of government is conducted in
accordance with the rule of law. Hayek's theory therefore offers
both a critique of contemporary arrangements and a programme
for realizing an alternative vision.

---

[87] Hayek, *The Political Ideal of the Rule of Law* (Cairo, 1955), 36.
[88] *The Constitution of Liberty*, 85.
[89] Ibid. esp. chaps. 11–14.
[90] Hayek, *Law, Legislation and Liberty. Vol. 3. The Political Order of a Free
People* (London, 1979), 112–13.

Hayek and liberalism

The value of Hayek's work as a representative theory of liberalism lies for us in its rigour and its comprehensiveness and in the fact that it is acutely aware of the importance of law. Furthermore, although Hayek's is a particular theory within the tradition of liberalism, the key themes which pervade his work—the supreme principle of liberty, the character of state power, and the relationship between the individual and the state—are themes which are central to the tenets of liberalism. In addition, despite the various differences amongst liberal theories, there is one theme of particular importance for our project on which many liberal theories seem agreed. This is the notion that, in order to protect the supremacy of the liberal conception of liberty, law must be non-purposive in character and must maintain neutrality with respect to different conceptions of the good life.

During the last 20 years major contributions have been made to liberal political philosophy. The most widely acclaimed of these has been John Rawls's *A Theory of Justice*, which was published in 1971 and rapidly assumed the status of a contemporary classic. Indeed it was this book more than any other which caused Laslett to retract his statement of 1956 that 'political philosophy is dead'.[91]

In *A Theory of Justice* Rawls seeks a method for rationally determining the principles of justice. He argues that the principles of justice are those which would be chosen by a rational agent situated behind a 'veil of ignorance'. The veil of ignorance operates so that the agent will not know his or her natural endowments, social situation, or conception of the good. Rawls argues that agents in this situation, which he calls 'the original position', will agree two fundamental principles of justice. These principles, in order of priority, are, first, that each person is to have an equal right to the most extensive basic liberty compatible with a similar liberty for all and, secondly, that social and economic inequalities are to be arranged so that they are both (*a*) to the greatest benefit of the least advantaged and (*b*) attached to offices and positions open to all

---

[91] For a discussion of this issue see Chap. 2 at pp. 29–30. For the identification of Rawls as the person who rendered the initial verdict obsolete see: P. Laslett and J. Fishkin (eds.), *Philosophy, Politics and Society (Fifth Series)* (Oxford, 1979), 1–2.

under conditions of fair equality of opportunity.[92] In the second part of his book, Rawls seeks to place flesh on these abstract principles by examining the basic structure of society that ideally satisfies them. The answer he arrives at is a 'constitutional democracy' which comprises a government which preserves equal basic liberties and promotes equality of opportunity and an economic system based on a market mechanism.

Rawls's work reaches somewhat different conclusions concerning justice and equality to that of Hayek. Following the work of Rawls, however, there has been a profusion of important contributions to liberal political philosophy. Theorists such as Nozick,[93] Dworkin,[94] and Ackerman[95] have all addressed major issues of equality, rights, and justice and do not necessarily agree with Rawls's work. Nozick, for example, formulates an entitlement theory of justice, in which a person's property holdings are just if they are acquired through some just act of original acquisition or by some just transfer.[96] From these principles he argues that the only form of the state which can be morally justified is a minimal state which is limited to the protection of citizens against force, theft, and fraud and to the enforcement of contracts. Nozick argues that any more extensive state, such as one which seeks justice through redistribution or prohibits certain activities for people's own good, will violate persons' rights and is morally unjustified. These conclusions thus accord more with Hayek's views on distributive justice[97] than with those of Rawls.[98]

Much of this recent literature has spawned a mass of critical commentary. Such studies have been carried out both from within liberal premises[99] and from various critics of liberalism.[100] I do

[92] J. Rawls, *A Theory of Justice* (Oxford, 1972), 302–3.
[93] R. Nozick, *Anarchy, State and Utopia* (Oxford, 1974).
[94] R. Dworkin, Taking Rights Seriously (Camb. Mass., 1977), Chap. 6; id., *A Matter of Principle* (Camb. Mass., 1985), chap. 8.
[95] B. Ackerman, *Social Justice in the Liberal State* (New Haven, 1980).
[96] Nozick, *Anarchy, State and Utopia*, 150–3.
[97] See esp. Hayek, *Law, Legislation and Liberty, Vol. 2. The Mirage of Social Justice* (London, 1976).
[98] For Nozick's critique of Rawls's theory see Nozick, *Anarchy, State and Utopia*, 183–231.
[99] In addition to Nozick's criticisms of Rawls, a vast literature has been spawned which examines such aspects of the rationality of Rawls's arguments as to whether people in the original position would in fact rationally choose Rawls's principles of justice. See, e.g. N. Daniels (ed.), *Reading Rawls. Critical Studies of a Theory of Justice* (Oxford, 1975). For critical studies of Nozick see, J. Paul (ed.), *Reading Nozick* (Oxford, 1982).
[100] This has mainly taken the form of a 'communitarian' critique. See M. Sandel,

not wish to underestimate the genuine differences which exist between writers such as Hayek and Dworkin, and Rawls and Nozick. What is interesting for our purposes, however, is to highlight those factors that provide a common thread within this body of work and which serves to identify the writers as working within a tradition of liberalism.

There is, for example, an important dimension which theories as apparently divergent as those of Rawls and Nozick share in common; namely, their method. Both theories are exercises in analytical moral philosophy which aspire to provide rational principles to support particular conceptions of just social arrangements. Both seek to argue logically from certain abstract premises. Rawls constructs his model so as to argue for the primacy of an equality of needs. Nozick develops a model which enables him to make primary a principle with respect to entitlement.[101] Once the major premises have been established the principles fall into place. The main point, however, is not simply that the premises are largely matters of choice. What is particularly interesting is the similarity in the method which they use to justify their principles. The method used is highly formal, abstract and individualistic. MacIntyre brings out its individualism thus:[102]

It is . . . clear that for both Nozick and Rawls a society is composed of individuals, each with his or her own interest, who then come together and formulate common rules of life. . . . Individuals are thus in both accounts primary and society secondary, and the identification of individual interests is prior to, and independent of, the construction of any moral or social bonds between them.

Liberalism and the Limits of Justice (Cambridge, 1982); id., 'The Procedural Republic and the Unencumbered Self' 1984 *Political Theory* 81; M. Walzer, *Spheres of Justice* (New York, 1983); A. Gutmann, 'Communitarian Critics of Liberalism' 1985 *Philosophy and Public Affairs* 308. Insofar as the communitarian critique is pitched against Rawls it has been complicated by Rawls's attempts to clarify or (as some have argued) amend the theoretical premises of *A Theory of Justice*. On this see Rawls, 'Justice as Fairness: Political not Metaphysical' 1985 *Philosophy and Public Affairs* 223; id., 'The Idea of an Overlapping Consensus' (1987) 7 *Oxford J. of Legal Studies* 1. See further Chap. 9, pp. 224–7.

[101] This point is clearly developed in A. MacIntyre, *After Virtue. A Study in Moral Theory* (London, 2nd edn., 1985), chap. 17. For an argument that Rawls and Nozick's theories are in fact commensurable see J. Stick, 'Turning Rawls into Nozick and Back Again' (1987) 81 *Northwestern Univ. L. Rev.* 363.

[102] Ibid. at p. 250.

This conception of the individual as autonomous and as existing prior to, and separate from, society is a common characteristic of liberal theories. It also tends to influence the shape of other aspects of the theory. When models are constructed from such premisses, for example, there is a tendency to view government as a restrictive and even as a repressive agency. Such models also share an essentially procedural conception of justice and view the primary function of the state as that of securing a framework of law through which individuals may pursue their own particular goals. In the work of Hayek and Nozick the limited role of the state as umpire is quite explicit. In Rawls it can be seen from his model of 'pure procedural justice'[103] and the assertion of an equal right to liberty as the primary principle. And in Dworkin it is evident in his views that 'government must be neutral on what might be called the question of the good life . . . [and] political decisions must be, so far as possible, independent of any particular conception of the good life, or of what gives value to life'.[104]

What unites such theorists, then, is their conception of the individual, the assertion of a particular conception of liberty as the supreme principle, a set of broadly shared attitudes on the character of state power and the relationship between the individual and the state, and an understanding that law should be non-purposive in character. The most basic criticism of this common liberal method is generally to be found in the view that humans are social beings who cannot be abstracted from a particular social and historical context in the manner that such theories propose. In the words of F. H. Bradley—someone who held views similar in many respects to Oakeshott—if we abstract those features which result from social context the exercise becomes 'a theoretical attempt to isolate what cannot be isolated'.[105] This is the view that is echoed by the communitarian critics who argue that the agency of reflection of liberal theories is that of the 'unencumbered self'[106] and that this model fails to appreciate the constitutive character of the self.

Finally, we should not leave the discussion of Hayek and Liberalism without noting certain recent developments in liberal

---

[103] A Theory of Justice, 88.
[104] Dworkin, A Matter of Principle (Camb. Mass., 1985), 191.
[105] Quoted in S. Lukes, Essays in Social Theory (London, 1977), 189.
[106] See Sandel, Liberalism and the Limits of Justice, 93–4.

theories which are particularly directed to the analysis of government and law and which, to some extent, derive their inspiration from Hayek's pioneering work. I am referring here to the recent growth in economic analysis of politics and law. An influential strand in the economic analysis of law seeks to transmit a particular message. This message is presented in a slightly different manner by different writers. In its most general and powerful form, however, the message is that, despite differences in vocabulary, detail, and specific subject-matter, there is an underlying unity to the various fields of the common law. This unifying character is to be found in the method of the common law. The common law method is such, it is argued, that there is a natural tendency for common law rules to produce efficient solutions to disputes.[107] Through this type of literature, generally based on the Chicago school of economics, we find the utilization of economic methodologies in support of Hayek's basic point about the common law as a spontaneous order.

Developments in the economic analysis of politics have perhaps had an even greater general significance than contributions to the economic analysis of law. These developments have taken a specific form through the theory of 'public choice'. Public choice theory arose from the fact that, although many welfare economists were concerned to examine the phenomenon of 'market failure', very few economists seemed to show an interest in applying their techniques to institutions other than the market; and, in particular, to political institutions. Public choice theory seeks to undertake this task. The theory challenges the assumption of orthodox welfare economics that the existence of market failure is sufficient reason for governmental intervention. It does so by applying assumptions about the utility maximizing behaviour of individuals to the arena of governmental decision-making and, as a result, challenges the assumption that government will act efficiently and in the public interest.

Public choice theory has developed both analytical and constructive dimensions. The analytical dimension provides us with theories of bureaucracy and politics. The theory of bureaucracy argues that

---

[107] See, e.g., R. Posner, *Economic Analysis of Law* (Boston, 2nd edn., 1977), 179; G. L. Priest, 'The common law process and the selection of efficient rules' (1977) 6 *J. of Legal Studies* 65.

bureaucracies have an in-built expansionary motivation which will result in operational ineffiencies.[108] The theory of politics argues, on the supply side, that political parties, in bidding for support, end up by promising more than they can deliver and that, on the demand side, this leads to inflated expectations since the electorate have incentives to vote for increased services because they do not pay for them directly and because there may be little correlation between tax payments and government benefits.[109] This analytical dimension of public choice theory therefore seeks to demonstrate that 'governmental failure' exists on a major scale. This is where the constructive dimension comes in. The constructive dimension argues that, in order to remedy government failure, it is essential to reform the framework of rules within which the business of politics is conducted. There has therefore emerged, within the framework of public choice, a theory arguing specifically for the establishment of constitutional limits to the scope of governmental action. The economic agenda of constitutional design has been called 'constitutional political economy'.[110]

What is interesting to note about both the theory of public choice and Chicago School economic analysis of law is that their analyses, although wrapped up in the analytical apparatus of modern economics, reach more or less identical conclusions to Hayek. Nevertheless, these economic theories of politics and law are a significant contribution to the understanding of liberal theories. In addition to reinforcing our general conceptions concerning the underpinnings of liberalism, economic theories, which are based on the assumption of 'rational economic man', highlight especially the notion of human beings as self-regarding creatures which under-pins liberal theories in general. These economic theories are also significant because ultimately they are founded on the objective of developing a new science of politics. They can therefore be viewed as an attempt to translate the methodological rigours of economic science to the sphere of political behaviour in which, as we have

[108] See, e.g., G. Tullock, *The Politics of Bureaucracy* (Washington, DC, 1965); W. A. Niskanen, *Bureaucracy and Representative Government* (Aldine-Atherton, 1971); and id., *Bureaucracy: Servant or Master?* (London, 1973).

[109] See, e.g., A. Downs, *An Economic Theory of Democracy* (New York, 1957); A. Breton, *The Economic Theory of Representative Government* (London, 1974).

[110] See, e.g., J. M. Buchanan, *The Limits of Liberty* (Chicago, 1975); G. Brennan and J. M. Buchanan, *The Reason of Rules. Constitutional Political Economy* (Cambridge, 1985).

seen,[111] the attempt to develop a scientific approach has not been entirely successful.

Tensions within liberalism

Classical liberalism has been subjected to severe criticism both from conservatives and communitarians. Such criticisms generally take the form of a challenge to the moral status of liberal theory. The conservative critique along such lines argues that liberalism is morally bankrupt. Liberals advocate the promotion of a free rather than a just society, based on the argument that, while we know what freedom is, we have no generally accepted notion of justice.[112] But conservatives claim that this sort of argument leads to the destruction of the moral foundations on which the social order is built: 'men cannot for long tolerate a sense of spiritual meaningless in their individual lives, so they cannot for long accept a society in which power, privilege, and property are not distributed according to some morally meaningful criteria'.[113] The conservative critique thus argues that the type of order which liberalism envisages 'tends to produce a sort of mindless hedonism which renders it defenceless against more vital tyrannies'.[114] The communitarian variant of this type of criticism is related. It suggests that the attempt to impose a neutral character on the liberal state and to purge its law of any substantive content can only serve to erode those moral and religious foundations which are essential for the survival of liberalism.[115]

There is, however, a more basic criticism of liberal theories. This criticism challenges the view of human nature and the human condition constructed by liberal theories. Liberal theories, it is suggested, start with the assumption of the priority of the individual over society and in particular the assertion of the primacy of individual rights. Such liberal theories tend then to adopt some variant of social contract theory or at least have

---

[111] See Chaps. 1 and 2.

[112] See Hayek, *Law, Legislation and Liberty. Vol. 2. The Mirage of Social Justice* (London, 1976).

[113] I. Kristol, ' "When virtue loses all her loveliness"—some reflections on capitalism and "the free society" ' in D. Bell and I. Kristol (eds.), *Capitalism Today* (New York, 1970), 8.

[114] J. Gray, *Hayek on Liberty* (London, 1986), 131; see also Kristol, *Two Cheers for Capitalism* (New York, 1978), chap. 7.

[115] See Sandel, 'The procedural republic and the unencumbered self' 1984 *Political Theory* 81.

inherited a vision of society in which an instrumental view of society—society as constructed by individuals for the fulfilment of essentially individual ends—is adopted. This view is generally called 'atomism'. Atomistic theories have been challenged by alternative theories which project a rather different view of human nature. This alternative view claims that individuals can only develop their characteristically human capacities within society and that 'living in society is a necessary condition of the development of rationality . . . or of becoming a moral agent in the full sense of the term, or of becoming a fully responsible, autonomous being'.[116] Social theories thus argue that freedom requires an understanding of the self and our self-understanding or identity can only be understood in relation to the practices of our society. Charles Taylor expresses it thus:[117]

The free individual . . . cannot . . . be concerned purely with his individual choices and the associations formed from such choices to the neglect of the matrix in which such choices can be open or closed, rich or meagre. It is important to him that certain activities and institutions flourish in society. It is even of importance to him what the moral tone of the whole society is—shocking as it may seem to libertarians to raise this issue—because freedom and individual diversity can only flourish in a society where there is a general recognition of their worth. They are threatened by the spread of bigotry, but also by other conceptions of life—for example, those which look on originality, innovation, and diversity as luxuries which society can ill afford given the need for efficiency, productivity, or growth, or those which in a host of other ways depreciate freedom.

These criticisms provide basic challenges not only to the classical liberalism of Hobbes and Locke but also to the more recent theories we have examined.[118] Hayek, however, constructs his theory in such a manner as to render such criticisms difficult to sustain. As we have seen, Hayek criticizes Oakeshott's traditionalism on the ground that it does not provide a framework for critical evaluation of social evolution. But Hayek also roots his theory in social evolutionary ideas. In so doing he is generally able to avoid criticisms laid against classical liberalism concerning both its

---

[116] C. Taylor, 'Atomism' in *Philosophical Papers. Vol. 2. Philosophy and the Human Sciences* (Cambridge, 1985), 187, p. 191.

[117] Ibid. 207.

[118] Although, in the light of Rawls's more recent writing, it is doubtful whether this argument can be applied to his work. See above n. 100.

atomistic conception of the human condition and the moral status of the theory. Nevertheless, although he may evade these basic criticisms of classical liberalism, Hayek, by rooting his liberal theory in an evolutionary framework, encounters a different problem. Is he able to construct a coherent theory?

There is undoubtedly a basic tension which permeates Hayek's liberal philosophy. This tension concerns the nature of the relationship envisaged in Hayek's theory between reason and tradition. Certain aspects of Hayek's theory, such as his model constitution,[119] seem essentially constructivist in nature, whereas other aspects stress the link between tradition and progress.[120] What his theory does not clearly specify is the method for determining the extent to which we observe cultural evolutionary achievements and the circumstances in which interference through institutional design is justified. Indeed, some have argued that the 'traditionalism of his general philosophy is so strong that it virtually disables him from that critical rationalism which is essential for the appraisal of particular traditions'.[121]

If correct, such criticisms suggest that Hayek, although circumventing the criticisms of classical liberalism, fails to maintain a coherent position. At the very least, the ambiguity of this method suggests that Hayek's evolutionary account of the development of law is value-laden. The theory of spontaneous social order, for example, has no necessary connection with the promotion of individual liberty in the sense that Hayek envisages. Hayek thus seems open to the criticism that he skews his account of moral and social development in order to render it harmonious with his ideological preference for a particular conception of liberty.

THE CHARACTER OF NORMATIVISM

This examination of the political theories of conservatism and liberalism may help us to appreciate the foundations of the normativist style in public law. From Oakeshott we can perhaps

---

[119] See above pp. 91–2.
[120] See esp. Hayek, *Knowledge, Evolution and Society* (London, 1984).
[121] See B. Barry, 'Hayek on Liberty' in J. Gray and Z. Pelczynski (eds.), *Conceptions of Liberty in Political Philosophy* (London, 1984), 280; B. M. Rowland, 'Beyond Hayek's Pessimism: Reason, Tradition and Bounded Constructivist Rationalism' (1988) 18 *Brit. J. of Pol. Sc.* 221.

better appreciate the concepts of authority, liberty, and law which pervade normativist thought. Through the distinctions he makes between civil association and enterprise association and between the state conceived of as *societas* and *universitas* we can begin to understand the intellectual foundations of the tension within normativist thought between law and administrative power. More generally, his theory provides us with a remarkable insight into the nature of the British constitution; the entire thrust of Oakeshott's work can be interpreted as laying down a view of the world in which the British constitution with its conventions, understandings, and practices which have evolved through a slow historical process actually makes sense. Seen in this light we can also discern distinct parallels between the thrust of Oakeshott's work and the idea of the common law mind.[122] From Hayek we see stated in forthright fashion the importance in normativist thought of the dignity of the individual and the primacy of individual freedom. We see also the clear link between the protection and promotion of those values and the normativist conception of law as a set of general, abstract, and purpose-independent rules. And from these connections we can begin to appreciate the significance which the idea of limited government under the rule of law plays in normativism.

There are, nevertheless, tensions between the conservative and liberal variants of the normativist style which are revealed by this study. These tensions can be detected at various levels. They can be seen in the centrality of the notion of traditions of behaviour in conservative thought as contrasted with (*pace* Hayek) the more rationalistic temperament of liberalism. They can be seen in the importance to conservatives of the notion of authority, a notion which in liberal thought is presented less positively and often as a potential threat to liberty. We see that the conservative is more likely to place his or her trust in the virtue and nobility of spirit of our rulers, whereas liberals, starting from the assumption that individuals are primarily motivated by self-interest, are anxious to formalize a body of principles and rules which are specifically designed to preserve individual liberty.

As we shall see later, such tensions are of importance. Nevertheless, they should properly be viewed as tensions *within* the normativist style in public law. Because, despite such tensions, there

---

[122] See Chap. 3, pp. 42–6.

	FORMS OF KNOWLEDGE	TYPES OF ORDER	FORMS OF THE STATE	CONCEPTION OF LAW
OAKESHOTT	Practical Knowledge	Moral Association	Societas	Imperium
	Scientific Knowledge (Rationalism)	Enterprise Association	Universitas	Dominium
HAYEK	Critical Rationalism	Cosmos	Nomocratic	Nomos
	Constructivist Rationalism	Taxis	Teleocratic	Thesis

Fig. 1: The Dualisms of Normativism

are common themes within conservative and liberal thought on matters which are of central importance to the normativist style. There are a number of matters to which attention might be drawn. The overlap between Oakeshott and Hayek on the critique of rationalism, for example, sets the scene for setting limits on the ability of government sensibly to re-order society. The parallels on organizational forms or modes of association—Oakeshott's distinction between moral and enterprise association as compared with Hayek's between *cosmos* and *taxis*—shapes the normativist understanding of the appropriate relationship between common law and statute law. The distinction which each of these writers make between forms of the state provide the normativist with a justification for viewing the positive state as a degenerate form. And finally the distinction which each writer makes between forms of law provides normativism with a distinct conception of law which may be used to identify degenerate forms of law. These distinctions, highlighted in Fig. 1, may be called the dualisms of normativism and occupy a central place in normativist thought.

6

Foundations of Functionalism

THERE are certain problems in seeking to identify the intellectual foundations of the functionalist style in public law with a particular political ideology. It is clear that, if normativist style has its roots in conservatism and liberalism, similarly one may say that the functionalist style has a certain affinity with a political theory of socialism. That statement must be qualified, however, if for no other reason than that there is no one theory of socialism to which the main adherents of a functionalist style would subscribe. It may therefore be more accurate to identify the functionalist style with those who adopt a collectivist social ontology. As a result, the foundations of functionalism may best be revealed by examining intellectual orientations rather than, in a strict sense, a political ideology. This is the method which I shall adopt. The three primary intellectual influences on the functionalist style which we shall examine are those of sociological positivism, evolutionary social theory, and pragmatism in philosophy.

Sociological positivism emerged mainly in the nineteenth century and particularly flourished in the French intellectual tradition. The aim of this school has been to pursue the attempt to elevate the study of social phenomena to the positive or scientific state. The emphasis has been on establishing laws governing these phenomena and creating a predictive science of social facts. In order to assess its influence we will consider the work of Auguste Comte and Emile Durkheim, as leading exponents of the tradition, and will also examine the application of their theories to the questions of government and law by considering the work of Léon Duguit.

The second influence we shall examine is the British attempt in the latter half of the nineteenth century to reconcile a tension between the romantic-historical and the positivist approaches to society by developing theories of social evolution. Although almost entirely forgotten now, during the late nineteenth century Herbert

Spencer was pre-eminent in this field. Spencer's organicist theories were pressed in the cause of libertarianism. Much of Spencer's rationalist, evolutionary spirit, however, was adopted by, and adapted to, the cause of a collectivist orientation in such forms as Fabianism and New Liberalism. After considering Spencer's work, the nature and significance of this movement for the shaping of the functionalist style will therefore be examined.

Finally, we will examine pragmatism which, particularly under the inspiration of C. S. Pierce, William James, and John Dewey, was very influential in the United States around the turn of the century. This pragmatic movement in philosophy also had a significant impact on the social theory of the time. We will consider in particular its impact on legal thought, primarily through the emergence, in the early decades of this century, of the American legal realist movement.

At first glance, these various theories appear strikingly different in terms of their methods and objectives. Nevertheless, I shall argue that each theme has played an important role in shaping the functionalist style in public law. It is also suggested that, provided we plunge below the surface of these theories, certain important links between them may be revealed. Although all these theories flourished during the latter half of the nineteenth century and the early decades of the twentieth, the links between them are not simply the product of historical circumstance. The most important links are political. For, while these theories pursued distinctive concerns, ideas drawn from each of them have been blended by political theorists to create an identifiable body of ideas with certain distinctive characteristics. The ideas were in effect harnessed to what may be called a theory of progressivism; that is, a belief which embraced socialism as an ideal but which argued that, with the coming of democracy, socialism could be achieved through a process of gradual evolution from the old order to the new. Thus, while there may be no one theory of socialism to which adherents of the functionalist style subscribe, the general thrust was in favour of a democratic evolutionary progress towards a socialist ideal.

SOCIOLOGICAL POSITIVISM

The tradition of sociological positivism is conditioned by the growth of modern science and the spread of the rationalist outlook.

The starting point for investigation may be taken to be the eighteenth-century revolutionary movements which gave impetus to beliefs that social progress was possible and that social organization could be reconstructed in accordance with rational principles. From this impetus various theories were proposed which sought to apply the empirical method of the natural sciences to the study of society. Sociological positivism was one such method. The founder of this method, which thrived in the nineteenth century, was Auguste Comte.[1] We will first consider the nature of Comte's thought and then examine its development by Durkheim. Finally, through an examination of the work of Léon Duguit, we will assess the contribution which sociological positivism may have for an understanding of government and law.

Comte's thought

The general objective of Comte's work was to establish a set of relations between the sciences. In part, these relationships were secured by appeal to the historical method. Comte argued that human thought passes through three stages: the theological, the metaphysical, and the positive. The theological stage he associated with militarism, the metaphysical with juristic thought, and the positive stage with industrialism. The specific task which Comte set himself was to develop a positive philosophy.

Comte's method was empirical. All reflections must be derived from experience; that is, from observation and from facts. According to Comte the different orders of experience each have their own laws. He identified six fundamental sciences: mathematics, astronomy, physics, chemistry, biology, sociology. These sciences, he argued, had developed in historical progression. Furthermore, the movement from one to another can be viewed as a movement from the abstract to the concrete. Although the laws governing the different orders are not strictly reducible to each other, Comte felt that the basis for sociology could be found in biology, the science preceding it in the hierarchy. He argued that the time was now ripe for the application of the positivist method to social phenomena and for the establishment of sociology, a term he seems to have invented.

[1] See, A. Comte, *Introduction to Positive Philosophy* (1830–42) (F. Ferre (ed.)) (Indianapolis, 1946); J. S. Mill, *Auguste Comte and Positivism* (1865: Ann Arbor, Mich., 1961); E. E. Evans-Pritchard, *The Sociology of Comte* (Manchester, 1970).

Comte argued that human behaviour is governed not primarily by the intellect but by the instincts and emotions. The intellect merely helps us choose the means by which we may best achieve ends dictated by our instincts. Among these instincts the egoistic, or self-regarding, are more powerful than the social, or other-regarding. However, although it is the egoistic instincts which force us to work, to acquire knowledge and to co-operate, eventually the altruistic instincts, strengthened by the power of the intellect, gain ground. For Comte the fundamental law of human evolution consists in the 'growing ascendancy of our humanity over our animality, brought about by a double process, namely the increase of power of the intellect over the instincts and of the other-regarding instincts over the self-regarding'.[2]

This evolutionary development was not the result of the growing significance of natural rights doctrines. Such ideas as natural rights belong to the metaphysical age and progress is to be found in positive laws. For Comte, this evolutionary movement lay in the growing division of labour in society. This division of labour was itself the product of the growing complexity of the social organism. It is the growing division of labour which reflects the scale of interdependencies in society and causes us to recognize that people are engaged in a common enterprise. Consequently, Comte believed that both the necessity of government and its functions may be deduced from the principle of the division of labour. The specialization of functions has a dispersive effect and a primary function of government becomes that of securing co-ordination amongst the parts.

Comte's work had a significant impact in Britain. His *Course of Positive Philosophy* was translated by Harriet Martineau who in 1853 commented that:[3]

We are living in a remarkable time, when the conflict of opinions renders a firm foundation of knowledge indispensable . . . The supreme dread of everyone who cares for the good of the nation or race is that men should be adrift for want of anchorage for their convictions . . . The work of M. Comte is unquestionably the greatest single effort that has been made to obviate this kind of danger.

[2] M. Ginsberg, *Essays in Sociology and Social Philosophy* (Harmondsworth, 1968), 272.
[3] H. Martineau, *The Positive Philosophy of A. Comte* (London, 1853). Quoted in G. Hawthorn, *Enlightenment and Despair* (Cambridge, 2nd edn., 1987), 79.

J. S. Mill, although critical of aspects of Comte's work and, in particular the French mania for system which Comte exemplified, nevertheless found Comte's empirical method, his historical approach and his conception of the hierarchy of the sciences, highly attractive.[4]

The contribution of Durkheim

The positive approach of Comte was developed by Emile Durkheim who adopted Comte's empirical and rationalist methods and fashioned them into an approach which provides a major foundation for the study of sociology today. Durkheim was particularly concerned with the issue of order in society. How was social cohesion possible? Durkheim sought to provide an answer to this question by demonstrating that society forms an integrated unity similar to that of living organisms. He suggested that the main cause of social differentiation was the increase in population density. While these changes had caused pressures, consensus was still possible. The source of consensus was to be found in the division of labour, which was the pre-eminent fact of social solidarity.[5]

Durkheim was especially concerned to try to measure changes in the basis of social solidarity. However, because the moral phenomena which lay at the roots of social solidarity could not directly be measured, Durkheim identified law as an external and visible index of changes in invisible moral phenomena. Different forms of law, it was argued, reflect different bases for social solidarity. Durkheim then sought to show that the movement from repressive to restitutive forms of law, from those based on penal sanctions to those aimed at restoration of relations before the law was violated, was indicative of a transition from a society based on 'mechanical solidarity', or shared values, to a society founded on 'organic solidarity', or functional interdependence.

Durkheim recognized that in modern societies social solidarity was no longer based on widely shared social values and that government and law had important functions to perform in organizing the 'collective conscience' of the new order and acting as an integrative mechanism respectively. The function of the state

---

[4] See Mill, *Auguste Comte and Positivism*.
[5] E. Durkheim, *The Division of Labour in Society* (trans. G. Simpson) (1893: New York, 1964).

was to plan the social environment so that individuals could more fully realize themselves. But this function could not be achieved by the state directly since it was too remote. Durkheim felt that these tasks should be performed by groups—such as professions and other occupational groups—which intermediated between the individual and the state. He expressed the hope that these corporate bodies would not only take on responsibilities for regulating economic activity but would also form a moral community for their members.[6]

Durkheim's identification of the fact of social solidarity captured the spirit of his times. This theme was a particularly influential one in French political thought during the late nineteenth and early twentieth centuries.[7] It is this idea of social solidarity that provided Léon Duguit with the basis of his theory of law and it is to his work that we now turn.

Duguit on government and law

Léon Duguit worked as a Professor of Law at the University of Bordeaux between 1886 and 1928. His work, the main fruits of which are to be found in his book, *Law in the Modern State*,[8] aimed to construct a science of public law entirely on empirical foundations. By eliminating all theological and metaphysical elements from his work, he sought to challenge the prevailing constitutional orthodoxy which was founded on the natural rights of the citizen and the inalienable sovereignty of the state. Here we may recognize Comte's influence in distinguishing the metaphysical stage associated with juristic thought from the stage of industrialism characterized by the rise of positivist thought. Duguit then founded the bedrock of his theory on the fact of social interdependence, and here we may discern the influence of Durkheim. That people are born free and equal is an a priori assumption, argued Duguit, whereas it is an incontestable fact that they were born as members of a collectivity. Duguit believed that the rights and duties of rulers and ruled could be founded on this fundamental fact. Since people

---

[6] Durkheim, *Professional Ethics and Civic Morals* (trans. C. Brookfield) (London, 1957).

[7] See J. E. S. Hayward, 'Solidarity: the social history of an idea in nineteenth-century France' (1959) 4 *International Review of Social History* 261; id., 'The official social philosophy of the French Third Republic: Léon Bourgeois and Solidarism' (1961) 6 *International Review of Social History* 19.

[8] L. Duguit, *Law in the Modern State* (trans. F. and H. J. Laski) (London, 1921).

were unable to exist outside society they were required, as a matter of prudence, to work for its preservation. This was the source of the basic duty to work for the preservation of social solidarity. It was from this basic duty that all rights were derived.

In adopting this positivist approach, Duguit thus rejected the metaphysical ideas of sovereignty and the personality of the state as legitimating principles. In seeking a legitimatory principle he embraced a functional approach. Duguit took the view that the state was simply an apparatus for performing certain functions. Consequently, the concept of sovereignty was replaced with that of 'public service'; the state exists merely to perform certain tasks which are necessary for the preservation and promotion of social solidarity.[9] This view of the state, together with the basic duty of working to preserve social solidarity, provides us with the essence of Duguit's approach. The basic duty provides us with the fundamental rule of conduct which may be called the rule of law; viz., that we must not only not injure, but must also work to promote, social solidarity.

From this approach, it can be seen that Duguit felt that, in general, citizens must, as a matter of fact, obey the state. The basic limitation on the obligation to obey the state arose from the fundamental purpose of the state. If the state acts in a manner not designed to promote social solidarity then, Duguit argued, this must be resisted. This follows from the fact that, having rejected the idea of the personality of the state, there can be no fundamental difference between rulers and ruled with respect to the rule of law; all are equally bound by it.

Finally, it is evident that Duguit's theory of law is far removed from those theories which are built on the assumption of the priority of individual rights. Duguit's theory is based on the fact that rights are derived from duties. Rights are therefore determined on a functional basis since there can be no liberty or property rights beyond those that contribute to maintenance of social solidarity.

For Duguit, then, the state must be viewed simply as a group of people issuing orders to others. Nevertheless, with the growth in the size and power of the public service state he recognized the dangers of subordination. Duguit advocated two main solutions to this problem. First, he proposed that, since the functions of the state

---

[9] Ibid., chaps. 1 and 2; id., 'Law and the State' (1917) 31 *Harvard Law Rev.* 1.

were such that it was no longer possible to impose a unified direction of society from the centre, there was a need for a territorial decentralization of power. Secondly, he suggested that the values of liberty and solidarity could be integrated through the promotion of associational and interest groups. Through such processes, it was felt, the basis of public law was no longer to be rooted in *command* but rather in *organization*.[10]

The French tradition of sociological positivism

In the French tradition of sociological positivism we are presented with an analysis which is empirical, positivist, and evolutionary and in which government and law lose their towering metaphysical status and become functional elements within a social organism.[11] That the orientation is rather different from the intellectual influences on the normativist style is fairly clear. In normativist language the style of sociological positivism is that of constructivist rationalism. But from the perspective of positivism things look different. Comte suggested that a society's political institutions provide an indication of the stage which has been attained by civilization. He would presumably have argued that the conservative variant of the normativist style lies in the theological stage of society, and the liberal variant is rooted in the metaphysical stage. From the Comtean perspective the functionalist style in public law should be viewed as a product of the scientific era.

The main criticism of sociological positivism is founded on the vagueness of the central concepts of the theory. The central idea of social solidarity, for example, is never clearly defined and is simply accepted as the foundation of the theory. By some mysterious process we simply awaken to the fact of interdependence and the 'ineluctable solidarity of things'.[12] In this way, sociological positivism is founded on a collectivist ideology in much the same

[10] Id., *Law in the Modern State*, 49.
[11] See, generally, D. G. Charlton, *Positivist Thought in France during the Second Empire, 1852–70* (Oxford, 1959).
[12] The phrase is taken from L. Bourgeois, *Solidarité* (1896: Paris, 7th edn., 1912), 6; quoted in J. T. Kloppenberg, *Uncertain Victory. Social Democracy and Progressivism in European and American Thought, 1870–1920* (Oxford, 1986), 301. Kloppenberg comments that Bourgeois's book 'became the bible of France's Radical Republicans during the years of their great political strength; it provided the rationale for an impressive array of social reforms enacted between 1896 and 1912'.

way as liberalism is based on an individualist ideology.[13] Consequently, sociological positivism can be criticized for giving the impression of setting out to demonstrate scientifically the truth of an approach which seemed already to have been assumed in the way the terms were defined.[14]

EVOLUTIONARY SOCIAL THEORY

Sociological positivism struck a resonant note in nineteenth-century Britain primarily because of its anti-metaphysical approach. As such it had an affinity both with utilitarianism and legal positivism. Utilitarianism substituted pleasure and pain for the attribution of natural rights in citizens and, through the felicific calculus, sought to place morals and politics on an empirical foundation. And, as we have seen, utilitarianism was closely associated with legal positivism.[15] The empirical method is seen most clearly in the work of John Austin who, in producing a science of positive law in terms of commands, sanctions, and habits, attempted to provide an explanation of law entirely in non-normative terminology.[16]

But positivism and utilitarianism, being nominalist and individualist in character, did not attempt to address directly the basic question of how order in society is achieved and maintained. These theories were based on the idea of the rational individual with certain desires rationally fitting means to ends, the ends themselves not being susceptible of rational calculation. Bentham's criticisms of social contract theory had been accepted but nothing was put in its place. For the utilitarian, apparently, it was enough to demonstrate the advantages offered by the social order. This might satisfy the legal practitioner or practical reformer but could not be sufficient for the political theorist for whom the issue of order is of central importance.

The existence of this gap may help us to explain the links between legal positivism, utilitarianism, and the influence of French sociological positivism. It may, for example, account for J. S. Mill's

---

[13] See H. J. Laski, 'M. Duguit's Conception of the State', in A. L. Goodhart *et al.* (eds.), *Modern Theories of Law* (London, 1933), 52 at pp. 63–7.
[14] See Hawthorn, *Enlightenment and Despair* (Cambridge, 1976), 122–4.
[15] See Chap. 1 p. 19.
[16] See Chap. 1, pp. 20–1.

interest in Comte.[17] But the existence of this gap also suggests one reason for the influence on the functionalist style in public law of a domestic form of evolutionary social theory which is not an obvious bedfellow of utilitarianism. This is the theory of social evolution which flourished in the nineteenth century from the stimulus of Darwin's *Origin of Species* and which is most closely associated with Herbert Spencer.[18]

Spencer and evolutionary theory

Herbert Spencer pursued a literary and journalistic career throughout the latter half of the nineteenth century and also found time to write books on such subjects as *The Proper Sphere of Government*,[19] *Social Statics*,[20] *First Principles*,[21] *Man Versus the State*,[22] *Principles of Ethics*,[23] and many others besides. His approach was positivist and rationalist and his general objective was to lay down a theory of social evolution. His influence throughout this period was extensive, not only in Britain but also in North America.[24]   Spencer believed that social evolution was part

---

[17] Mill, *Auguste Comte and Positivism* (1865: Ann Arbor, 1961).

[18] See J. W. Burrow, *Evolution and Society. A Study in Victorian Social Theory* (Cambridge, 1968); D. Wiltshire, *The Social and Political Thought of Herbert Spencer* (Oxford, 1978); W. H. Greenleaf, *The British Political Tradition. Vol. 2. The Ideological Heritage* (London, 1983), chap. 3.

[19] (London, 1843).

[20] *Social Statics: Or The Conditions Essential to Human Happiness Specified, and the First of Them Developed* (1851: Farnborough, Hants, 1970).

[21] (London, 1862).

[22] (1884: Harmondsworth, 1969).   [23] (London, 1892).

[24] One index of Spencer's popularity in the United States is seen in the fact that, between 1860 and 1903, a total of 368,755 copies of his books had been sold: see H. I. Sharlin, 'Spencer, Scientism and American Constitutional Law' (1976) 33 *Annals of Science* 457, p. 464. See generally, R. Hofstader, *Social Darwinism in American Thought 1860–1915* (Boston, rev. edn. 1955). Spencer entered the folklore of American constitutional law as a result of Justice Holmes's infamous dissent in the case of *Lochner* v. *New York* (1905) 198 US 45. In this case, in which a statute regulating hours of work in bakeries was struck down by the Supreme Court, Justice Holmes tried to reveal the thought processes of the majority in stating (at pp. 75–6): 'This case is decided upon an economic theory which a large part of the country does not entertain . . . [A] constitution is not intended to embody a particular economic theory, whether of paternalism and the organic relation of the citizen to the State or of laissez-faire . . . General propositions do not decide concrete cases . . . The Fourteenth Amendment does not enact Mr Herbert Spencer's Social Statics.'

Later Holmes, who was himself very interested in evolutionary theories, when referring to Spencer, stated that he doubted 'if any writer of English except Darwin had done so much to affect our whole way of thinking about the universe' *Justice Oliver Wendell Holmes, Vol. 1. The Shaping Years* (Cambridge, Mass., 1957), 156.

of the processes of evolution at large and that societal arrangements were the outcome of natural causes. His theories linked the idea of progress with advances in technological knowledge and, by showing how progress follows natural laws, he sought to place the development of political organization on a scientific footing. He argued that there is an inexorable tendency towards the differentiation of things and that, as a result, societies become more differentiated. This, he argued, was conducive to liberty. In industrial society free action flourishes and diversity of opinion is tolerated.

Spencer's ideological orientation was therefore libertarian: societies evolve from homogeneity to heterogeneity; industrial society is highly differentiated and its government exhibits limitation of scope and diffusion of authority; as civilization advances, so does government decay. Spencer propounded the law of equal freedom which was not unlike the first of Rawls's principles of justice: 'Every man is free to do that which he wills provided he infringes not the equal freedom of any other man.'[25] Unlike Rawls, however, this principle of liberty is not tempered by any principle of justice which recognizes a principle of equality. It will come as no surprise to discover, then, that Spencer was highly critical of statutory intervention, arguing that it stifled liberty and led to rigidity and uniformity: 'Society, a living growing organism, placed within apparatuses of dead, rigid, mechanical formulas, cannot fail to be hampered and pinched.'[26]

If Spencer is taken as the model it seems clear that Victorian evolutionary social theory was far from being collectivist in its orientation. Further, if we include Maine amongst the evolutionists then it is also a tradition which was antagonistic to an Austinian, positivistic conception of law.[27] Yet, despite Maine's hostility both to utilitarianism and legal positivism, J. S. Mill was an early admirer of Maine's work.[28] Furthermore, Mill thought Spencer 'one of the most vigorous as well as boldest thinkers that English speculation has yet produced, full of the true scientific spirit'.[29]

---

[25] H. Spencer, *Social Statics*, 76–8, 87–8, 103; for Rawls's principles of justice see Chap. 5 pp. 93–4.
[26] Quoted in Greenleaf, *The British Political Tradition. Vol. 2. The Ideological Heritage* (London, 1983), 74.   [27] H. S. Maine, *Ancient Law* (London, 1861).
[28] See S. Collini, D. Winch, and J. W. Burrow, *That Noble Science of Politics* (Cambridge, 1983), 145.
[29] See Greenleaf, *The British Political Tradition*, vol. 2 at p. 48.

These views are significant for our purpose because Mill played a pivotal role in British nineteenth-century thought. In Barker's words, 'it is Mill who serves, in the years between 1848 and 1880, as the bridge from laissez-faire to the idea of social readjustment by the State, and from political Radicalism to economic Socialism'.[30] When, after 1880, we began to see emerging new philosophies to provide the intellectual underpinning for the foundations of the welfare state that were being laid between 1880 and 1914, Mill might have supplied the economic doctrine, but the conceptions of order and progress utilized the methods, if not the ideologies, of the social evolutionists.

Harnessing the evolutionists' methods while jettisoning their ideologies was scarcely a difficult exercise since the libertarian theory patently did not hold together. Spencer's argument was that although societies become more differentiated and heterogeneous this tends, not to chaos, but new forms of equilibrium. This argument, however, seemed to defy the second law of thermo-dynamics which suggests that energy tends to become dissipated and order to dissolve. The ambiguities and contradictions in Spencer's theory gradually became apparent and, as Hawthorn comments: 'Towards the end of the century he became in England a living monument to vanished assumptions.'[31] It was left to the newer ideologies, in particular Fabianism and New Liberalism, to utilize the evolutionary method to different effect.

Fabianism

The Fabian Society, founded in 1884, is committed to what Sidney Webb once called 'the inevitability of gradualism'. The Fabians did not accept that under capitalism the necessary contradictions would manifest themselves in a growing class struggle. They believed in the prospect of a gradual and constitu-tionally achieved transition to socialism. The Fabians were particu-larly influential during the first forty or so years of their history, a period in which the leading lights were the Webbs, G. B. Shaw, Graham Wallas, and H. G. Wells and, less consistently, Bertrand Russell, G. D. H. Cole, Harold Laski, and R. H. Tawney. It was, however, Sidney and Beatrice Webb—a remarkable partnership between a natural bureaucrat and a natural aristocrat—who

[30] E. Barker, *Political Thought in England 1848–1914* (London, 1915), 215.
[31] Hawthorn, *Enlightenment and Despair*, 91.

provided the Fabians with their centre of gravity. In addition to their work for the Fabian Society and the Labour party, and the prodigious nature of their social inquiry work, they were responsible for founding—as institutional outlets for their ideas—the London School of Economics in 1895 and the *New Statesman* in 1913.

In effect the Fabians sought to weld the methods of both utilitarianism and evolutionary theory to a collectivist ideology. First, they exploited the ambivalence of utilitarianism. Benthamism seemed to provide no basis for determining whether the principle of utility aimed to maximize an individual's happiness or the happiness of all. In effect, the Fabians skewed utilitarianism in favour of the principle of social solidarity. One consequence was that, while Bentham was concerned with legal and constitutional reform, the Fabians were more interested in social and economic reform; and specifically with the social control of socially created values. Secondly, the Fabians pressed evolutionary theory in service of a collectivist ideal. Behind both the economics and politics of Fabianism lay an organic theory of society and the view that progress is tied to advances in technical knowledge.[32] The most direct link between the Fabians and Spencer is Beatrice Webb, who was brought up under his tutelage, absorbed his scientific method of viewing 'all social institutions exactly as if they were plants or animals—things that could be observed, classified and explained', but who eventually shook herself 'completely free from *laisser-faire* bias'.[33]

The Fabians inherited both the positive scientific spirit and a conception that progress follows natural laws from the evolutionists, but they adapted it to French sociological positivism based on the principle of social solidarity. Consider, for example, Kloppenberg's assessment of Sidney Webb: 'Although he passed through a Comtean phase that permanently altered his perspective from liberal individualism to organic collectivism, he had shed the positivist's confidence in ultimate certainties as inconsistent with

[32] 'Owing mainly to the efforts of Comte, Darwin, and Herbert Spencer, we can no longer think of the ideal society as an unchanging State. The social ideal from being static has become dynamic. The necessity of the constant growth and development of the social organism has become axiomatic' S. Webb, 'The basis of socialism: historic' in B. Shaw *et al.* (eds.), *Fabian Essays in Socialism* (London, 2nd edn., 1920), 28, at p. 29.
[33] B. Webb, *My Apprenticeship* (Harmondsworth, 1938), vol. 1, p. 56; and see Greenleaf, *The British Political Tradition*, vol. 2 at p. 393.

empiricism and democracy by the time he proclaimed himself a socialist in 1886.'[34] Certainly the empiricist strain runs deeply through the work of the Fabians. Scientific analysis of society was considered an essential preliminary to the effective reform of social and political arrangements.

For Fabianism, the emergence of democracy which was taking place in the political sphere had to be accompanied by the spread of socialism in the economic sphere. The policies of the Fabians were described by Beatrice Webb during the 1890s as 'essentially collective ownership wherever practicable; collective regulation everywhere else; collective provision according to need for all the impotent and sufferers; and collective taxation in proportion to wealth'.[35] The State, albeit in an anti-metaphysical sense, was thus viewed as being of central importance. Through its control and regulatory functions it was viewed as the primary mechanism for transforming the anarchic tendencies of individualism to the collective good. A variety of models were suggested for the forms which these political institutions might take.[36] But running through all these was the belief that an advanced state could not be run without a bureaucracy. The complexity of the issues meant that these matters could not be dealt with by popular vote. Nor could they be formulated by the amateur civil servant. What was required in order to achieve a more efficient and expert government in 'a highly differentiated and systematically co-ordinated social order'[37] was a professionalized administrative élite.

The Fabians, then, were pioneers of social engineering or what might be termed 'evolutionary rationalism'. Their vision was of a functionally differentiated society in which 'the individual is now created by the social organism of which he forms a part'[38] and in which a state, founded on democracy tempered by respect for the expert, is required to co-ordinate the social order. This is the society

[34] Kloppenberg, *Uncertain Victory*, 203.
[35] B. Webb, *Our Partnership* (London, 1948), 107; quoted in Greenleaf, *The British Political Tradition*, 374.
[36] H. G. Wells, *A Modern Utopia* (London, 1905); S. and B. Webb, *A Constitution for the Socialist Commonwealth of Great Britain* (Cambridge, 1920). G. Wallas, *The Great Society: A Psychological Analysis* (London, 1914).
[37] S. and B. Webb, *A Constitution for the Socialist Commonwealth of Great Britain*, 202.
[38] S. Webb, 'The basis of socialism', 53.

which Graham Wallas, adapting the term from Durkheim, labelled 'the great society'.[39]

The Fabians recognized the dangers that lay in the establishment of a powerful centralized bureaucracy. The answers they provided took both institutional and ethical forms. The institutional response was—in common with Duguit—to suggest that there should be a broad territorial diffusion of power. Sidney Webb, for example, highlighted 'the important part to be played in the Socialist State by its various democratically organised and practically autonomous Local Governing Bodies'.[40] The ethical response was provided by Graham Wallas who recognized that, in order to prevent the all-powerful state from becoming the servile state, the development of a strong public service ethic was fundamental. Here, however, Wallas highlighted a particular weakness within Fabianism. Their vision expected the civil service 'to know more and do less than any other body in public life. . . . It is to be competent where those who control cannot be competent, yet it is not to control. It is to enable those who do not know and cannot know enough for policy-making to make policy, yet it is to have no policies of its own.'[41]

That particular weakness also serves to reflect a more basic tension within the Fabian model of evolutionary rationalism. This tension is that between élitism and egalitarianism. It is concisely expressed by Kloppenberg: 'Did the Webbs want ethical regeneration or institutional efficiency? Did they want a democratic society or a society organized by experts? In short, did they want to reform Great Britain or run it?'[42]

New liberalism

Both the strength and limitation of Fabianism is to be found in its tendency to examine the benefits of collectivism in terms of economic efficiency. There was, however, also an ethical strain to the progressive ideas of this period. This dimension to progressive thought was well brought out by the school of 'New Liberalism'

[39] Wallas, *The Great Society*.
[40] S. Webb, 'Introduction' in G. B. Shaw (ed.), *Fabian Essays in Socialism* (London, 2nd edn., 1920), p. xxiii. See also A. M. McBriar, *Fabian Socialism and English Politics, 1884–1918* (Cambridge, 1966), 108–9.
[41] R. Barker, 'The Fabian State' in B. Pimlott (ed.), *Fabian Essays in Socialist Thought* (London, 1984) 27, p. 33.
[42] Kloppenberg, *Uncertain Victory*, 205.

120   Foundations of Functionalism

which was associated in particular with T. H. Green[43] and
L. T. Hobhouse.[44] The thought of 'New Liberalism' was shaped by
the fact that during the period 1880–1914 a great deal of
interventionist legislation had been enacted, much of which had
been the responsibility of Liberal governments. Yet this wave of
social legislation could not easily be reconciled with the tenets of
classical liberalism. Was not this type of legislation a threat to
freedom? It was within this milieu that the thinkers of New
Liberalism sought to develop a self-consciously modernist philosophy.
This movement was inspired by philosophical Idealism. It
therefore rejected empiricism and was particularly critical of
utilitarianism. The British Idealist thinkers who shaped the New
Liberalism of the period nevertheless otherwise shared many of its
roots with the Fabians. In the words of Vincent and Plant:[45]

These thinkers, including Sir Henry Jones, Bernard Bosanquet,
D. G. Ritchie, William Wallace, E. Caird, and Lord Haldane, fundamentally
changed the conception of the role of the state within the Liberal tradition
of political thought. They developed a theory of the state which was a long
way removed from the rational calculative tendencies of utilitarianism and
provided a justification for the role of the state in the spheres of economic
life and welfare which went beyond what has usually been countenanced
within Liberalism, whether based on utilitarianism or Lockean theory. The
Idealists achieved this by means of a complex theory which gave the state a
particular moral significance. They saw the role of the state not merely as a
set of instrumentalities for securing material welfare but as the focus of
a sense of community and citizenship, an institution in which a good
common to all classes and recognizable to all interest groups could be
articulated. The purpose of the state was to promote the good life of its
citizens and to develop the moral nature of man.

[43] T. H. Green, *Lectures on the Principles of Political Obligation* (London,
1907). See M. Richter, *The Politics of Conscience: T. H. Green and His Age*
(London, 1964); I. M. Greengarten, *Thomas Hill Green and the Development of
Liberal–Democratic Thought* (Toronto, 1981).
[44] L. T. Hobhouse, *Liberalism* (London, 1911); id., *Social Evolution and
Political Theory* (New York, 1911); id., *Development and Purpose: An Essay
towards a Philosophy of Evolution* (London, 1913); id., *The Metaphysical Theory
of the State* (London, 1918). See J. A. Hobson and M. Ginsberg, *L. T. Hobhouse:
His Life and Work* (London, 1931); Collini, *Liberalism and Sociology.
L. T. Hobhouse and Political Argument in England 1880–1914* (Cambridge, 1979).
[45] A. Vincent and R. Plant, *Philosophy, Politics and Citizenship. The Life and
Thought of the British Idealists* (Oxford, 1984), 1–2.

Green was the pivotal figure in the movement. He viewed society not as an aggregate of isolated atoms but as an organism for the realization of common purposes. From this starting point he developed a theory of the common good and of human freedom which could be coupled to the collectivist tendencies of the age. The foundation of this approach was a positive conception of liberty; freedom as an actual capacity for doing or enjoying something rather than simply the absence of external constraint:[46]

When we speak of freedom, we . . . do not mean merely freedom from restraint or compulsion. We do not mean merely freedom to do as we like irrespectively of what it is that we like. We do not mean a freedom that can be enjoyed by one man or one set of men at the cost of a loss of freedom to others. When we speak of freedom as something to be highly prized, we mean a positive power or capacity for doing or enjoying something worth doing, and that, too, something that we do or enjoy in common with others.

This notion of freedom is positive in the sense that it is directly related to self-realization. The objective is to transform instincts and desires in such a way that they can be fitted to the overall goals of a person's deliberative life. That is, liberty should not be viewed as the absence of compulsion but as the empowerment of all members of society to make the best of themselves.

This notion of freedom is also evolutionary. What Green in effect was arguing is that, since Liberals had won the battle for civil and parliamentary freedom and for freedom of trade, the challenge now was that of self-realization. And, to render this possible, it was essential for the state to provide a basic platform of entitlements. This sentiment was succinctly stated by Herbert Samuel:[47]

[L]iberty was not a matter only of national independence, or of constitutional democracy, or of freedom of thought and religion . . . [T]here could be no true liberty if a man was confined and oppressed by

[46] Green, 'Liberal legislation and freedom of contract' (1880) in *Works*, vol. 3, 365, at p. 371. Cf. Mill, *On Liberty* (1859) (G. Himmelfarb (ed.), Harmondsworth, 1974). For the importance of the debate in the twentieth century see: I. Berlin, *Four Essays on Liberty* (Oxford, 1969), chap. 2; C. Taylor, *Philosophical Papers, Vol. 2* (Cambridge, 1985), chap. 8.

[47] H. Samuel, *Memoirs* (London, 1945), 25. Quoted in Vincent and Plant, *Philosophy, Politics and Citizenship*, at p. 73. See also id., *Liberalism: an Attempt to State the Principles and Proposals of Contemporary Liberalism in England* (London, 1902), in which Samuel specifically defends the principles of New Liberalism against the views of Herbert Spencer.

poverty, by excessive hours of labour, by insecurity of livelihood . . . To be truly free he must be liberated from these things also. In many cases, it was only the power of law that could effect this. More law might often mean more liberty.

From this foundation, the New Liberalism developed distinctive views on the idea of citizenship and on the positive functions of the state.[48] The movement also contributed illuminating insights into such matters as governing institutions and rights and duties. Institutions are viewed as expressions of collective purposes which maintain vitality so long as they are able to maintain a clear sense of purpose.[49] People are viewed as having a 'station' or 'groove' in society;[50] notions which imply a distinctive balance between rights and duties inherent in an individual's social role or function. Further, rights are rooted in society; contrary to the beliefs of classical liberalism, the idea of rights existing prior to, or apart from, society was regarded as nonsensical. Finally, some looked to the 'increasing ordering of economic organisation by the conscience of the community, and a great extension of public control in the use of private property and in industrial relations'.[51]

Many of these themes run through Green's *Lectures on the Principles of Political Obligation*.[52] In these lectures his purpose 'is to consider the moral function or object served by law, or by the system of rights and obligations which the state enforces'.[53] Although built on customs and habits, institutions were nevertheless the repositories of ideas of the common good; the challenge was to avoid institutional sclerosis by ensuring that they continued to meet contemporary needs. The function of law, then, was to provide the conditions for the development of our capacities and powers towards the moral end of self-realization. And the capacity of institutions to achieve this end was the criterion of their moral development and progress. Civic institutions were therefore the public expression of private morality.

Similar themes can be seen in the work of writers such as Bosanquet and Hobhouse. Bosanquet's book, *The Philosophical*

---

[48] See, e.g., H. Jones, *The Principles of Citizenship* (London, 1919).
[49] J. H. Muirhead and H. J. W. Hetherington, *Social Purpose: A Contribution to a Philosophy of Civic Society* (London, 1922).
[50] See Vincent and Plant, *Philosophy, Politics and Citizenship*, 28.
[51] Hetherington, *Life and Letters of Sir Henry Jones* (London, 1924), 137; quoted in Vincent and Plant, *Philosophy, Politics and Citizenship*, 32.
[52] (London, 1924; preface by B. Bosanquet.)   [53] Ibid. at p. 29.

Theory of the State,[54] was, for example, designed to challenge the individualism of such thinkers as Bentham, Mill, and Spencer who posit a basic antagonism between the individual and the state. Bosanquet argues that such individualism is based on a false understanding of the self. The true self must be understood as engaging in the world in a specific way as part of a community. Hobhouse wrote *The Metaphysical Theory of the State*[55] specifically to criticize Bosanquet's idealist theory on the ground that it provided too expansive a role for the state. This, however, has been felt to be rather ironical since, although he is critical of idealism and maintains a formal commitment to empirical rationalism, it is Hobhouse who in fact calls for the greater degree of state intervention.[56]

Hobhouse 'presented a kind of fusion of Spencer and Green'[57] insofar as he believed in the scientific importance of the idea of evolution but felt that the most highly evolved society is one 'in which the efforts of its members are most completely coordinated to common ends, in which discord is most fully subdued to harmony.'[58] Within this process Hobhouse recognized the importance of Green's positive conception of liberty: 'liberty without equality is a name of noble sound and squalid result'.[59] Hobhouse's evolutionary method was, however, also reminiscent of Comte since he argued that it was the growing domination of mind over the conditions of life that enables us to appreciate the importance of the collective framework of society. The result was a 'rather unusual derivation of idealist conclusions from empiricist premises'.[60]

Evolutionary theory and collectivism

As we have seen, during the late nineteenth and early twentieth century there were influential strands of opinion which harnessed an evolutionary approach to a collectivist objective. Our concern here is not to try to disentangle New Liberalism from Fabian

[54] (London, 1899).
[55] (London, 1918).
[56] Collini, 'Hobhouse, Bosanquet and the State: Philosophical Idealism and Political Argument in England 1880–1918' (1976) 72 *Past and Present* 87.
[57] Greenleaf, *The British Political Tradition*, 163.
[58] Hobhouse, *Social Evolution and Political Theory* (New York, 1911), 23.
[59] Hobhouse, *Liberalism* (London, 1911), 48.
[60] P. Weiler, 'The New Liberalism of L. T. Hobhouse' (1972–3) 16 *Victorian Studies* 143.

124   *Foundations of Functionalism*

socialist thought.[61] Some of these differences were rooted in the extent to which the writers embraced positivism or Idealism. But, more important than their differences for our purposes is the fact that these movements shared many basic principles and common objectives. When, for example, Sidney Webb talked of a 'fourfold path of collective administration of public services, collective regulation of private industry, collective taxation of unearned income, and collective provision for the dependent sections of the community' as being the pathway to socialism, he outlined a programme with which many New Liberals in practice agreed. Furthermore, Webb himself indicated that 'much of what is claimed as the progress of socialism might be equally well described as a merely empirical development from the principles of Canning, Peel, Bentham and Gladstone'.[62]

But what, in particular, these movements had in common was an evolutionary or organicist method. During the latter half of the nineteenth century the emphasis in social and political thought shifted from an atomistic to an organic conception of society. This shift primarily reflects the influence of the processes of scientific discovery on the social thought of the period. And here the Darwin theory of evolution was most influential. The influence of Darwinian theory on Victorian social thought is often thought of in terms of 'the survival of the fittest' and the notions of struggle and competition which became known as 'Social Darwinism'.[63] But it is evident that its influence was much more broad-ranging. What in effect happened after 1880 was that the biological approaches of those such as Darwin and Spencer were transformed by Fabians and New Liberals. This essentially came about by positing a correlation between ethics and evolution and harnessing an evolutionary approach in service of a collectivist ideal.[64]

[61] Those interested in the debate can track it through: A. M. McBriar, *Fabian Socialism and English Politics 1884–1918* (Cambridge, 1966); H. V. Emy, *Liberals, Radicals and Social Politics, 1892–1914* (Cambridge, 1973); M. Freeden, *The New Liberalism: An Ideology of Social Reform* (Oxford, 1978); P. F. Clarke, *Liberals and Social Democrats* (Cambridge, 1978).

[62] S. Webb, 'Modern Social Movements' in *The Cambridge Modern History of the World*, vol. XII (Cambridge, 1919), 760. See the discussion in Freeden, *The New Liberalism*, 49, 71.

[63] See J. A. Rogers, 'Darwinism and Social Darwinism' (1972) 32 *J. of the History of Ideas* 267.

[64] See Freeden, 'Biological and evolutionary roots of the New Liberalism in England' 1976 *Political Theory* 487.

It is this attempt by Fabians and New Liberals to conjoin ethical and evolutionary considerations that led to the most sustained criticism of their theories. Such criticisms are perhaps most clearly and tersely summed up in Hawthorn's assessment of Hobhouse:[65]

Hobhouse's theory was . . . a *bricolage.* Out of the morally serious upper middle-class English air he took empiricism and Idealism, the assumption of pre-determined progress and a belief in benevolent intervention, the general English notions of biological evolution and a Comtean conviction in positive altruism and put them together in the service of a liberal socialist ideal.

These criticisms of Hobhouse might, with little modification, also be applied to the general movements we have examined. Certainly Hobhouse can be taken as a representative figure since, in addition to being a leading light of New Liberalism, he also held the first Chair of Sociology to be established in Britain—at the London School of Economics, which was founded by the Webbs.

New Liberalism and Fabianism were not the only movements of socialist thought which were influential during this period. One should, for example, mention guild socialism which was much more concerned than Fabianism about the problems of establishing a strong, centralized bureaucracy and which promoted a pluralist theory of the state.[66] But many of the ideas of guild socialism also ran within channels which have already been discussed; the guild socialist's conception of the state, for example, shared certain similarities with the views of Duguit. Certainly, the theories developed in the period between 1880 and 1914 have had a very important influence on twentieth-century British social democratic thought.[67] And within this period, despite the tension between an empiricist and an idealist temperament, the dominant theme was that of evolution.

[65] Hawthorn, *Enlightenment and Despair*, 106–7; see also Kloppenberg, *Uncertain Victory*, 305–6.
[66] See, H. Magid, *English Political Pluralism: the Problems of Freedom and Organisation* (New York, 1941); D. Nicholls, *The Pluralist State* (London, 1975); Laski, *The Foundations of Sovereignty and Other Essays* (London, 1921). On Laski's pluralism see Chap. 7, pp. 169–72.
[67] See A. Ulam, *Philosophical Foundations of English Socialism* (Cambridge, Mass., 1951); A. Warde, *Consensus and Beyond* (Manchester, 1981); F. Inglis, *Radical Earnestness: English Social Theory 1880–1980* (Oxford, 1982). ·

PRAGMATISM

The final influence on the functionalist style of public law to consider is that of pragmatism. The philosophy of pragmatism flourished in the United States at roughly the same period that the social movements of Fabianism and New Liberalism emerged in Britain. Its influence in the United States was largely the result of the work of C. S. Peirce, William James, and John Dewey who, by challenging the prevailing conceptions of knowledge, tried to redirect the course of philosophy.

Pragmatism may appropriately be referred to as a *via media*[68] between, on the one hand, an empiricism and positivism that may lead to inhumanism and, on the other, a rationalistic Idealism that may become out of touch with contemporary realities.[69] When viewed in this light its theoretical position and its influence in relation to the social movements of Fabianism and New Liberalism may be revealed. Pragmatism can be viewed as appealing to many who located themselves at the convergence between liberalism and socialism, since it sought to temper and transcend the positivism and empiricism associated with Fabianism and the idealism identified with New Liberalism. Pragmatism sought to force philosophers to confront doubt. The pragmatist's solution to many of the problems of philosophy is simply that of not providing any systematic solution at all.

Pragmatism is essentially a method of settling philosophical disputes by tracing their practical consequences. This may be viewed as an empiricist attitude but, according to William James, pragmatism represents empiricism 'both in a more radical and in a less objectionable form than it has ever yet assumed'. The pragmatist, continues James, 'turns away from abstraction and insufficiency, from verbal solutions, from bad *a priori* reasons, from fixed principles, closed systems, and pretended absolutes and origins. He turns towards concreteness and adequacy, towards facts, towards action and towards power'.[70] With pragmatism

---

[68] The phrase is taken from Dewey who wrote that William James set out to find 'a *via media* between natural science and the ideal interests of morals and religion' (quoted in Kloppenberg, *Uncertain Victory*, 26).

[69] See W. James, *Pragmatism* (London, 1907), Lecture 1, 'The present dilemma in philosophy'.

[70] Ibid., Lecture 2, p. 25.

truth and usefulness become fused: 'ideas . . . become true just in so far as they help us to get into satisfactory relations with other parts of our experience.'[71]

Beyond empiricist epistemology

Pragmatism may be viewed as a critique of an empiricist epistemology, which is based on the Cartesian distinction between mind and matter.[72] Pragmatism rejects the conventional dualisms between mind and body and subject and object and articulates a view of truth as being grounded in human experience. The philosophers of pragmatism resisted the idea that experience could be frozen at a particular moment in time and analysed in chunks. James emphasized the essential quality of *continuity* of experience; it is a stream of thought or consciousness.[73] Dewey challenged the idea that experience was exclusively concerned with knowledge:[74]

In the orthodox view, experience is regarded as a knowledge-affair. But to eyes not looking through ancient spectacles, it assuredly appears as an affair of the intercourse of a living being with its physical and social environment.

Dewey here accentuates the idea that experience is relational, that it is not exclusively private and subjective. This point is further reinforced by Peirce who argued that all language, all inquiry and all knowledge is essentially social in character. On this aspect of Peirce's work Bernstein comments:[75]

The alternative paradigm of inquiry or knowledge that Peirce . . . develop[s] . . . is a view of inquiry as a self-corrective process which has no beginning or end points and in which any claim is subject to further rational criticism . . . Our claims to knowledge are legitimised not by their origins . . . but rather by the norms and rules of inquiry itself. These very norms, rules and standards are themselves open to rational criticism. The fallibility of all knowledge is not a sign of its deficiency but rather an essential characteristic of knowledge, for every knowledge claim is part of a

---

[71] Ibid. 26.
[72] We might note that both Oakeshott and Hayek also criticize Cartesian rationality: see Oakeshott, *Rationalism in Politics*, 16–20; Hayek, *Rules and Order*, chap. 1. See Chap. 5, pp. 65 and 86.
[73] James, *The Principles of Psychology* (New York, 1890).
[74] J. Dewey, 'The need for a recovery of philosophy' in R. J. Bernstein (ed.), *John Dewey: On Experience, Nature and Freedom* (New York, 1960), 23.
[75] Bernstein, *Praxis and Action* (Philadelphia, 1971), 175–7.

system of signs that is open to further interpretation and has consequences that are to be publicly tested and confirmed. . . . This shift of orientation from the foundation paradigm to that of inquiry as a continuous self-corrective process requires us to rethink almost every fundamental issue in philosophy.

The pragmatists thus argue that all knowledge is hypothetical and fallible; that the meaning of concepts must be rooted in their social context; that we should focus on the consequences rather than the origins of knowledge; that all distinctions and boundaries to inquiry are relative to the stage of development of the inquiry; and that the standards or norms of inquiry are developed as part of the process of inquiry. Pragmatism challenges the dominance in philosophy of the idea of the 'mental eye'; of the idea of analysing perception and knowledge in terms of the model of mental seeing.[76] In its place pragmatism poses the analogy of the craftsman who is involved in making or doing, not by reference to some ideal model, but in accordance with the cumulative product of experience.

The work of Dewey

Within political theory the work of John Dewey has been particularly influential.[77] Dewey's thought was mainly influenced by Hegel, although his appreciation of the organic unity of life also caused him to be attracted to the lessons of Darwinian biology.[78] Dewey rejected the fundamental dualisms of philosophy. He argued that thought does not arise out of abstract logical puzzles but from specific problems which we encounter in practice. He thus suggested that ideas should be viewed not as mirrors of reality but plans of action. Theory could only be completed in practice and, as a result, Dewey argued that philosophy must abandon abstract metaphysics and apply itself to social engineering.

In the political sphere Dewey maintained an organic rather than an atomistic conception of society. As we have seen, 'this notion of society as a organism, whether derived from Hegelian, Comtean, or

---

[76] For a more recent pragmatic critique of this idea of foundational philosophy see: R. Rorty, *Philosophy and the Mirror of Nature* (Princeton, 1980).

[77] See, e.g., Dewey, *The Ethics of Democracy* (New York, 1888); id., *Democracy and Education* (New York, 1916); id., *The Public and its Problems* (New York, 1927); id., *Liberalism and Social Action* (New York, 1935).

[78] See Morton G. White, *The Origin of Dewey's Instrumentalism* (New York, 1943); Bernstein, *John Dewey* (New York, 1966), esp. chap. 2 'From Hegel to Darwin'.

Law, the realists argued, was not a matter of abstract logic but a practical exercise in social engineering. Since law should be viewed basically as an instrument for realizing certain practical objectives many felt that a genuine scientific study of law must examine its functioning through the experimental methods of the social sciences. But some in the movement were uneasy about viewing realism primarily as an appeal to a social scientific approach to law. This group preferred to focus their work on the myth of legal certainty and to challenge the idea of legal formalism by undermining the conception of the judicial process implicit in the case method.[89]

Both aspects of the legal realist movement seem to have been influenced by pragmatism. The gist of the critique of legal formalism had, in all its essentials, already been presented by James and Dewey. In 1891, in an essay called 'The moral philosopher and the moral life', William James had set out the essence of the realist's case. James argued here that abstract rules provide us with only limited assistance in arriving at moral decisions because 'every real dilemma is in literal strictness a unique situation'. The reason for this, continued James, is that 'the exact combination of ideals realized and ideals disappointed which each decision creates is always a universe without precedent, and for which no adequate previous rule exists'.[90] As James graphically put it, in every moral decision 'some part of the ideal is butchered'.[91] It does not require a great deal of insight to appreciate the significance of James's theory for the judicial process. Similar messages can readily be derived from Dewey's work. In an essay published in 1915, for example, Dewey examined the nature of practical judgment, which he defined 'a judgment respecting the future termination of an incomplete and in so far indeterminate situation'.[92] Dewey then identified the characteristics of practical judgments in terms of their tentative and hypothetical character and suggested that we may often misjudge what is to be done either because we have overlooked relevant facts or misinterpreted them or because we have misjudged the best course of action to be followed. In essays of this sort the

---

[89] See, e.g., J. Frank, *Law and the Modern Mind* (New York, 1930).

[90] *The Will to Believe. The Works of William James* (F. H. Burkhardt *et al.* (eds.)) (Camb., Mass., 1979), 158.

[91] Ibid. 154.

[92] Dewey, 'The Logic of Judgments of Practise' (1915) 12 *J. of Philosophy* 505, 514. See also Dewey, 'Logical Method and Law' (1924) 10 *Cornell L.Q.* 17.

pragmatist's conception of practical judgment captures the essence of the legal realist's criticism of legal formalism.

The influence of pragmatism on the realist's call for a social scientific approach to the study of law can also be readily detected since a basic tenet of pragmatism was to view practical judgment as an instrumental method of inquiry which was validated by society. From this perspective law should be viewed as an instrument for meeting certain social goals. When so viewed, what becomes necessary is a study of how best those goals might, through law, be realized. When viewed in this light Robert Summers's thesis that the legal realist movement should best be seen as part of a tradition of 'pragmatic instrumentalism' in American jurisprudence seems basically correct.[93]

By the late 1930s the legal realist movement seemed to have lost its way. One reason for this may be that it was overtaken—and, perhaps, undermined—by political developments. Roosevelt's New Deal programme was an exercise in regulatory government and led to a major growth in regulation by administrative agencies. The realists, insofar as they advocated training and expertise in the specialized areas of law, generally supported this programme and a number of prominent realists left law schools to work for Roosevelt in Washington. But realism itself never developed an adequate theorization of regulatory law; the public law dimension to its theory was largely missing.[94] As the political culture changed so, it seemed, did the power of their critique.

There is a final point about realism which, given the nature of our exercise, needs to be mentioned. Realism directed its challenge to the attempt to construct an autonomous science of law which was rooted in legal positivism. In its place, realism posited a predictive science of law rooted in the experimental methods of social science. These methods, however, seemed to be largely based on positivist conceptions of social science. In the light of our discussion in Chapter 2, it could be argued that in so doing they failed to get to the root of the problem.

The value of pragmatism

Pragmatism may be viewed as the philosophy of the new world of interdependence. Philosophy, so this argument goes, had taken

---

[93] R. S. Summers, *Instrumentalism and American Legal Theory* (Ithaca, 1982).
[94] See Duxbury, *Patterns of American Jurisprudence* (forthcoming), chap. 2.

the wrong step with Cartesian dualisms. The key task of pragmatism was therefore to root philosophy within a social world in which ideas can be validated only in practice. The pragmatists, and Dewey in particular, have been criticized for being overly optimistic about the power of creative intelligence to reconstruct social institutions through a programme of educational reform. Pragmatism here underestimated the strength of the social and economic forces that might work to distort and undermine this ideal. Dewey's response to such criticism, I suspect, would have been that he was certainly not naïve about the nature of those forces but that, if there is to be hope for humanity, there is no alternative but to be optimistic.[95]

In general, the philosophy of pragmatism appears to have a particular value for the functionalist style in public law, which may be seen most clearly in pragmatism's rejection of a systematic and comprehensive philosophy. The value of this approach became most evident in the period after the First World War, which many regard as marking the terminus of the era of belief in continuous evolutionary progress of human society. By embracing pragmatism, functionalists felt they could adopt a legal method without necessarily absorbing the more optimistic beliefs of the evolutionists about the inevitability of progress. This was especially the case when pragmatism was conjoined to a legal positivist outlook. From this perspective, legal realism may be viewed as a continuation, albeit in a non-systematic fashion, of John Austin's project of producing an entirely non-normative account of law.[96]

THE CHARACTER OF FUNCTIONALISM

The foundations of the functionalist style in public law are to be found in the intellectual movements of sociological positivism, evolutionary theory, and pragmatism which flourished in the late nineteenth and early twentieth centuries. That this functionalist style contains different orientations should be clear from the differences in approach and nuance between these movements. There is, for example, a distinct positivist and empiricist strain which emerges in the functionalist style and whose roots can be seen in sociological positivism, the Fabian aspects of evolutionary theory, and that interpretation of pragmatism which views the

---

[95] See Bernstein, *John Dewey*.   [96] On Austin see Chap. 1 pp. 20–1.

application of the methods of pragmatic instrumentalism to the judicial role as a continuation of Austin's positivist project. On the other hand an Idealist and more rationalistic strain of the functionalist style also exists. This version of functionalism connects with the movement of New Liberalism and highlights the Hegelian aspects of pragmatism associated, in particular, with Dewey.

There are therefore different aspects of the functionalist style which can most readily be seen as tensions between empiricism and rationalism or positivism and idealism. These tensions took specific political form in the tensions between Fabianism and New Liberalism; the former being essentially a movement founded on ideas of organization and efficiency and the latter projecting a specific moral dimension as an emancipatory movement. Such tensions can emerge in a variety of forms. One specific historical illustration can be seen in the famous Report of the Royal Commission on the Poor Law in 1909. The Royal Commission was split on the subject and the Majority and Minority Reports embody two different social theories of poverty. The Majority Report, of which Helen Bosanquet was a signatory, encapsulated the ideas of New Liberalism whereas the Minority Report, signed by Beatrice Webb, represented the views of the Fabians.[97]

Despite such differences and tensions, it is nevertheless suggested that these are best viewed as variations *within* the functionalist style of public law thought. This functionalist style views law not as a phenomenon which exists on an altogether different plane to government but rather as an instrument which is part of the apparatus of government. Functionalism in public law views this apparatus of government as serving to promote a distinct set of purposes. These purposes are those most readily associated with the objectives of the positive state which emerged towards the end of the nineteenth century and which are summed up in the idea of government as institution which promotes progressive evolutionary change. Consequently, the functionalist approach tends to be built on an organicist conception of society, generally embraces a positive conception of liberty, and looks on democracy as an achievement of great moral as well as evolutionary importance.

[97] For a discussion see Vincent and Plant, *Philosophy, Politics and Citizenship*, 122–31.

These characteristic ideas of functionalism are found running throughout the theories of sociological positivism, evolutionary social theories, and pragmatism. Since ideals from these intellectual movements also filtered into the political movements for social democracy or evolutionary socialism it is not surprising that the functionalist style is closely associated with a socialist tendency. Here we can discern some lines of connection between philosophy and politics, between thought and life. Thus, the functionalist style tends to incorporate an empiricist rather than a metaphysical view of law. It is less concerned with what law *is* than with what law *does*. But this philosophical disposition also tends to be harnessed to a political orientation which seeks to democratize political institutions and is supportive of reforms pioneered through social legislation.

Pragmatism has been an especially important influence on the functionalist style. Its practical orientation makes its message more accessible for lawyers. But its influence is attributable to more than its accessibility. What perhaps is most important is its attempt, as its proponents themselves viewed it, to chart a middle course between empiricism and rationalism, and between positivism and idealism. Pragmatism thus has many continuities with the positivist and evolutionary theories which have influenced the functionalist style in public law. These connections can be woven at many different levels. John Stuart Mill, for example, emerges as a critically important link throughout these movements. Mill, rooted in positivism and utilitarianism, seemed to be converted in his later years to the socialist cause.[98] His influence can clearly be seen in both Fabianism, where his analysis of the unearned increment reached a receptive audience, and New Liberalism, which developed his later concerns about distributive justice.[99] Mill's influence on pragmatism is also evident. William James, for example, dedicated *Pragmatism* to J. S. Mill 'from whom I first learned the pragmatic openness of mind and whom my fancy likes to picture as our leader'.

Connections of this nature could be woven many times over. T. H. Green's emphasis on the centrality of experience exerted a

[98] J. S. Mill, 'Chapters on Socialism' (1879) 25 *Fortnightly Review* 226, 525. These writings were published posthumously and had been written ten years earlier.
[99] See Freeden, *The New Liberalism*, 42–52.

profound influence on both James and Dewey.[100] Hobhouse's
views on epistemology were heavily influenced by James.[101] And it
has even been argued that the pragmatists simply 'extended Spencer
to argue that, since all human activity could be interpreted as the
outcome of the instinct for survival, so therefore could thinking
be'.[102] A major conduit for the translation of many of these ideas
into legal thought was Oliver Wendell Holmes. In addition to being
well versed in organicist theories, during the 1870s Holmes was,
along with Peirce and James, a member of 'The Metaphysical
Club'.[103] Holmes can be viewed as the grandfather of the American
legal realist movement; his statement that 'the life of the law has
not been logic: it has been experience'[104] has, for example, become
one of the most celebrated legal aphorisms of recent times.

Running alongside these personal connections, however, were
material changes affecting these societies during the late nineteenth
century. In Kloppenberg's words:[105]

After 1870 industrialization and urbanization entered a new phase, which
economic historians have designated the second industrial revolution to
distinguish it from the coming of industry to Britain over a century earlier.
This second wave struck more rapidly and spread more broadly than its
predecessor. By 1920 the United States, Germany, and France had joined
Britain as substantially industrialized nations . . . During these years the
economies of all four nations evolved in different ways from the
comparative chaos of entrepreneurial capitalism to the more advanced
stage of organized capitalism. . . . American and European societies became
increasingly interdependent, by which I mean that complex urban-
industrial societies involved individuals in unprecedently complex patterns
of relations extending beyond personal and community ties to distant
bonds no less real because of their obscurity. . . .

The industrialized and urbanized mode of life involved the replacement
of magic and mystery by precisely calculable and strictly functional
procedures, a less obvious but equally pervasive fact of modern life.

The changes, which were taking place in the economy and society
during the period of formative influence on the functionalist style,

---

[100] See Dewey, *Liberalism and Social Action* (New York, 1935), 23–6.
[101] See Hobhouse, *The Theory of Knowledge* (London, 1896).
[102] Hawthorn, *Enlightenment and Despair*, 206.
[103] See M. H. Fisch, 'Justice Holmes, the Prediction Theory of Law, and
Pragmatism' (1942) 39 *J. of Philosophy* 85 at 88.
[104] O. W. Holmes, *The Common Law* (Boston, 1881), 1.
[105] Kloppenberg, *Uncertain Victory*, 153, 155.

provide us with a further dimension to consider. The functionalist style can be viewed as an attempt to develop a legal style compatible with the technically orientated, interdependent, and functionally ordered society which was emerging. From this perspective we can see a direct contrast with the normativist style.

When considering the character of the normativist style,[106] we identified a characteristic tendency of normativism to construct a set of dualisms, particularly between types of order, forms of the state, and conceptions of law. The objective in doing so is to identify their 'true' nature or ideal character and distinguish or highlight the corrupt forms which have entered modern political consciousness as a result of rationalistic errors. Within that normativist framework the functionalist style in public law is to be identified with that side of the dualist divide that is associated with error, distortion, and corruption. From the functionalist perspective, however, these dualisms are artificial; and recall here the fact that a powerful theme in pragmatism is to reject all dualistic thinking. Furthermore, from the functionalist perspective, the normativist style must be seen as a nostalgic response to these facets of modern society.

The rationalization of modern life, suggest those who adopt the functionalist style, must be directly confronted. They reject the normativist criticism that they are 'constructivist rationalists' whose views are founded on the 'synoptic delusion'. 'There are many "collectivists"', argued Ginsberg, 'who are well aware of the limitations of our knowledge and of the difficulties that hinder the growth of an enlightened common will. Humility of spirit is no monopoly of the individualists, nor is the *hubris* of the specialist confined to the collectivists'.[107] Indeed, some would go further and criticize the liberal variant of normativism on the ground that that doctrine is based on what might be called 'the Rationalist Fallacy' in political thinking; that human beings act on rational motives.[108] By contrast, they argue, the functionalist style is rooted in the rejection of such metaphysical assumptions and in the application of the scientific method to the problems of politics, government, and law.

[106] Chap. 5, pp. 101–4.
[107] Ginsberg, *Essays in Sociology and Social Philosophy* (Harmondsworth, 1971), 124.
[108] See, e.g., G. Wallas, *Human Nature in Politics* (London, 1908).

7

Traditions of Public Law Thought

MY argument has been that the positions adopted within public law by commentators, advocates, and judges are rooted in certain categories of thought. I have identified the main styles of public law thought, which I call normativism and functionalism, in an ideal-typical form.[1] In this form these styles are inventions; they are constructed to permit us to obtain initial insights into the dominant categories of public law thought. As I suggested, these styles are fluid and that, within them, certain tensions may be evident. In order to understand them better we therefore need to examine their influence; and this process of investigation also leads to elaboration. I have first tried to show how their origins are to be found in certain political ideologies.[2] Through this exercise we may obtain an insight into the richness of these styles. In addition to appreciating their complexity, however, we have also seen something of their internal tensions. This is hardly surprising since these styles are not fixed and intractable. Their various facets are constantly being adapted in the light of changing circumstances and requirements.

Having examined the foundations of these styles of public law thought, we should now seek to test our understanding of them by reference to our experience of the subject. The two dominant styles of public law thought which have been identified in ideal-typical form may be viewed as models. They should be thought of as models rather than theories because they are orientated to action and to practice. These models are constructions which are aimed directly at influencing the development of law. The question is: can we detect their influence in our traditions of public law? Are these categories of thought manifest in the languages of advocacy and judgment within public law?

---

[1] Chap. 4.   [2] Chaps. 5 and 6.

THE DOMINANT TRADITION IN PUBLIC LAW

On this issue, my contention is that the dominant tradition of public law thought is to be found in a conservative variant of the normativist style. We have already seen many of its characteristics in considering approaches to the study of public law. It may be found in formalism and the analytical method in public law and in the belief that public law is concerned with the 'order of things'.[3] And we have explored its ideological roots through an examination of the political philosophy of Michael Oakeshott.[4]

This conservative variant of normativism has, I believe, provided both the authoritative framework for determining the boundaries of the subject and supplied the basic language through which we reflect on issues raised within the subject. Its status is such that those who work within this dominant tradition have generally felt able to get on with their work without having to reflect on its theoretical foundations. This normativist approach sets the principal agenda for, and method of, inquiry. Indeed, it could be argued that it is only problems which are set within this framework that are viewed by the legal community as being properly legal. Other approaches are marginalized as being 'theoretical' (that is, not sufficiently practical) or perhaps more properly the concern of another discipline.

The dominant tradition of conservative normativism has, during this century, come to operate hierarchically, defensively, and complacently. Having become established, people tend to work within the tradition for reasons which are never properly articulated. Indeed, it is through this sort of process that public law comes to be seen as concerned with 'the order of things'. The tradition is then perpetuated through the standard textbooks and is transmitted in teaching by asking students to 'do it my way'. In these respects there are some similarities between the way in which Kuhn views the paradigm of 'normal science' operating in the natural sciences and the way in which this dominant tradition has been established in public law.[5]

---

[3] See Chap. 1, pp. 13–23; Chap. 3, pp. 42–6.

[4] See Chap. 5, pp. 64–83.

[5] On Kuhn see Chap. 2 pp. 31–2. Notwithstanding such similarities I agree with Bernstein that, although Kuhn's work helps us to overthrow the simplistic picture of science that has been used as a model by some social scientists, there are differences between the natural and human sciences and that Kuhn's framework should be used

We must now turn to examine the making and shaping of this dominant tradition of conservative normativism in British public law.

DICEY'S THEORY OF PUBLIC LAW

We begin with A. V. Dicey, Vinerian Professor of English Law at Oxford University between 1882 and 1909. Dicey lived during a period of great political and economic change, a period in which the range and the functions of government expanded greatly and in which legislation was used explicitly as a method of changing social conditions. As we have seen,[6] Dicey recognized that, in this social context, the function of the academic lawyer could not be simply to venerate the ancient constitution. Rather, the duty of the constitutional lawyer must be to analyse the legal foundations of the British constitution in a methodical manner. 'We are compelled', wrote Dicey, 'to search for the guidance of first principles.'[7]

Dicey is generally regarded as the high priest of orthodox constitutional theory. Both the form and the substance of his approach rapidly assumed an authoritative status and have played a major role in shaping the dominant tradition. In part, this achievement was because of Dicey's role as a codifier and purveyor of the analytical method. During the 1930s, for example, Sir Ivor Jennings readily acknowledged that Dicey was 'the first to apply the juridical method to English public law'.[8] The method has become so ensconced in public law thought that today we seem incapable of recognizing any work which predates Dicey; it is as though he invented the subject.[9] But Dicey's influence is not confined to his

strictly and confined to the understanding of natural science. See Bernstein, *The Restructuring of Social and Political Theory*, 93–106.

[6] Chap. 1, pp. 14–17.
[7] Dicey, *Introduction to the Study of the Law of the Constitution* (1885) (London, 8th edn., 1915), 34.
[8] W. I. Jennings, *The Law and the Constitution* (London, 1933), p. x.
[9] The acid test is the fact that virtually all recent work by public lawyers which purports to be both historical and critical commences with Dicey. See, e.g., P. McAuslan and J. F. McEldowney (eds.), *Law, Legitimacy and the Constitution* (London, 1985), esp. chaps 1 and 2; I. Harden and N. Lewis, *The Noble Lie. The British Constitution and the Rule of Law* (London, 1986) which begins with a section on 'Dicey and the rule of law'; and P. P. Craig, *Public Law and Democracy in the United Kingdom and the United States of America* (Oxford, 1990), where the first substantive chapter (chap. 2) is devoted to an analysis of Dicey.

method. His theory of public law was also influenced by a particular outlook or political ideology. As Keeton acknowledges, Dicey 'inherited an outlook upon the constitution which owed something to Burke, Blackstone and Bagehot, and which saw in the English system the climax of political achievement'.[10]

It is this combination of method and values that underpins conservative normativism. Dicey is important precisely because he expressed both the form and substance of normativism in a clear and simple manner. In Keeton's words, 'it was left to Dicey to formulate in general principles the assumptions on which political association was founded'.[11]

Sovereignty, democracy, and law

Dicey identified three guiding principles which underpinned the British constitution: the legislative sovereignty of Parliament; the universal rule throughout the constitution of ordinary law; and the role which constitutional conventions play in the ordering of the constitution.[12] His objective in the *Law of the Constitution* was to explain these principles and to illustrate their interlocking nature.

Dicey considered the sovereignty of Parliament, from a legal point of view, to be 'the dominant characteristic of our political institutions'.[13] This doctrine requires some explanation. First, Parliament 'in the mouth of a lawyer' means 'the King, the House of Lords, and the House of Commons; these three bodies acting together may be aptly described as the "King in Parliament", and constitute Parliament'.[14] It is only when thus defined that Parliament 'has, under the English constitution, the right to make or unmake any law whatsoever; and, further, that no person or body is recognised . . . as having the right to override or set aside the legislation of Parliament'.[15]

Dicey's identification of sovereignty as a basic principle is based in part on the work of earlier writers and in part on the use of historical examples to demonstrate both the breadth of Parliament's authority and the absence of any competing legislative authority. His method is therefore essentially empirical. He was not particularly concerned with 'speculative difficulties of placing any limits

---

[10] G. W. Keeton, *The Passing of Parliament* (London 1952), 6.
[11] Ibid.   [12] Dicey, *Law of the Constitution*, 34.
[13] Ibid. 37.   [14] Ibid.   [15] Ibid. 37–8.

whatever on sovereignty'.[16] So far as Dicey was concerned Parliamentary sovereignty was 'a legal fact'[17] and his purpose was to demonstrate that 'Parliament does constitute such a supreme legislative authority or sovereign power as, according to Austin and other jurists, must exist in every civilised state.'[18]

Dicey's outlook thus seems positivist and his concept of sovereignty seems absolutist and authoritarian. That, however, would not be an entirely faithful reading. To appreciate why we must understand that Dicey's theory was tempered both by his conception of democracy and by the adoption of a normativist conception of law.

In order to appreciate the significance of Dicey's views on democracy we should recall, in particular, the fact that political opinion during the last decades of the nineteenth century was dominated by a concern with the rise of democracy. In 1885 Sir Henry Maine echoed the conservative dissent:[19]

The delusion that democracy . . . is a progressive form of government, lies deep within the convictions of a particular political school; but there can be no delusion grosser . . . All that has made England famous and all that has made England wealthy, has been the work of minorities, sometimes very small ones. It seems to me quite certain that, if for four centuries there had been a very widely extended franchise and a very large elected body in this country, there would have been no reformation of religion, no change of dynasty, no toleration of Dissent, not even an accurate Calendar. The threshing-machine, the power-loom, the spinning-jenny, and possibly the steam-engine, would have been prohibited. . . . [W]e may say generally that the gradual establishment of the masses in power is the blackest omen for all legislation founded on scientific opinion, which requires tension of mind to understand it, and self-denial to submit to it.

In Sir Ernest Barker's words, Maine 'was the tragic voice, sonorous behind the mask of Cassandra, which uttered the feelings that had gathered since the extension of the suffrage in 1867'.[20] Spencer similarly was sceptical and argued that the doctrine of the divine right of kings would be replaced by the divine right of

[16] Dicey, *Law of the Constitution*, 58.
[17] Ibid. 37.   [18] Ibid. at p. 59.
[19] H. S. Maine, *Popular Government* (London, 1885), 97–8.
[20] E. Barker, *Political Thought in England 1848–1914* (London, 1915), 170. Note also that Maine's *Ancient Law* constituted an attack on the analytical method in jurisprudence. See, Dicey, *Lectures on the Relation between Law and Public Opinion in England during the Nineteenth Century* (London, 1905), 459.

Parliament as the new superstition.[21] Even Bagehot was uneasy about the 'leap in the dark' made in 1867:[22]

[O]ur statesmen have the greatest opportunities they have had for many years, and likewise the greatest duty. They have to guide the new voters in the exercise of the franchise; to guide them quietly, and without saying what they are doing, but still to guide them. . . . They settle the conversation of mankind. . . . The common ordinary mind is quite unfit to fix for itself what political question it shall attend to; it is as much as it can do to judge decently of the questions which drift down to it, and are brought before it . . . And in settling what these questions shall be, statesmen have now especially a great responsibility if they raise questions which will excite the lower orders of mankind; if they raise questions on which the interest of those orders is not identical with, or is antagonistic to, the whole interest of the State, they will have done the greatest harm they can do. . . . Just when it is desirable that ignorant men, new to politics, should have good issues, and only good issues, put before them, these statesmen will have suggested bad issues. They will have suggested topics which will bind the poor as a class together; topics which will excite them against the rich; topics the discussion of which in the only form in which that discussion reaches the ear will be to make them think that some new law can make them comfortable . . .—that Government has at its disposal an inexhaustible fund out of which it can give to those who now want without also creating elsewhere other and greater wants.

Bagehot, then, was anxious for the education of the new political class and was greatly concerned whether our system of government, which was possible 'because England was a deferential country',[23] could survive the change. Dicey, however, was not quite so pessimistic. He certainly feared 'class legislation'[24] and he recognized the tendency of social legislation to destroy the moral fibre of the nation.[25] But he took a more optimistic view than Bagehot and

---

[21] H. Spencer, *The Man versus the State* (1884: Harmondsworth, 1969), pp. 151, 254.

[22] W. Bagehot, *The English Constitution* (1867: London, R. H. S. Crossman (ed.) 1965) 'Introduction to the Second Edition, 1872', pp. 274–5.

[23] Ibid. at p. 270.

[24] Speaking to the annual conference of the British Constitutional Association in 1908 Dicey remarked: 'We dread the passing of laws, and still more the administration of the law, in accordance, not with the deliberate and real will of the majority of the nation, but with the immediate wishes of a class, namely the class of . . . wage earners. *We fear class legislation*', quoted in W. H. Greenleaf, *The British Political Tradition*, vol. 2 (London, 1983), 284.

[25] Dicey, *Law and Opinion*, 256: 'The beneficial effects of State intervention, especially in the form of legislation, is direct, immediate, and, so to speak, visible, whilst its evil effects are gradual and indirect . . . State help kills self-help.'

believed that constitutionalism could be maintained by the British practice of 'democracy tempered by snobbishness'.[26]

The other constraint on the absolutist interpretation of the sovereignty concept arose from Dicey's normativist conception of law. Dicey felt that 'a real limit to the exercise of sovereignty is imposed not by the laws of man but by the nature of things'.[27] He believed that liberty was best preserved by maintaining the balance implicit in the guiding legal principles of the constitution. Consequently, while Parliamentary sovereignty is 'an instrument well adapted for the establishment of democratic despotism',[28] on a true understanding of the interlocking nature of the concept of sovereignty with the principles of the rule of law it is conducive to the promotion of liberty. This is because, first, 'the sovereignty of Parliament, as contrasted with other forms of sovereign power, favours the supremacy of law' and, secondly, 'the predominance of rigid legality throughout our institutions evokes the exercise, and thus increases the authority of Parliamentary sovereignty'.[29]

Parliamentary sovereignty was felt to be compatible with the rule of law primarily because 'the commands of Parliament . . . can be uttered only through the combined actions of its three constituent parts' and that, 'unlike a sovereign monarch who is not only a legislator but a ruler, that is, head of the executive government, has never hitherto been able to use the powers of the government as a means of interfering with the regular course of law'.[30] The rule of law upholds Parliamentary sovereignty because the 'rigidity of the law constantly hampers . . . the action of the executive, and . . . the government can escape only by obtaining from Parliament the discretionary authority which is denied to the Crown by the law of the land'.[31]

Dicey's formulation of the idea of the 'rule of law', while evoking the idea of Parliament and the courts as being the true fountains of law within the British constitution, is not without its ambiguities. He felt that the concept had three meanings. First, the 'absolute supremacy . . . of regular law as opposed to the influence of arbitrary power'. Secondly, it meant equality before the law, or 'the equal subjection of all classes to the ordinary law of the land

[26] Dicey, *Law and Opinion*, 57.
[27] *Law of the Constitution*, p. xxvi.
[28] *Law and Opinion*, 305.
[29] *Law of the Constitution*, 402.
[30] Ibid. 402, 405.
[31] Ibid. 406.

administered by the ordinary Law Courts'. Finally, the concept was a formula for expressing the fact that, in our system, 'the principles of private law have . . . been by the action of the Courts and Parliament so extended as to determine the position of the Crown and of its servants'. That is, 'the constitution is the result of the ordinary law of the land' and that 'the law of the constitution . . . [is] not the source but the consequence of the rights of individuals'.[32] Running throughout these meanings there endures a normativist conception of law. Within the first meaning we see a conception of law founded on general rules; an idea that Dicey had signalled earlier with his references to 'rigid legality'. The second meaning appeals to a principle of universality. And the third constitutes an expression of the common law tradition.

Also implicit within, but fundamental to, Dicey's conceptual structure is the idea of the separation of powers. The principle of the separation of powers is, for example, clearly evident in his views on administrative law. By administrative law Dicey meant a special body of rules, institutions and procedures which, as with the French system of *droit administratif*, is established to determine the rights, powers, liabilities, and immunities of public officials and of private individuals in their dealings with public bodies. He regarded this system as inimical to the rule of law for a number of reasons: first, because it undermined the principles of equality and universality of law; secondly, because it placed the State in a privileged position and would therefore threaten the historic achievement of bringing the Crown under law; and, thirdly, insofar as it resulted in the establishment of special courts, it infringed the principle of the separation of judicial and ministerial powers.

The idea of the separation of powers also seems to influence Dicey's belief that Parliamentary sovereignty favours the supremacy of law. The idea here is that Parliament will set the framework of general rules for society, the executive will govern within those rules and an independent judiciary will resolve disputes over the meaning of those rules and will, in particular, keep the executive within the boundaries of law. We see here the importance of Parliament as an expression of 'self-correcting democracy'.[33] Dicey's theory thus seems constructed on the idea of balances within parliamentary mechanisms. Here we may discern a connec-

[32] Ibid. 198–9.
[33] Craig, *Public Law and Democracy*, chap. 2.

tion with the Whig imagery of balance which dominated constitutional writing a century earlier. But, like Millar, Dicey's idea of balance is not that of a balance between the different estates; it is a balance within Parliament which ultimately reflects a balance in society in general.[34] This vision is particularly evident in Dicey's views on the role of conventions. Dicey maintained that conventions are mainly rules governing the exercise of the Crown's prerogative powers and privileges of the Houses of Parliament. These conventional rules all have one ultimate object: 'Their end is to secure that Parliament, or the Cabinet which is indirectly appointed by Parliament, shall in the long run give effect to the will of the power which in modern England is the true political sovereign of the State—the majority of electors or . . . the nation.'[35]

Continuity and change within Dicey's theory

I have stressed the view that Dicey's importance can be traced to his role both in codifying certain ideas and in adapting the analytical method to public law. We may now assess the significance of his role by examining the themes of continuity and change in relation to his twin principles of Parliamentary sovereignty and the rule of law.

There is an important strand in English thought, which is traceable to Hobbes's idea of *civitas*, and which believes that the only way to preserve society is by acknowledging a perpetual sovereign power. This is a political idea and it is one which we have seen expressed in a contemporary form in Oakeshott's idea of *respublica*.[36] Dicey does not, apparently, endorse this view since, as a result of his analytical method, he makes a formal distinction between a political and legal concept of sovereignty. There is, however, a major difficulty with this distinction. One crucial characteristic of sovereignty is that it is apparently indivisible. Either the Queen-in-Parliament is sovereign or the sovereign electorate delegates its power to that body. If the delegation is absolute and unconditional then the electorate cannot be sovereign; if it delegates its power on trust then Parliament cannot be sovereign.[37] This formal distinction does not therefore seem

---

[34] See Chap. 1, pp. 8–10.   [35] *Law of the Constitution*, 424.
[36] Chap. 5, pp. 72–3.
[37] See H. J. Laski, *A Grammar of Politics* (London, 5th edn., 1967), 54.

convincing. If then, as I have already suggested we must,[38] we challenge the formal distinctions of the analytical method, Dicey can be seen as being deeply rooted within this tradition of thought. I have already mentioned that Dicey finds support for the principle of Parliamentary sovereignty in the work of earlier writers. Amongst these writers Blackstone is undoubtedly pre-eminent. On the power and jurisdiction of Parliament, Blackstone had this to say:[39]

It hath sovereign and uncontrollable authority in making, conforming, enlarging, restraining, abrogating, repealing, reviving, and expounding of laws, concerning matters of all possible denominations, ecclesiastical or temporal, civil, military, or criminal: this being the place where that absolute despotic power, which must in all governments reside somewhere, is entrusted by the constitution of these kingdoms. . . . It can, in short, do everything that is not naturally impossible; and therefore some have not scrupled to call its power, by a figure rather too bold, the omnipotence of Parliament. True it is, that what the Parliament doth, no authority upon earth can undo. So that it is a matter most essential to the liberties of this kingdom, that such members be delegated to this important trust, as are most eminent for their probity, their fortitude, and their knowledge; for it was a known apophthegm of the great lord treasurer Burleigh, 'that England could never be ruined but by a Parliament' . . . To the same purpose the president Montesquieu, though I trust too hastily, presages; that as Rome, Sparta, and Carthage have lost their liberty and perished, so the constitution of England will in time lose its liberty, will perish: it will perish whenever the legislative power shall become more corrupt than the executive.

The first half of this quotation is well known to lawyers and is often quoted. When the fuller text is consulted, however, it seems evident that Blackstone himself makes no clear distinction between political and legal ideas of sovereignty. Blackstone's idea of sovereignty addresses both the legal idea of the unlimited legislative power of the Queen-in-Parliament and the political idea of vesting absolute power in a single institution. Blackstone should be viewed as working within this Hobbesian tradition.

Similarly with Dicey. When his general writing is examined it is clear that, notwithstanding the analytical distinction he makes in

---

[38] Chap. 2.
[39] W. Blackstone, *Commentaries on the Laws of England* (London, 1776), Bk. I, pp. 160–1. Quoted in Dicey, *Law of the Constitution*, 39–40.

Law of the Constitution, Dicey worked within this tradition. Dicey's position on this question is seen most clearly in his attitude to federalism. In 1915 Dicey wrote that although federalism possessed a 'vague, and therefore the strong and imaginative, charm' there is 'good reason to fear that the federalisation of the United Kingdom, stimulating as it would the disruptive force of local nationalism, might well arouse a feeling of divided allegiance'.[40] Dicey argued, not only that belief in the inherent excellence of federalism was a 'delusion',[41] but that it also ran against the grain of English history:[42]

> Federalism, as the dissolution of the United Kingdom, is absolutely foreign to the historical and, so to speak, instinctive policy of English constitutionalists. Each successive generation from the reign of Edward I. onwards has laboured to produce that complete political unity which is represented by the absolute sovereignty of the Parliament now sitting at Westminster. . . . To every foreign country, whether it were numbered among our allies or among our rivals, the federalisation of Great Britain would be treated as a proof of the declining power alike of England and of the British Empire.

I do not consider that Dicey's beliefs on the nature of political authority can be, or should be, divorced from his conception of legal sovereignty. In Bernard Crick's words 'the legal doctrine of sovereignty . . . was almost consciously confused with the empirical, pseudo-historical doctrine: that political stability, indeed law and order themselves, depended on parliamentary sovereignty'.[43] From this perspective Dicey's views on sovereignty are on all fours with Oakeshott's. Both are elaborations of conservative normativism.

Dicey's views on the rule of law also merit detailed scrutiny. The contemporary difficulty has been well expressed by Judith Shklar who suggests that:[44]

> It would not be difficult to show that the phrase 'the Rule of Law' has become meaningless thanks to ideological abuse and general over-use. It may well have become just another one of those self-congratulatory rhetorical devices that grace the public utterances of Anglo-American

---

[40] *Law of the Constitution*, Introduction, pp. lxxxviii, xc.
[41] Ibid., p. lxxiv.
[42] Ibid., pp. xc–xci.
[43] B. Crick, 'The Sovereignty of Parliament and the Irish Question' in D. Rea (ed.), *Political Co-operation in Divided Societies* (London, 1983), 229 at pp. 232–3.
[44] J. N. Shklar, 'Political Theory and the Rule of Law' in A. C. Hutchinson and P. Monahan (eds.), *The Rule of Law. Ideal or Ideology?* (Toronto, 1987), 1.

politicians. No intellectual effort need therefore be wasted on this bit of ruling-class chatter.

Despite having certain sympathies with that view, Shklar dismisses her initial inclinations. She recognizes that historically the concept has had a significant place in the vocabulary of political theory and notes that legal theorists continue to invoke the concept and argue about its meaning. She therefore engages in a diagnostic experiment of identifying historically distinct meanings of the concept in order to use them as a measure against contemporary political usage.

Shklar argues that the rule of law originally had two quite distinct meanings. We might refer to these as the ancient and modern conceptions. The ancient conception, which Shklar attributes to Aristotle, is the 'rule of reason'. In this conception the single most important condition for the rule of law is the *character* of those who engage in legal judgments:[45]

Justice is the constant disposition to act fairly and lawfully . . . It is part of such a character to reason syllogistically and to do so his passions must be silent. In the course of forensic argument distorted syllogisms will of course be urged upon those who judge. That indeed is the nature of persuasive reasoning, but those who judge, be they few or many, must go beyond it to reason their way to a logically necessary conclusion. To achieve that they must understand exactly just how forensic rhetoric and persuasive reasoning work, while their own ratiocination is free from irrational imperfections. For that a settled ethical character is as necessary as is intelligence itself.

Within this conception those called upon to exercise legal judgment must be able to recognize the claims of others as if they were their own. On the shoulders of this group rests the responsibility for preserving the basic standards of the polity. On such character depends the security of society. Although this conception seems to focus on courts, where 'justice is activated into legality',[46] its impact is more wide-ranging:[47]

[I]n the structure of the politics the presence of men with such a mind-set, most usually middle-class moderates, has the effect of inhibiting the self-destructive proclivities that tend to afflict most regimes. The rule of reason depends decidedly on the capacity of the sane to persuade others to practise some degree of self restraint and to maintain the legal order that best fits the ethical structure of the polity.

[45] Ibid. at p. 3.   [46] Ibid. at p. 4.   [47] Ibid. at p. 3.

By way of contrast, the modern conception of the rule of law, which Shklar attributes to Montesquieu, is not so much the rule of reason as a set of institutional constraints. It is a principle of limited government based on the ideas that what was required was 'a properly equilibrated political system in which power was checked by power in such a way that neither the violent urges of kings, nor the arbitrariness of legislatures could impinge directly upon the individual'.[48] The modern conception is therefore closely associated with the idea of the separation of powers and the principle that public officials should not violate a private sphere of conduct.

There are basic differences between the ancient and modern conceptions. The ancient conception has enormous ethical and intellectual scope but applies to only a few people; the modern conception concerns a limited number of protective arrangements which concern every member of society. The modern conception is built on a principle of equality before the law; the ancient conception is entirely compatible with a slave society.

The key question we need to address is whether Dicey's notion is rooted in an ancient or modern conception of the rule of law. Shklar regards Dicey's work as constituting the most influential restatement of the rule of law since the eighteenth century. She therefore considers it most unfortunate that his statement amounted to an 'outburst of Anglo-Saxon parochialism'.[49] By this she meant, first, that Dicey began by finding the rule of law inherent in the remote English past, in the depth of the early Middle Ages. He therefore ascribed its validity to its antiquity; on its having grown, rather than being constructed as in the written constitutions of continental Europe.[50] And, secondly, she points to the importance to Dicey of the idea that all cases were judged by the same body of people, following a single body of rules. It was through this process that Dicey felt that England had escaped the threat to liberty presented by administrative law. Shklar argues that, with Dicey, the concept was 'both trivialized as the peculiar patrimony of one and only one national order, and formalized, by the insistence that only one set of inherited procedures and court practices could sustain

---

[48] J. N. Shklar, 'Political Theory and the Rule of Law' in A. C. Hutchinson and P. Monahan (eds.), *The Rule of Law. Ideal or Ideology?* (Toronto, 1987), 4.

[49] Ibid. at p. 5.

[50] But compare Dicey's criticism of the idea of the ancient constitution: *Law of the Constitution*, 17. See Chap. 1, p. 15.

it'.[51] Dicey thus suggested that, rather than the purposes of juridical rigour, it was the forms that were significant for freedom.

Shklar is undoubtedly accurate in her general assessment. What I should like to highlight, however, is the fact that, notwithstanding Dicey's formalism, his theory is suffused with the ideas of the ancient conception of the rule of law. Aspects of Dicey's concept of the rule of law, such as the principle of equality before the law, undoubtedly reflect the modern conception. But I think that contemporary interpretations of Dicey as a positivist who was concerned to freeze late nineteenth century political principles[52] obscures more than it illuminates.

In putting this case we should first recollect the third pillar in Dicey's concept of the rule of law. This pillar, which constituted a defence of the common law tradition, seems to be firmly rooted in the ancient conception, for the rather simple reason that this conception of the rule of law is clearly reflected in the common law tradition itself. This tradition of the common law mind and the doctrine of the ancient constitution has already been examined.[53] When considering these ideas we saw, in Sir Edward Coke's idea of the law as 'the golden metwand' and his articulation of the 'artificial reason' of the common law, as clear an expression of the ancient conception of the rule of law as one could expect to find. Coke's juridical ideas lived on through Hale and Mansfield and his political ideas filter through the work of Blackstone and Burke. Notwithstanding Dicey's curt rejection of the vulgar Whig idea of the ancient constitution,[54] I believe that it is through the influence of this tradition on Dicey that we are able to make sense of his thought.

We may most easily reveal the power of these influences on Dicey's thought by posing what from a contemporary perspective seems to be a major difficulty with Dicey's theory: how do we reconcile the twin principles of parliamentary sovereignty and the rule of law? How can an absolutist doctrine of sovereignty rest in harmony with the idea of the rule of law? From the standpoint of mainstream contemporary jurisprudence the issue seems irreconcilable. The issue seems resonant of the classic Hart–Fuller debate in which—to re-interpret—Hart posits sovereignty as the criterion of

[51] Shklar, 'Political Theory and the Rule of Law', 6.
[52] See, e.g., Harden and Lewis, *The Noble Lie.*
[53] Chap. 3, pp. 42–50.   [54] See *Law of the Constitution*, 16–19.

identity of law *against* Fuller's conception of the rule of law as embodying the essence of law.[55]

Dicey, however, believed that, on a true appreciation of the constitution, the principles should be viewed as being complementary. I have already tried to explain his views by reference to his ideas about democracy and law. Here we might examine another layer of the onion. My argument is that this harmonious interpretation can be fully understood only by interpreting Dicey's entire theory in the light of the ancient conception of the rule of law. The primary stumbling block is the concept of sovereignty. On this issue we might first note that Dicey, in seeking the support of earlier writers for his conception of sovereignty, refers mainly to Coke, Hale, and Blackstone. The significance of this lies not only in the fact that these are all writers who themselves adopted the ancient conception of the rule of law. It also rests on their shared view of Parliament as 'the highest and greatest court over which none other can have jurisdiction in the kingdom'.[56] That is, Parliament was seen as a vital element in a juridical order which was permeated with the cultural values of the ancient conception of the rule of law. At this point we must remind ourselves that Shklar includes as part of this ancient conception the idea of 'middle-class moderates' within the structure of politics who are able to persuade others to practise self-restraint and maintain a legal order that best fits the ethical structure of the polity. This is precisely how Dicey viewed Parliament and expected it to act. Keeton, for example, suggests that Dicey felt that Parliament was in no danger of abusing its powers 'because it was a combination of diverse elements, linked together by an intricate system of "checks and balances" . . . and also because Englishmen possessed, to a markedly greater degree than other peoples, a mysterious political instinct'.[57] Gladstone may have been slightly closer to the mark in suggesting that the public schools were part of the constitution.[58] From this perspective, the discord between Dicey and Maine seems rooted in a

---

[55] For references see Chap. 5 n. 43.
[56] Sir Matthew Hale, in Dicey, *Law of the Constitution*, 40.
[57] Keeton, *The Passing of Parliament*, 6.
[58] Quoted in C. Turpin, *British Government and the Constitution* (London, 1985), 16.

disagreement on the possibility of educating the new political class in the culture of the constitution.[59]

Dicey should not, I believe, be viewed primarily in a modern light as a legal positivist. In codifying the British constitution he attempted, whether consciously or not, to blend the languages of ancient and modern: tradition and reason; artificial reason and will; Coke and Hobbes; the modern institutional forms and the culture of the ancient constitution. In that sense he expressed the anxiety of Victorians who were 'wandering between two worlds, one dead, the other powerless to be born'.[60]

The frailty of Dicey's theory

In 1914, just after the commencement of the First World War that many have suggested marked the beginning of the end of the old order in British society, Dicey wrote an extended introduction to the eighth edition of *Law of the Constitution*. In this—his last—introduction Dicey sought to 'compare our constitution as it stood and worked in 1884 with the constitution as it now stands in 1914'.[61] His views are illuminating.

Dicey felt, first, that during the previous 40 years 'faith in parliamentary government has suffered an extraordinary decline'.[62] The main reason why this is so is that 'our English [sic] executive is, as a general rule, becoming more and more the representative of a party rather than the guide of the country'.[63] New political conventions have arisen to meet the wants of a new time, the general tendency of which has been 'to increase the power of any party which possesses a parliamentary majority' and 'to place the control of legislation, and indeed the whole government of the country, in the hands of the Cabinet'.[64] Dicey thus identifies the growth in power of the party machine as the source of the problem: 'Coalitions, log-rolling, and parliamentary intrigue are in England diminishing the moral and political faith in the House of Commons.'[65]

[59] On Maine's influence on Dicey, see R. C. J. Cocks, *Sir Henry Maine: A Study in Victorian Jurisprudence* (Cambridge, 1988), 146–7.

[60] M. Arnold, *The Poems of Matthew Arnold* (London, 1950), vol. 2, p. 214. Quoted in Kloppenberg, *Uncertain Victory*, 25.

[61] *Law of the Constitution*, p. xvii.   [62] Ibid., p. xcii.

[63] Ibid., p. lvii.   [64] Ibid., p. lv.   [65] Ibid., p. xcviii.

In passages which resonate with the spirit of Bagehot, 'a man of genius',[66] Dicey argues that the 'rule of a party cannot be permanently identified with the authority of the nation or with the dictates of patriotism'[67] and that 'while popular government may be under wise leadership a good machine for simply destroying existing evils, it may turn out a very poor instrument for the construction of new institutions or the realisation of new ideals'.[68] The limitations in practice of his belief in 'democracy tempered by snobbishness'[69] are finally conceded:[70]

> The time has come when the fact ought to be generally admitted that the amount of government . . . which is necessary to the welfare or even to the existence of a civilised community, cannot permanently co-exist with the effective belief that deference to public opinion is in all cases the sole or the necessary basis of a democracy.

The distrust which Dicey felt concerning this tendency of party government to destroy the balance of parliamentary institutions caused him to advocate the use of various institutional control devices. He did not openly support the maintenance of the power of the House of Lords to veto legislation but he seemed to do so implicitly since he expressed concern that the authority of the Lords had been 'gravely diminished'.[71] He did, however, explicitly propose the introduction of proportional representation arguing that it 'may sometimes secure a hearing in the House of Commons for opinions which, though containing a good deal of truth, command little or comparatively little popularity'.[72] Dicey also recommended the use of the referendum, on the ground that it 'may diminish the admitted and increasing evil of our party system'.[73]

Dicey's concerns in 1914 also extended to apprehension about the principle of the rule of law:[74]

> The ancient veneration for the rule of law has in England suffered during the last thirty years a marked decline. The truth of this assertion is proved by actual legislation, by the existence among some classes of a certain

---

[66] *Law of the Constitution*, p. civ. For Bagehot's views see above p. 143.
[67] Ibid., p. xliii.   [68] Ibid., p. xciii.   [69] Above n. 26.
[70] Dicey, *Law of the Constitution*, p. xlii.   [71] Ibid., p. c.
[72] Ibid., p. cii. See also, V. Bogdanor, *The People and the Party System. The referendum and electoral reform in British politics* (Cambridge, 1981), esp. pp. 11–16, 77–9.
[73] Ibid.   [74] Ibid., p. xxxviii.

distrust both of the law and the judges, and by a marked tendency towards the use of lawless methods for the attainment of social or political ends.

The reference here to distrust of the judiciary once again accentuates Dicey's adoption of the ancient conception of the rule of law. Law bolstered the moral order of society and judges, as custodians of those values, were deserving of respect and trust. Dicey viewed the intrinsic connection between law and morality as a vital part of the rule of law.[75] The new class of citizens whom democracy has empowered 'partly because of the fairness and regularity with which the law has been enforced for generations in Great Britain, hardly perceive the risk and ruin involved in a departure from the rule of law'.[76]

The tendency of recent legislation also provided cause for concern. Modern legislation had increasingly vested quasi-judicial powers in officials and excluded or indirectly diminished the authority of the courts. Dicey recognized that this practice was 'due, in part, to the whole current of legislative opinion in favour of extending the sphere of the State's authority' since the courts themselves, being obliged to act in accordance with 'the strict rules of law', were unsuited to 'manage a mass of public business'.[77] Dicey thus felt that 'the law of England is being "officialised" . . . by statutes passed under the influence of socialistic ideas'.[78] This process directly undermined the rule of law: 'such transference of authority saps the foundation of that rule of law which has been for generations a leading feature of the English constitution.'[79] Nor did he see much hope in the extension of parliamentary redress: 'any man who will look plain facts in the face will see in a moment that ministerial liability to the censure not in fact by Parliament, nor even by the House of Commons, but by the party majority who keep the Government in office, is a very feeble guarantee indeed against action which evades the authority of the law courts.'[80]

Finally, Dicey conceded that in the years since 1885 the French system of *droit administratif* had become increasingly judicialized

---

[75] 'Till a time well within the memory of persons now living, it would have been very difficult to find any body of men or women who did not admit that, broadly speaking, a breach of the law of the land was also an act of immorality' ibid., p. xli.
[76] Ibid.   [77] Ibid., p. xxxix.   [78] Ibid., p. xliv.
[79] Dicey, 'The development of administrative law in England' 31 *L.Q.R.* 148, 150.
[80] Ibid. 152.

and that the entirely negative portrayal of 1885 may no longer be justified. He thus concluded, perhaps from pessimism about the nature of general trends, on a surprising note:[81]

It is at least conceivable that modern England would be benefited by the extension of official law. Nor is it quite certain that the ordinary law Courts are in all cases the best body for adjudicating upon the offences or the errors of civil servants. It may require consideration whether some body of men who combined official experience with legal knowledge and who were entirely independent of the Government of the day, might not enforce official law with more effectiveness than any Division of the High Court.

In later life Dicey therefore felt that developments in society and politics were threatening the idea of the British constitution which he had sought to formulate in 1885. The harmony of the guiding principles of the constitution had been threatened by the rise of party government and by the acquisition of powers by government. Dicey's 1914 *Introduction* may be read as a lament; having adopted an optimistic view of the impact of democracy on the workings of the British constitution he realized his error and wished to realign himself with Bagehot's—if not Maine's—more pessimistic position. His work is thus marked with a bitter irony which permeated not only the substance of his theory but also its method. *The Law of the Constitution*, as we have seen,[82] commences with a sneer at 'the religious enthusiasm of Burke' and 'the fervent self-complacency of Hallam'[83] and proposes analysis, rather than veneration, of the constitution. In his final commentary, however, he is to be found mourning the loss of faith:[84]

This [contemporary] condition . . . greatly puzzles the now small body of surviving constitutionalists old enough to remember the sentiment of the mid-Victorian era, with its prevalent belief that to imitate the forms, or at any rate to adopt the spirit of the English constitution, was the best method whereby to confer upon the people of any civilised country the combined blessings of order and of progress.

Dicey and the shaping of the dominant tradition

Dicey has played a major role in the shaping of twentieth-century thought in public law. His work is rooted in the conservative variant of normativism. In the interpretation of Dicey which I have

[81] *Law of the Constitution*, p. xlviii.   [82] Chap. 1, p. 14.
[83] *Law of the Constitution*, 3.   [84] Ibid., p. xciii.

presented the themes that recur in Oakeshott—anti-rationalism, the importance of tradition, and the value of practical experience— can be seen to play major roles in Dicey's theory. They share common views on the idea of knowledge and of the character of political and legal experience. More specifically, they hold very similar views on the issues of authority and law.

In Oakeshott's view the establishment of the authority of the ruler is the paramount consideration in establishing the polity and the admiration which he expresses for Hobbes is rooted in the latter's replacement of reason by will as the foundation of political authority. This perspective, I have argued, forms a major influence on Dicey's views on sovereignty. Oakeshott's belief in the importance of will rather than reason in establishing political authority flows from his views on rationalism. His conception of civil association as a form of moral association and his idea of *jus* of *lex* should not therefore be viewed rationalistically. He believed that rationality, as distinct from rationalism, required fidelity to the knowledge we have acquired of how to conduct specific activities. His views on civil association and the rule of law should be understood as expressions of the values of the ancient conception of the rule of law. This, for example, is why he believed Hobbes (and himself) to be an authoritarian but not an absolutist. As I have already suggested, Dicey's views on both the rule of law and the constitution in general should be interpreted in the light of his belief in the ancient idea of the rule of law. I have also suggested that both Oakeshott and Dicey, in upholding authority and law, apparently blend will and reason or, in the terms of the modern jurisprudential debate, Hart and Fuller. More strictly, they should be seen as blending Hobbes and Coke, since the idea of reason Dicey and Oakeshott each have in mind is the artificial reason and practical knowledge of the common law.

These values permeate their views on the nature of parliament, the judiciary, and liberty. Oakeshott, for example, argues that parliamentary government and democratic (rationalist) politics belong to quite different traditions:[85]

The truth is . . . that the institutions of parliamentary government sprang from the least rationalistic period of our politics, from the Middle Ages,

[85] M. Oakeshott, 'Scientific Politics' (1947–8) 1 *The Cambridge Journal* 347, 357.

and (despite the cloud of false theory with which recent centuries have
enveloped them) were connected, not with the promotion of a rationalist
order of society, but (in conjunction with the common law) with the
limitation of the exercise of political power and the opposition to tyranny
in whatever form it appeared. The root of so-called 'democratic theory' is
not the rationalist optimism about the perfectibility of human society, but
scepticism about the possibility of such perfection and the determination
not to allow human life to be perverted by the tyranny of a person or fixed
by the tyranny of an idea.

These views, which are reminiscent of those of Maine and Bagehot,
were also held by Dicey, notwithstanding his initial optimism about
accommodating democracy to parliamentary government. He
believed that parliamentary government could go a great way
towards securing personal liberty but 'neither parliamentary
government nor any other form of constitution . . . will ever of itself
remove all or half the sufferings of human beings. Utopias lead to
disappointment just because they are utopias'.[86]

Dicey and Oakeshott's view of the role of the judiciary is
similarly rooted in a scepticism of a scientific approach to
adjudication. As Dicey says, 'the appeal to precedent is in the law
courts merely a useful fiction by which judicial decision conceals its
transformation into judicial legislation'.[87] These are not the words
of a proto-realist. His views must be interpreted within the
tradition within which he worked. What Dicey is saying, and with
which Oakeshott would agree,[88] is that the common law system of
precedent satisfies the requirements of both continuity and innovation and, more generally, the common law tradition retains the
value of political experience.

These traditions of government and law have served to protect
our liberties. Here, it scarcely needs stating, we have in mind a
traditional, negative conception of liberty. Dicey, for example,
suggested that the meaning which T. H. Green gave to the concept
of liberty 'was lending support to the current growth of state
intervention and "social despotism".'[89] And the continuing vitality

---

[86] *Law of the Constitution*, p. xciii.
[87] Ibid. 18.
[88] For Oakeshott's view of adjudication see Chap. 5, pp. 73–4.
[89] Quoted in Greenleaf, *The British Political Tradition*, 138.

of these traditions rested on 'public opinion'[90] or 'the prevailing educated moral sensibility of a people'.[91]

These values of conservative normativism underpin the dominant tradition of public law. They shape orthodox views on such matters as sovereignty and liberty, the authority of the judiciary, and the relationship between common law and statute, particularly when the statute in question may be classified as social legislation. That we do not see clearly the value system which gives meaning to our orthodox construction of the subject is in part because of the method of this orthodoxy. The analytical method, which has also been taken from Dicey, and forms part of this orthodoxy supposedly separates fact from value; parliamentary sovereignty, for example, is viewed as part of 'the order of things' rather than a concept derived from a particular political theory. This method constitutes a barrier to understanding. Nevertheless, notwithstanding the adoption of an analytical method, the dominant tradition is both anti-rationalist and anti-formalist in conception.

While Dicey played a major role in shaping this tradition, his particular views are not to be equated with it. Although strongly influenced by Dicey, the tradition comes to take on a life of its own. What specific meanings Dicey himself intended when writing the *Law of the Constitution* matters little. The fact that he appeared to revise his views between 1885 and 1914 is not necessarily important. Although Dicey's theory played a major role in shaping the dominant tradition, his views are subsequently re-invented in the light of the requirements of this tradition.

DICEY AND HIS TIMES

As we have already seen when we considered the foundations of functionalism,[92] the period between 1880 and 1914, during which Dicey wrote, was one of major social and economic change. This period of the second industrial revolution is marked especially as a period of rapid industrialization and urbanization. These changes also had a significant impact at the political level as government

[90] Dicey, *Law and Opinion*.
[91] Oakeshott, *On History* (Oxford, 1983), 160. Note also that Bagehot states that: 'Public opinion . . . is the opinion of the bald-headed man at the back of the omnibus.' (*The English Constitution*, 247). In the Clapham version, this formulation is used as a criterion of reasonableness in the common law.
[92] Chap. 6, p. 136.

sought to introduce reforms to accommodate these changes. As Maitland, who was a contemporary of Dicey, recognized, one repercussion of the consequent growth in the quantity and complexity of government business was that there was 'a tendency . . . on the part of parliament to confine itself to the work of legislation, of framing general rules of law, and of entrusting the power of dealing with particular cases to the king's ministers, to boards of commissioners, to courts of law'.[93] In other words, there was a growth in the use of 'framework legislation', with Parliament establishing a general framework for controlling or regulating an area of activity and granting to governmental agencies both rule-making powers to put flesh on the framework or quasi-judicial powers to resolve disputes that arose in the course of implementing these schemes. The vesting of such powers in governmental bodies was certainly not new. What was significant, however, was not so much the practices themselves but rather their scale.

One might have thought that these trends would not present major difficulties since one apparent virtue of the British constitution was its flexibility. Dicey, however, did not respond to these developments in the role of government by proposing legal arrangements which might ensure that the values of individual liberty were reconciled with these new powers of government. Instead, he developed a concept of the rule of law, drawing on aspects of both the ancient and modern conceptions, which seemed incompatible with the extensive use of these governmental powers. Through this conservative normativist theory Dicey attempted to stem the tide of government growth in a collectivist direction.

Dicey's efforts in this direction were as effective as Canute's. This is not to say that his efforts did not have an impact. The effect, however, seemed to be quite contrary to his intentions. By denying the existence of administrative law in the face of the structural pressures for the growth in administration, the influence which Dicey's theory had on political and legal thought served to shield us from the realities and to prevent us from addressing the issues raised by these developments in a constructive fashion. Rather ironically, given the 'note of condescension, almost of contempt, [which] characterises Dicey's exposition of continental constitu-

---

[93] F. W. Maitland, *The Constitutional History of England* (Cambridge, 1908), 385.

tions',[94] almost all studies undertaken of the French system of *droit administratif* have cast doubt on the superiority of the British approach and have concluded that the French system provides greater protections than our own.[95]

Dicey's approach, nevertheless, lived on in the minds of lawyers. Writing in 1935 Ivor Jennings suggested that Dicey's 'authority to-day is greater than that of any other public lawyer'.[96] But in pressing Dicey's theory into the service of a tradition his thought was transposed into a crude form. C. K. Allen has suggested, for example, that: 'It is evidently difficult for a generation brought up on the early editions of Dicey's *Law of the Constitution* to relinquish the belief that *droit administratif* is the sinister embodiment of all the distempers of the commonwealth which the Rule of Law has so proudly repulsed.'[97] More generally, almost in a caricature of Dicey's views, a belief grew during the early decades of the twentieth century that, because of the destruction in the balances in parliamentary mechanisms wrought by the rise of party government, the courts formed the last bastion in the protection of liberties immanent in constitutional arrangements. A version of this approach may be seen, for example, in the words of Farwell LJ in *Dyson* v. *Attorney-General*:[98]

If ministerial responsibility were more than the mere shadow of a name, the matter would be less important, but as it is, the Courts are the only defence of the liberty of the subject against departmental aggression.

In such forms it seems but a short step from saying that the courts are also our only effective guardians against the evils of socialism.

By the 1920s, the tone of constitutional debate had shifted from one of complacency and self-satisfaction about our matchless constitution to one of growing unease. In William Robson's words, 'the complacent contrast between happy Englishmen free from *droit administratif* and unhappy Frenchmen subject to its terrors

---

[94] Keeton, *The Passing of Parliament*, 7.
[95] In addition to Dicey's own views in 1914 (above pp. 155–6) see, e.g., C. K. Allen, *Bureaucracy Triumphant* (Oxford, 1931), 2–3, 48–9; A. Denning, *Freedom Under Law* (London, 1949), chaps. 3 and 4; C. J. Hamson, *Executive Discretion and Judicial Control* (London, 1954).
[96] Jennings, 'In praise of Dicey 1885–1935' (1935) 13 *Public Admin.* 123, p. 133.
[97] Allen, *Bureaucracy Triumphant* (Oxford, 1931), 96.
[98] *Dyson* v. *Attorney-General* [1911] 1 K.B. 410, at 424.

quietly faded out of the picture'.[99] It came to be replaced by the
view that a 'new despotism' was arising from the growing practice
of vesting legislative and judicial powers in the Executive. And it is
around this issue that the debate in the inter-war years was
polarized.

THE NORMATIVIST CHALLENGE

In concluding the lament that constituted his 1914 Introduction,
Dicey tried to end on an optimistic note. He found it in the fact that
the State, 'united for once in spirit' and 'with the fervent consent of
the people of every land subject to the rule of our King' had entered
on an arduous conflict, not for territory or glory but 'for the sake of
enforcing the plainest rules of international justice and the plainest
dictates of common humanity'. From this event Dicey detected a
'good omen for the happy development of popular government'.[100]
Here again Dicey seems wide of the mark. Not only did the First
World War produce a major crisis of authority for the old order,[101]
but it also resulted in the harnessing by the State, on an
unprecedented scale, of the power and resources of the nation
towards the war effort. This experience was not lost on socialists. If
the government could acquire broad discretionary powers under
the Defence of the Realm Acts 1914–18 to deal with the emergency
could not also a socialist government to meet the peacetime
emergencies of poverty and sickness? As Harold Laski wrote in
1925: 'Anyone who studies the record of war-control of industry
from 1914 to 1918, will be amazed at the mass of material we
possess upon the necessary mechanisms of regulation.'[102]

It was in the context of this post-war challenge to the authority of
the old order, together with the war-time experience of collectivistic
state organization, that normativist lawyers swapped complacency
for extreme concern. The issue was recognized by many even before
the war was concluded. One illustration of the normativist concern,

[99] W. A. Robson, 'Administrative Law in England 1919–1948' in G. Campion
(ed.), *British Government Since 1918* (London, 1950), p. 85, at 86.
[100] *Law of the Constitution*, pp. civ–cv.
[101] See, e.g., J. A. G. Griffith, 'The Political Constitution' (1979) 42 *MLR* 1,
pp. 3–5.
[102] Laski, *A Grammar of Politics* (1925: London, 5th edn., 1967), 489.

both in analysis and prescription, may be found in Lord Shaw's dissent in *R* v. *Halliday* in 1917:[103]

The increasing crush of legislative efforts and the convenience to the Executive of a refuge to the device of Orders in Council would increase th[e] danger [of transition to arbitrary government] tenfold were the judiciary to approach any such action by the Government in a spirit of compliance rather than of independent scrutiny. That way also would lie public unrest and public peril.

In the immediate post-war period, the main legal concern lay with local authorities which across the country were coming under Labour control. Many of these Labour controlled authorities began to use their powers in novel ways by, for example, paying more generous sums in Poor Law relief[104] or in adapting general powers to develop municipal enterprise.[105] In policing these activities the courts were particularly vigilant. The *cause célèbre* of the period is *Roberts* v. *Hopwood*,[106] a case in which the House of Lords upheld the decision of the district auditor to surcharge members of Poplar Borough Council for maintaining a minimum wage for its employees which was not only in excess of wage rates in the area but was also paid to men and women alike. Not only do we find Lord Sumner in this case denying that elected members 'are to be guided by their personal opinions on political, economic, or social questions in administering the funds which they derive from levying rates'[107] but Lord Atkinson denounces the councillors for being guided 'by some eccentric principles of socialistic philanthropy, or by a femininist ambition to secure equality of the sexes in the world of wages'.[108] Here we might note that Atkinson is largely following Dicey who talked of 'the delusion that wages can be raised by legislation'.[109]

But after the formation of the first Labour government in 1924 matters potentially became much more serious, since socialists then

---

[103] [1917] A.C. 260, 287. For others see G. Hewart, *The New Despotism* (London, 1929), pp. 143–8; J. Willis, *The Parliamentary Powers of English Government Departments* (Cambridge, Mass., 1933), 30–1.

[104] See J. Redlich and F. W. Hirst, *A History of Local Government in England* (London, 1958), pp. 223–31.

[105] See, e.g., *Attorney-General* v. *Fulham Corporation* [1921] 1 Ch. 440.

[106] [1925] AC 578. See P. Fennell, '*Roberts* v. *Hopwood*: the Rule against Socialism' (1986) 13 *J. of Law & Society* 401.

[107] Ibid. at p. 604.   [108] Ibid. at p. 594.

[109] Dicey, *Law of the Constitution*, p. lxiii.

came to be vested with the power of legislation. This normativist concern came to a head with the publication in 1929 by Lord Hewart, the Lord Chief Justice, of a book entitled *The New Despotism*.[110] In this book, Hewart warned against the danger of 'organised administrative lawlessness' which was arising from the forms in which new statutory powers were being acquired by government departments. Hewart claimed that this was 'a persistent and well-contrived system, intending to produce, and in practice producing, a despotic power which . . . places Government departments above the Sovereignty of Parliament and beyond the jurisdiction of the Courts'.[111] The importance of the book is attributable to the status of its author. For here we find the head of the common law courts, echoing the spirit of Coke, Hale, and Mansfield and working largely within Dicey's framework, expressing anxiety about the challenge to the supremacy of the 'ordinary law' posed by statutory developments.

These efforts of the judiciary were supported by a number of academics, such as C. K. Allen[112] and Sir John Marriott.[113] Their chorus was in harmony with the principals on the judicial stage: 'To any but those who desire to see a Sidney Webbian England', wrote Allen, 'it is essential that the bureaucratic mind be confined to its proper function, which is that of the lieutenant, not the captain.'[114] Recent tendencies in vesting powers in government departments, however, 'makes the executive not merely a deputy but a plenipotentiary'.[115]

Through such thought and writing the spirit of Dicey was fashioned into orthodoxy in public law. Most of the key actors mentioned had close connections with Dicey, as a pupil or colleague, and to some extent they formed a fairly distinctive group of conservative libertarians. Hewart had held both Law Officer positions in the post-war Liberal Government (although it should be said that his arguments in *The New Despotism* did not seem to

---

[110] Hewart, *The New Despotism*.

[111] Ibid. at p. 14.

[112] Allen, *Law in the Making* (London, 1927); id., *Bureaucracy Triumphant* (London, 1931); id., *Democracy and the Individual* (London, 1943); id., *Law and Orders* (London, 1945).

[113] J. Marriott, *English Political Institutions* (Oxford, 4th edn., 1948); id., *The Mechanism of the Modern State* (Oxford, 1927).

[114] *Bureaucracy Triumphant*, 22.

[115] *Law in the Making*, 325.

trouble him much in that capacity)[116] and Marriott, an Oxford academic, also become a prominent Conservative MP. More personal links can be traced through Sir Ernest Benn, the founder of the Society for Individual Freedom, who, in addition to being a good friend of Allen, was also the publisher of Hewart's *The New Despotism*.[117] But, although the core of this group was quite small and tight-knit, the influence of their ideas was widely felt.

THE FUNCTIONALIST RESPONSE

The normativist crusade did not go unchallenged. In the inter-war period a group of public lawyers and political scientists developed a distinctive functionalist style of public law. Their basic objective was to challenge Dicey's theory of the constitution. They sought both to contest his method and to expose the political values on which his theory rested. But their primary thrust constituted an attack on Dicey's twin principles of parliamentary sovereignty and the rule of law.

The challenge to Dicey's theory

Given the concerns of the 1920s, it comes as no surprise that the initial challenge was over the issue of administrative law. In 1928 William Robson published *Justice and Administrative Law*,[118] a landmark text which he later described as an attempt 'to dispel the illusion held by all the leading lawyers, politicians, civil servants and academics who had been brought up on Dicey's *Law of the Constitution* that in Britain there was no administrative law'.[119] In this book Robson argued that 'no modern student of law or political science has today the slightest doubt that there exists in England a vast body of administrative law' and that 'the problem is not to discover it but rather to master its widespread ramifications

---

[116] As Solicitor-General, for example, Hewart had been responsible for the conduct of the Government's case in *Halliday supra* n. 103. Furthermore, Hewart was hardly a distinguished holder of the office of Lord Chief Justice. R. M. Jackson in *The Machinery of Justice in England* (Cambridge, 7th edn., 1977) referred to Hewart as 'the worst English judge in living memory' (p. 475).

[117] See Greenleaf, *The British Political Tradition*, vol. 2 at pp. 307–8. Benn was also responsible for publishing Keeton's book, *The Passing of Parliament*.

[118] W. A. Robson, *Justice and Administrative Law* (London, 1928).

[119] Robson, '*Justice and Administrative Law* reconsidered' 32 *Current Legal Problems* 107 (1979).

and reduce it to some kind of order and coherence'.[120] Robson was, in one sense, simply echoing the words of Maitland that 'if you take up a modern volume of the reports of the Queen's Bench division, you will find that about half the cases reported have to do with rules of administrative law' and that you must 'not neglect their existence in your general description of what English law is' otherwise 'you will frame a false and antiquated notion of our constitution'.[121] The fact that Robson felt the need to propound this view so strongly, and that Maitland's thoughts seemed to have been almost entirely neglected, serve to indicate that conservative normativism had by the 1920s become established as the dominant tradition.

Robson's aims in *Justice and Administrative Law* were to examine the extent and nature of administrative adjudication and to provide an intellectual foundation for the development of a system of public law. He argued that, although courts of law exist to determine rights and departments of state are charged with the implementation of policy, court judgments can be viewed as the expressions of judicial conceptions of social policy and departmental policies do not in general ignore the issue of private rights. Here we see a characteristic attempt, evident on a range of fronts, to break down the dualisms of normativism.[122] Robson recognized that, throughout history, courts have performed administrative functions and administrative bodies have undertaken judicial functions. With the growth in government activity since the late nineteenth century the administration had, for a variety of reasons, become charged with judicial duties. While the challenge could not be ignored, Robson felt that it would not be resolved by recourse to conceptualistic argument. Robson's solution was to enhance the judicial process and cultivate the judicial spirit *within* the administration by developing a rational system of administrative courts.

Robson's text, which focused mainly on administrative adjudication, was complemented by the work of Willis on delegated legislation.[123] Willis's treatise provided a powerful corrective to Hewart's book. It argued that there was a long history of use of

[120] *Justice and Administrative Law* (3rd edn., 1951), 32.
[121] Maitland, *Constitutional History of England* (Cambridge, 1908), 505–6.
[122] On the dualisms of normativism see, e.g., Chap. 4 pp. 59–61, Chap. 5, Fig. 1, p. 103.
[123] Willis, *The Parliamentary Powers of English Government Departments* (Cambridge, Mass., 1933).

such powers; that, with the widening of the sphere of government, the use of delegated legislative powers was necessary for the efficient conduct of business in the modern state; that the civil service was best placed to provide the expertise which was necessary to make effective use of these powers; and that the way in which the powers were actually used in practice was such as to refute any claim of a 'new despotism'. In Willis's use of history, his recognition of the roots of social change, and his orientation to practice, we can see similarities with Robson's approach. Willis's work also shares Robson's view of courts as framers of judicial policy on social and political questions and it contains a number of pointed criticisms of the normativist style.[124]

Such writing on administrative law was bolstered in respect of constitutional law by the work of Ivor Jennings, whose book, *The Law and the Constitution*, subjected Dicey's constitutional principles to critical examination:[125]

Looking back to the Constitution of 1884 which [Dicey] was analysing . . . , I do not think that his interpretation was in every respect correct. Since then there have been fundamental changes, and few of his principles appear to me to be applicable to the modern Constitution.

Jennings argued that Dicey's ideas on sovereignty were overly conceptualistic and that his concept of the rule of law was based on an individualistic, *laissez-faire* philosophy. For Jennings a constitution is 'only an organisation of men and women' and is a 'transient thing, changing like the colours of the kaleidoscope'. Consequently 'an examination of its working involves an examination of the social and political forces which make for changes in the ideas and habits of the population'.[126] Jennings thus began *The Law and the Constitution* with an examination of the functions of government and, in an approach reflecting the influence of sociological positivism, commenced with an outline of the growing interdependence of society founded in the increasing division of labour.

In general Jennings sought to re-orientate the focus of public law away from Dicey's concern with individual rights and towards an

---

[124] See, e.g., ibid. at p. 51: 'To a lawyer a statute does not speak the living language of the day. Lawyers' ears are attuned to the accents of the forgotten past, new commands are faintly apprehended through the fog of the Common Law.'
[125] 'Preface to the First Edition' (1933) (London, 2nd edn., 1938), p. xv–xvi.
[126] Ibid., p. xiv.

examination of the powers and functions of public authorities. Dicey believed that the constitution was based on principles of private law, which had been extended to determine the position of the Crown.[127] Jennings, however, criticized Dicey for never considering the *powers* of public authorities.[128] Rather than replicate a private law focus, Jennings emphasized that 'the attitude of the modern public lawyer is essentially different from that of the private lawyer'.[129]

The functionalist style

The style of writing exemplified by Jennings, Robson, and Willis displays a number of common patterns. Their method is empirical and historical, it is imbued with a scientific temperament, and implicit in their approach is an evolutionary conception of progress. This style of writing focuses on facts rather than abstractions: this explains the differences in the views of Dicey and Jennings on the subject of sovereignty; it is the reason for the disagreement between Dicey and Robson over whether or not we have administrative law; and it is reflected in Willis's argument against Hewart that the test of the existence of the 'new despotism' was to be found in the way in which the powers were actually used rather than how the form of the power cut across abstract constitutional principles.

This empiricist orientation and scientific temperament is also harnessed to a progressive outlook. Robson's choice of a quotation from Whitehead for the epigraph of *Justice and Administrative Law* is indicative of the general mood:

The period has been one of unprecedented intellectual progress . . . We do not go about saying that there is another defeat for science, because its old ideas have been abandoned. We know that another step of scientific insight has been gained.

The basic objective of these writers was to project an image of public law. In general public law should ensure that the legal framework within which government operated provided an effective and equitable structure for the implementation of the public good, as expressed in the positive functions of the state. From this perspective delegated legislation and administrative adjudication

---

[127] Dicey, *Law of the Constitution*, 199.
[128] Jennings, *The Law and the Constitution*, 54.   [129] Ibid. at p. xi.

was not a symptom of despotic power but of the changing role of the state.

The use of framework legislation and the practice of delegated legislation were thus viewed essentially as methods of efficiently allocating legislative tasks. By relieving it of responsibility for details, Parliament was thereby able to concentrate on major issues of policy. Furthermore, in the modern era of science and specialization, executive expertise is better able than Parliament to deal with complex and technical matters of detail. Or, as Bernard Shaw more eloquently put it, 'The ocean of Socialism cannot be poured into the pint pot of a nineteenth century parliament.'[130]

This functionalist approach also stressed the need for a rational system of administrative adjudication. The courts of law, they argued, are procedurally ill-equipped for this task since their formality, cost, speed, and complexity made them inaccessible to, or intimidating for, the ordinary citizen. Further, the judiciary do not possess the expertise or technical knowledge and are not provided with the training to deal effectively with the disputatious issues arising under social legislation. But the functionalists also argue that the ideology which informs the common law approach is hostile to the positive aims of modern government, that the judiciary display a philosophical, cultural, or political bias when reviewing administrative action and therefore that new institutions with new personnel are required to develop a new jurisprudence for the modern age.[131]

The functionalist style of legal writing was greatly influenced by the work of Harold Laski. From 1915 Laski had worked to construct a theory of the state appropriate to modern times. The various elements of this work[132] were pulled together in 1925 in his book, *A Grammar of Politics*. His objective was to challenge what he called 'the liberal theory of the state' which 'assumed that in

---

[130] Quoted in Greenleaf, *The British Political Tradition*, vol. 2, p. 369.

[131] The classic texts on these issues are: H. J. Laski, 'Judicial review of social policy in England' 39 *Harv. L. Rev.* 839 (1926); *Report of the Committee on Ministers' Powers*, Cmd. 4060, Annex V, 'Note by Professor Laski on the judicial interpretation of statutes'; Willis, 'Three approaches to administrative law: the judicial, the conceptual and the functional' 1 *Univ. of Toronto L.J.* 53 (1935); Jennings, 'The courts and administrative law—the experience of English housing legislation' 49 *Harv. L. Rev.* 426 (1936).

[132] See Laski, *Studies in the Problem of Sovereignty* (London, 1917); id., *Authority in the Modern State* (New Haven, Conn., 1919); id., *The Foundations of Sovereignty and Other Essays* (London, 1921).

political society where anarchy was to be avoided there must be a supreme authority which gives orders to all and receives orders from none'.[133] This liberal theory is, of course, the Hobbesian theory which we have associated with conservative normativism. Laski argued that, while this theory provided for social order, it was deficient insofar as it was unable to provide an adequate technique for coping with peaceful social change.

In the *Grammar* Laski, before turning his attention to the issue of sovereignty, commenced his analysis, significantly, with an examination of the purpose of social organization and suggested that, when viewed purposively, the State 'becomes an organisation for enabling the mass of men to realise social good on the largest possible scale'.[134] It is from this functional perspective, or 'realistic view of the State',[135] that he considered the issue of sovereignty. Here Laski was highly critical of the abstract legal idea of absolute legal sovereignty, arguing that it could not form a realistic basis for political relationships. Authority in the state is inherently federal since the state is simply one association amongst many. This idea of authority was linked to his conception of rights. Rights, which constitute the groundwork of the State, inhere in individuals by virtue of their being members of society: 'A State which neglects them fails to build its foundations in the hearts of its citizens.'[136] From these ideas of sovereignty, authority, and rights Laski developed a sophisticated conception of law:[137]

To those for whom law is a simple command, legal by virtue of the source from which it comes, it is not likely that such complexities as these will be popular. We are urging that law is, in truth, not the will of the State, but that from which the will of the State derives whatever moral authority it may possess. That is, admittedly, an abandonment of simplicity. It assumes that the rationale of obedience is in all the intricate facts of social organisation and in no one group of facts. It denies at once the sovereignty of the State, and that more subtle doctrine by which the State is at once the master and servant of law by willing to limit itself to certain tested rules of conduct. It insists that what is important in law is not the fact of command but the end at which that command aims and the way it achieves the end. It sees society, not as a pyramid in which the State sits crowned upon the summit, but as a system of co-operating interests through which, and in

---

[133] Laski, *A Grammar of Politics* (1925: 5th edn., 1967), p. iii.
[134] Ibid. 25.   [135] Ibid. 29.
[136] Ibid. 40.   [137] Ibid. 286–7.

which, the individual finds his scheme of values. It argues that each individual scheme so found gives to the law whatever of moral rightness it contains. Law, that is to say, is made valid by my experience of it, and not by the fact that it is presented to me as law. Such experience, indeed, is rarely separate in kind (though it is always unique in degree) because it is shared with others in the effort to make an impact upon society. It appears as an interest which seeks the objectivity of realisation. It strives to suffuse the law with its sense of need. . . . Law then emerges as the evaluation of the interests by the interweaving of interests. It is a function of the whole social structure and not some given aspect of it. Its power is determined by the degree to which it aids what that whole social structure reports as its desires.

The influences on Laski's political and legal thought are many and various. His ideas on sovereignty and social organization seem to have been influenced by sociological positivism and by Duguit in particular.[138] His pluralist view of the nature of the State seems inspired by Maitland.[139] His view on the role of the state in the fulfilment of individual personality and his related theory of rights seems greatly indebted to T. H. Green.[140] Laski's political theory can in general be seen as the product of a pragmatic revolt in politics.[141] Finally, as the quotation demonstrates, his views on law are greatly influenced by Holmes, Gray, and Pound.[142] While Laski was thus influenced by many of the strands of thought which we have identified as foundations of functionalism, his views have, in turn, held great sway over the development of the functionalist style in public law.

We can, at numerous points, see the clear imprint of Laski's method and approach on the work of these lawyers.[143] In effect his

---

[138] See, e.g., Laski, 'M. Duguit's Conception of the State' in A. L. Goodhart (ed.), *Modern Theories of Law* (London, 1933), 52. Laski also translated Duguit's *Law and the Modern State* (London, 1921).

[139] See, e.g., Maitland, Introduction to O. von Gierke, *Political Theories of the Middle Ages* (Cambridge, 1900). His views were also influenced by Figgis. See, J. N. Figgis, *Churches in the Modern State* (London, 1913).

[140] See, e.g., *Grammar*, 39.

[141] The influence of William James is especially evident: see, e.g., *Grammar*, 23, 261, 400, 544.

[142] See, e.g., O. W. Holmes, *The Common Law* (Boston, 1881); J. C. Gray, *The Nature and Sources of the Law* (New York, 1909); R. Pound, 'Liberty of Contract' (1909) 18 *Yale L.J.* 454; 'Law in Books and Law in Action' (1910) 44 *American Law Rev.* 12; 'The Scope and Purpose of Sociological Jurisprudence' (1911) 24 *Harv. L. Rev.* 591; (1911) 25 *Harv. L. Rev.* 140; (1912) 25 *Harv. L. Rev.* 489.

[143] Perhaps the clearest influence is to be found in Jennings, *The Law and the*

agenda of constructing a theory of the state appropriate to the modern world is transformed by the public lawyers into an agenda for building a modern theory of public law. Laski himself led the way, not only in general theoretical orientation but also in the detailed study. He believed that the implementation of politics constituted its essence, that 'a working theory of the state must, in fact, be conceived in administrative terms'.[144] His thoughtful articles during the early 1920s on delegated legislation, administrative discretion, and judicial review of social legislation[145] seem to point the way for Jennings, Robson, and Willis.

Laski's study of judicial review is particularly interesting since its primary focus is a study of *Roberts* v. *Hopwood*.[146] He concludes the study with the observation that it 'is an easy step from the *Poplar* judgment to the conclusion that the House of Lords is, in entire good faith, the unconscious servant of a single class in the community'.[147] This has two resonances. First, Laski is counterposing Dicey's normativist concern with 'class legislation'[148] with his functionalist concern with 'class adjudication'. Secondly, his formulation, particularly in an American law review, reverberates with Holmes's classic dissent in *Lochner* v. *New York*.[149] Through this latter resonance we can see the connection between the functionalist style and American legal realism.

The functionalist style in public law exhibits tendencies to examine critically the reasoning processes of courts and to expose the value assumptions on which they rest.[150] It is highly critical of

---

Constitution, where both his structure (cf. chap. 1 'The Functions of Government' with the *Grammar's* first chapter, 'The Purpose of Social Organisation') and his views on such matters as legal sovereignty (chap. IV) the rule of law (chap. II, sect. I and Appx. II) and the nature of law (Appx. III) can all be read as an elaboration of Laski's thought. Jennings, of course, acknowledged this debt: 'Most of the ideas in this book have been discussed with Professor H. J. Laski' (Preface p. xvi).

[144] *Grammar*, 35.

[145] See Laski, 'The problem of administrative areas' in *The Foundations of Sovereignty* (London, 1921), 30; 'The Growth of Administrative Discretion' (1923) 1 *J. of Public Admin*. 92; 'Judicial Review of Social Policy in England' (1926) 39 *Harv. L. Rev*. 839.

[146] See above n. 106.   [147] 39 *Harv. L. Rev*. 832 at 848.

[148] See above n. 24.   [149] See Chap. 6, n. 24.

[150] In addition to the works cited above at n. 131, consider the following from Robson's *Justice and Administrative Law* (London, 3rd edn., 1951), 514: 'Beneath the perfect propriety of judicial utterances such as these one can discern a deep-seated dislike of the rent tribunals; a distrust of their ability to do their work properly without legal knowledge; and a firm intention to keep them strictly within

abstract theorizing, believing that positivist legal theory 'is an exercise in logic and not in life'.[151] It adopts a sociological approach to evaluating the meaning and purpose of law and the style is rooted in a social scientific approach.[152] And a particularly important strand to the style was the emphasis on facts and data gathering, rather than conceptualization, to good decision-making; it therefore had a tendency to place greater trust in administrative bodies than courts. The functionalist public lawyers of the inter-war years were our equivalent of the American legal realists.[153] Just as there were variations within the Realist movement, so also differences of emphasis were to be found in Britain. Some writing of Jennings, for example, seems more in tune with Pound's sociological jurisprudence, which views social interests rather than legal rules and principles as the building blocks of the legal order.[154] But the shared pragmatic approach is clearly evident.

the letter of their jurisdiction. . . . The supposition of what Parliament would have done if it had intended to allow the tribunals to interfere with the standard rent is based on a major premiss which in this instance is scarcely inarticulate.'

[151] Laski, *Grammar*, p. vi. The Holmesean formulation (see Chap. 6, p. 136) is often reflected in functionalist writing. See, e.g., Willis, *Parliamentary Powers*, 5: 'the English lawyer, with his strange but quite intelligible aptitude for divorcing life from law . . . , failed to realise the significant changes going on beneath the trappings of legal theory.' We might also note that Robson's allusion (ibid.) to the 'inarticulate major premiss' is also to Holmes.

[152] 'The most fertile field of investigation in the social sciences appears to be presented by the ground which lies between law, economics, political science and psychology, a territory which so far has been almost unexplored' (Robson, *Justice and Administrative Law* (London, 1st edn., 1928), p. xiv). 'I could not go on recommending to my students books which appeared to me to be out of date. I was therefore compelled to assume many things without explanation, including the general methodology of public law. For historical reasons that subject has become divided into three branches in England, known respectively as constitutional law, political science and the most important part of jurisprudence' (Jennings, *Law and the Constitution*, p. ix).

[153] Roger Cotterrell has recently asked: 'Why has [American legal] realism . . . had little impact on normative legal theory in Britain . . . ?' (*The Politics of Jurisprudence* (London, 1989), 202). The question raises more questions about the nature of jurisprudence in Britain than about the impact of realism on British legal thought.

[154] Pound, 'A Survey of Social Interests' 57 *Harv. L. Rev.* 1 (1943). And cf. id., 'Call for a Realist Jurisprudence' 44 *Harv. L. Rev.* 697 (1931); K. N. Llewellyn, 'Some Realism about Realism—Responding to Dean Pound' 44 *Harv. L. Rev.* 1222 (1931).

Networks and linkages

If the nodal point of normativism was in Oxford, that of the functionalist style was the London School of Economics and Political Science. This is hardly surprising since the School had been established in 1895 by Sidney Webb with the aim of contributing 'to the improvement of society by promoting the impartial study of its problems and the training of those who were to translate policy into action'.[155] Evolutionary rationalism was built into its foundations and was reflected in the character of its early work. This can be seen, for example, by the fact that Graham Wallas, a prominent Fabian,[156] and L. T. Hobhouse, a leading light in New Liberalism,[157] occupied the first chairs of Political Science and Sociology respectively. Consider also Hawthorn's assessment of Ginsberg, who succeeded to Hobhouse's Chair:[158]

Unlike Hobhouse, he had no teleology, but he did have faith in an historical progression towards the universalisation of morals, towards a greater influence upon men of their consciences (and thus of their own independently critical rationality), and towards a clearer distinction between individual and collective responsibilities (evident in the steady separation of morals, religion and law). If moral progress was not, as for Hobhouse, pre-ordained, it seemed nevertheless to be occurring. But Ginsberg realised that it was a conditional matter, and the task of sociology as he saw it was to discern and specify the conditions under which it could continue. This of course was exactly Durkheim's view . . .

Ginsberg's framework, which was in accord with the spirit of work being done by Hobson in economics, Tawney in economic history, and Laski in political science, seems equally applicable to the functionalist style of Robson, Jennings, and Willis. Furthermore, functionalism as a method of social investigation, which is also traceable to Durkheim, seemed particularly influential at the LSE. Tawney's *The Acquisitive Society*,[159] for example, constituted a sustained argument on the need to organize society on the basis of

---

[155] LSE, *Calendar 1987–88* (London, 1987), 19; and see Chap. 6, p. 117.
[156] Chap. 6, p. 116.
[157] Chap. 6, p. 120.
[158] G. Hawthorn, *Enlightenment and Despair*, 168.
[159] R. H. Tawney, *The Acquisitive Society* (London, 1921). Tawney, a Balliol graduate from the period in which T. H. Green's influence was still profound (see Greenleaf *The British Political Tradition*, vol. 2, pp. 440–1) held the Chair of Economic History at LSE from 1931 until 1949.

functions rather than rights and Malinowski did much to pioneer the functionalist method in anthropology.[160]

It was in this intellectual environment that the characteristics of the functionalist style were fashioned. And it is by bringing this institutional dimension into focus that we may fully appreciate the influence of Laski, who was Professor of Political Science at LSE from 1926 to 1950. The linkages are too numerous to relate but it is worthy of note that, in addition to acknowledging the help of Hobhouse, Wallas, Ginsberg, and Tawney in producing the *Grammar*, Laski also mentions Holmes, Frankfurter, and Pound.[161] We can see here the personal link between Fabianism and New Liberalism as political movements, the positivist and functionalist methods in social science, on the one hand, and, on the other, the sociological and realist movements in American law. Holmes, the grandfather of realism, maintained a remarkable correspondence with Laski.[162] Frankfurter, the fact-orientated administrative lawyer and eminent New Dealer, was the sponsor of Laski's appointment at Harvard University in 1916.[163] It may not be going too far to suggest that Laski was the primary conduit through which early twentieth-century developments in American legal thought were filtered into British public law thought.[164]

Jennings and Robson obtained teaching appointments at the LSE in the 1920s and were greatly influenced by Laski. Pragmatic instrumentalist thought would appear to have had a significant influence on the general intellectual milieu in which Jennings and Robson worked. When, for example, *The Modern Law Review*, based at the LSE, was founded in 1937, the *Review* published as its

---

[160] See R. Firth (ed.), *Man and Culture: An Evaluation of the Work of Malinowski* (London, 1957). Malinowski was Professor of Social Anthropology at the LSE during the 1920s.

[161] *Grammar*, 'Preface to First Edition'.

[162] See *Holmes-Laski Letters* (M. De W. Howe edn.) (London, 1953).

[163] K. Martin, *Harold Laski* (London, 1953), 23. It is also worthy of note that, although Laski does not appear to have had a hand in it, Frankfurter was the supervisor at Harvard of Willis's dissertation on delegated legislation: see R. C. B. Risk, 'John Willis—A Tribute' (1985) 9 *Dalhousie L.J.* 521, 526.

[164] Consider, e.g., the assessment of Felix Cohen: 'In the field of jurisprudence, this became a struggle to bring a scientific outlook into the law, and thus to make of law a more effective tool in the cause of social justice. Fellow soldiers in this struggle, Harold J. Laski, Felix Frankfurter, and Louis D. Brandeis, were devoted friends of Morris R. Cohen and Oliver Wendell Holmes. The interplay of these friendships offers a bright page in the development of American legal thought' Foreword, 'The Holmes–Cohen Correspondence' (1948) IX *J. of the History of Ideas* 3 at 5.

first article an essay by Felix Cohen, a prominent American legal realist, called 'The problems of a functional jurisprudence'.[165] Despite these various influences we should also recognize that, perhaps because of the growing differentiation of law as a separate discipline (a process recognized by Ginsberg and associated with a positivist outlook), the methods of the social sciences are often not rendered explicit in the functionalist style in public law. For this reason, their message is not always expressed as clearly as it could be. The imprint is, nevertheless, clearly discernible.

THE GROWTH OF ADMINISTRATIVE LAW

Now that the shape of the functionalist style has been outlined, we must consider the influence which it has had on the development of public law this century. As we have seen, during the early decades of this century debate in public law focused on the issues arising from the growth in the legislative and judicial powers of the Executive. These issues came to a head with the appointment of the Committee on Ministers' Powers in 1929. The committee was appointed to consider powers of delegated legislation and quasi-judicial decision and to report on any safeguards needed 'to secure the constitutional principles of the sovereignty of Parliament and the supremacy of the Law'.[166] The terms of reference themselves provoked concern, causing Robson to comment that the Donoughmore Committee 'started life with the dead hand of Dicey lying frozen on its neck'.[167] Nevertheless, the function of the Committee was not all that it might appear. It was, after all, established by a Labour government, it included Laski amongst its membership and, being appointed two days before Hewart's book was published, could be viewed as a means of deflecting the pressures from the normativist legal lobby.

In these circumstances, the conclusions of the Committee were all

---

[165] (1937) 1 *MLR* 5. The title of the *Review* indicated that it was designed to be forward-looking and present a challenge to the traditional values of law. On the founding of the MLR see: C. Glasser, 'Radicals and Refugees: The Foundation of The Modern Law Review and English Legal Scholarship' (1987) 50 *MLR* 688.

[166] *Report of the Committee on Ministers' Powers*, Cmd. 4060, 1932 (Donoughmore Report).

[167] Robson, *Justice and Administrative Law* (3rd edn., 1951), 423.

too predictable. Robson argued that the Committee had three broad courses of action open to it:[168]

It could (in theory at least) have recommended a return to the eighteenth century position, illustrated by the Lord Chief Justice when he expressed hope that 'the worst of the offending sections' in Acts of Parliament be repealed or amended. It could have accepted the proposals which I put forward to rationalise and institutionalise the administrative jurisdiction in a boldly-conceived system of administrative courts separated to a large extent from the ordinary routine of departmental administration and free from indirect ministerial interference. Or thirdly, it could accept the patchwork quilt of ill-constructed tribunals which at present exists, and endeavour to remedy some of their more obvious defects.

Presented in this way, it is almost inconceivable to anyone understanding the function of such committees that it would pursue any other than the last alternative. The Committee's report thus concluded that these practices were necessary in modern circumstances but they suggested that, because of haphazard evolution, the practices lacked coherence and the system should therefore be regularized and checked. From a functionalist perspective the Committee's value was, first, as a pressure-release valve and, secondly, that it 'disposed once and for all of this conspiratorial theory of executive power'.[169] From a normativist perspective the Report seemed to be the occasion for less satisfaction. Keeton, for example, in the 1950s argued that:[170]

[F]ew reports have assembled so much wisdom whilst proving so completely useless, as the Report of the Committee on Ministers' Powers ... [I]n no important respect did the report influence, much less delay, the onrush of administrative power, and the supercession of the ordinary forms of law which is today taking place. . . . Its report restored to the public a sense of security, which had been badly shaken by Lord Hewart's book, and which subsequent events have proved to be false.

Nevertheless, while the Report may have rejected the reactionary normativist ideology it is also the case that it did nothing to challenge the dominant legal culture. Orthodox legal views on the

[168] Robson, 'The Report of the Committee on Ministers' Powers' (1932) 3 *Political Quarterly* 346 at 359.
[169] Robson, 'Administrative Law' in M. Ginsberg (ed.), *Law and Opinion in England in the Twentieth Century* (London, 1959), p. 193 at 198. (We might note also how this functionalist tract takes its cue from Dicey.)
[170] Keeton, *The Passing of Parliament*, 1–2, 10.

nature of social legislation and the relationship between that legislation and the common law remained untouched by the Report.[171] The anti-rationalist, anti-systematizing characteristics of conservative normativism were retained intact.

Although the Donoughmore Report dealt not only with delegated legislation but also with administrative adjudication, the latter subject continued to exercise concern. It was this issue which lay at the heart of Dicey's concern about *droit administratif*. Dicey had feared that if the use of administrative tribunals was extended and regularized, particularly if judicial review were excluded, Britain would rapidly develop an independent and formalized system of administrative law. This is precisely what Robson, Jennings, and Willis were advocating since they argued for the rationalization of our haphazard arrangements for tribunals with an appellate jurisdiction vested in an administrative appeal tribunal which would be separate from the High Court.[172] And, as we have seen, this development was rejected by the Donoughmore Committee.

As the century progressed the tribunal network mushroomed, with an exponential growth rate most conveniently tracked in the successive editions of Robson's book.[173] Of the arrangements for health service tribunals, for example, Robson commented: 'The complexity of this labyrinthine system of adjudication is fantastic. It is difficult to discover any intelligible principles which would justify, or even explain, the existence of so many different tribunals.'[174] This is precisely as the normativist tradition would wish. In this form they are to be conceived of as *ad hoc*, dispute-resolving mechanisms. Without a set of intelligible principles to guide them, or a rational institutional structure to supervise them, tribunals cannot develop a system of administrative law.

Nevertheless, in the period after the Second World War, as the Labour government made significant advances in laying down its programme for a welfare state, there was a growing unease about

[171] But see Cmd. 4060, Annex V, 'Note by Professor Laski on the judicial interpretation of statutes'.
[172] Donoughmore Report, Cmd. 4060, vol. 2 Evidence, p. 51; Robson, *Justice and Administrative Law*, 3rd edn., chap. 6; Jennings, 'The Report on Ministers' Powers' 10 *Public Admin.* 333 at 348–51 (1932); Willis, *Parliamentary Powers* at pp. 171–2.
[173] In the first edition (1928) of *Justice and Administrative Law* the chapter describing administrative tribunals ran to 70 pages; in the second edition (1947) it had increased to 132; and in the third (1951) it amounted to 228.
[174] Ibid. (3rd edn.), 143.

the scale of administrative activity. These issues came to a head with the Crichel Down affair in the 1950s, which led to a general 'moral panic' about administrative power.[175] One of the reverberations was the establishment in 1955 of the Franks Committee, charged with the task of examining the working of the system of administrative tribunals and inquiries.[176] At this stage, we should record, the ideological dimension of conservative normativism altered its tack. If the growth of administrative adjudication could not be prohibited, it was argued that it must be regularized by integrating it into the ordinary law of the land, thereby ensuring that it develops in harmony with traditional common law principles.[177]

The Report of the Franks Committee in 1957 was recognized by Robson as 'an important landmark in our constitutional history', largely because it accepted that administrative tribunals are 'a valuable and permanent part of the machinery of justice' and went much further 'than the grudging admission of the advantages possessed by tribunals accorded by the Donoughmore Report'.[178] Nevertheless, on the subject of the clash between the normativist and functionalist styles of public law—which emerged in the Franks Committee's investigations over the question of whether any body responsible for supervising administrative tribunals should be detached from or integrated into the Supreme Courts[179]— the Committee came down firmly in favour of integration.

By this stage, then, the Diceyan argument that in Britain we had no administrative law had clearly been rejected. The rejection of Dicey's view does not, however, constitute a rejection of conservative normativism. Conservative normativism lived in the analytical method, which is rooted in the divorce of fact from value, and law from politics, and which ran hand-in-hand with the recognition of the universal supervisory jurisdiction of our superior courts of law. The patchwork quilt of administrative decision-making powers reinforced the idea that this was not a new system of law in the

---

[175] See P. Hennessy, *Whitehall* (London, 1989), pp. 502–4.

[176] Report of the Committee on Tribunals and Enquiries (1957) (Franks Report).

[177] See Allen, *Bureaucracy Triumphant*; id., 'Administrative Jurisdiction' 1956 *Public Law* 13. See also A. Denning, *Freedom under the Law* (London, 1949) chaps. 3 and 4.

[178] Robson, 'Administrative Justice and Injustice: A Commentary on the Franks Report' 1958 *Public Law* 12 at 17.

[179] Cf. Franks Report, *supra* note 176, Minutes of Evidence, pp. 491–2 (Robson), 523–4 (Society of Labour Lawyers); pp. 304–9 (Inns of Court Conservative and Unionist Society), Appx. 1, pp. 3–4 (Allen).

making and the formalism of normativism led to the idea that to the extent that we had administrative law, the subject consisted wholly or mainly of delegated legislation and administrative adjudication; that is, the forms of administrative action classifiable in terms of a conception of a formal separation of powers. In general, the project of conservative normativism has been to ensure that the decisions of 'inferior tribunals' are subject to review by the superior courts applying the common law.

There have been those in positions of authority who have expressed doubt about the possibilities of this normativist project. In 1956, for example, Sir Patrick Devlin commented that:[180]

The common law has now, I think, no longer the strength to provide any satisfactory solution to the problem of keeping the executive . . . under proper control. The responsibility for that now rests with Parliament and is to be discharged . . . in two ways. The first is by keeping a close watch on the powers that are granted to the executive . . . The other is by controlling the way in which the executive exercises the powers which it is given. Since that cannot be effectively done under the law as it stands, there must be created a new body of law of the sort that has come to be called administrative law.

Others, even during the 1950s, adopted a more optimistic note. Clive Schmitthoff, for example, contended that:[181]

[T]he most significant legal development of the past fifty years is the almost complete absorption of administrative law into the fold of the common law. This development is an event of the first magnitude, which is comparable to the incorporation of the law merchant into the common law in the eighteenth century.

Schmitthoff's views, expressed in 1951, seem somewhat premature. It was not until the 1960s that the courts rid themselves of the most debilitating restraints of formalism and assumed a more active supervisory role.[182] During the 1970s, the consolidation of this role was achieved by procedural reforms providing for a simplified

---

[180] P. Devlin, 'The Common Law, Public Policy and the Executive' 1956 *Current Legal Problems* 1, 14–15.
[181] C. Schmitthoff, 'The Growing Ambit of the Common Law' (1951) 29 *Can. Bar Rev.* 469, 470.
[182] The landmark cases of this period are *Ridge* v. *Baldwin* [1964] AC 40; *Padfield* v. *Minister of Agriculture* [1968] AC 997; *Anisminic* v. *Foreign Compensation Commission* [1968] 2 QB 862.

application for judicial review.[183] And in the early 1980s, this procedure was established as an essentially exclusive procedure for the determination of public law rights.[184] By 1982 Lord Diplock signalled the success of the project in commenting, obiter dictum, that:[185]

[T]he progress towards a comprehensive system of administrative law . . . I regard as having been the greatest achievement of the English courts in my judicial lifetime.

The functionalist style in public law, it would therefore appear, has maintained its life only as a dissenting tradition. Its methods and values have rarely been able to challenge the dominance of conservative normativism.

[183] See Order 53, R.S.C. (1977); Supreme Court Act 1981, s. 31. See L. Blom-Cooper, 'The new face of judicial review: administrative changes in Order 53' 1982 *Pub. Law* 250. Scottish reforms, along similar lines, were introduced in 1985: see, A. W. Bradley, 'Applications for judicial review—the Scottish model' 1987 *Pub. Law* 313.
[184] See, *O'Reilly* v. *Mackman* [1983] 2 AC 237; C. F. Forsyth, 'Beyond *O'Reilly* v. *Mackman*: the foundations and nature of procedural exclusivity' 1985 *Camb. LJ* 415; H. Woolf, 'Public law—private law: why the divide?' 1986 *Pub. Law* 220.
[185] *R.* v. *I.R.C., ex parte National Federation of Self Employed* [1982] A.C. 617, 641.

8

Contemporary Thought in Public Law

THE existence during the inter-war period of the normativist and functionalist styles of public law has been generally recognized. It has even been accepted that the adversaries—Hewart and Allen on one side and Robson and Jennings on the other—may 'be grouped together as exponents of a particular type of political thought'.[1] What is particularly interesting about the inter-war debate was that both Hewart and Robson were breaking with long-standing tradition. This tradition, as J. A. G. Griffith explains, insisted on there being two levels of presentation:[2]

On one level was advanced the view of the constitution handed down from Blackstone to Bagehot and Dicey. This consisted of a series of comfortable, liberal–democratic doctrines about the nature and functioning of the constitution, and disregarded the close political, social and class linkages between the different groups of public authorities, the inaccessibility of the courts to all but a handful of people . . . The other level was that of the day-to-day reality. The 'what actually happens' constitution. This reality was not to be written about. Time and again, it was usual to hear learned exposition about 'the theory of the constitution'. And occasionally when the lecturer had closed his bible it was possible to persuade him to speak a little about the reality of power in a capitalist parliamentary democracy.

Griffith suggests that Hewart and Robson, 'with opposed political positions, opposed philosophies, and opposed remedies' were both breaking that tradition in talking about the exercise of power in the real world. As a result, 'neither was easily forgiven'.[3]

---

[1] G. W. Keeton, *The Passing of Parliament* (London, 1952), 10. See also, C. R. Harlow and R. W. Rawlings, *Law and Administration* (London, 1984), chaps. 1 and 2.

[2] J. A. G. Griffith, '*Justice and Administrative Law* Revisited' in Griffith (ed.), *From Policy to Administration. Essays in Honour of William A. Robson* (London, 1976), 200 at pp. 204–5.

[3] Ibid. 205.

Some may argue, however, that the study of public law has emerged from its early ideological state and has now established itself as a distinct discipline. Griffith, for one, would disagree. 'It is', he proposes, 'a tradition no less strong today.'[4] This is, of course, a view with which I agree.[5] Contemporary work in public law is largely based on the first level identified by Griffith. Much of this work is analytical and therefore seems to take the form of a technical contribution to an objective discipline. As I have indicated, however, this formalism is invariably underpinned by a normativist orientation. As we have seen, Dicey sought to draw a distinct line between law and politics and suggested that the duty of the public lawyer 'is to state what are the laws which form part of the constitution, to arrange them in their order, to explain their meaning, and to exhibit where possible their logical connection'.[6] But, as we have also seen, secreted within this formalism is a normativist conception of law.[7]

This analytical approach to the subject has been bolstered in the post-war period by the influence of the Oxford school of linguistic philosophy, which has, mainly through the work of H. L. A. Hart,[8] had a profound impact on post-war British jurisprudence. When viewed sociologically, however, this linguistic movement can be seen as fulfilling a culturally conservative role. As Ernest Gellner has argued: 'Linguistic Philosophy . . . tries to make us take the world for granted and to think only about the oddity of philosophy emerging in it, rather than to think philosophically about it.'[9] We certainly need to try to render explicit the concepts we use, but we should also be concerned with trying to evaluate them and the purposes for which they are used.

Consequently, most who today write within an orthodox analytical framework are actually adopting a normativist approach and thereby incorporating its values. I shall try to illuminate this point by taking a distinguished example. During the 1980s the most important work in public law of Professor Sir David Williams of Cambridge University has been (if we exclude work on civil liberties) three articles on delegated legislation, administrative

---

[4] Ibid. at p. 204.   [5] See Chap. 3.
[6] Dicey, *Law of the Constitution*, 31. See Chap. 1, p. 17.
[7] Chap. 7 pp. 141–6.
[8] H. L. A. Hart, 'Definition and Theory in Jurisprudence' (1954) 70 *L.Q.R.* 37; id., *The Concept of Law* (Oxford, 1961).
[9] E. Gellner, *Words and Things* (London, 1959), p. 85.

tribunals, and public local inquiries.[10] To invoke Quentin Skinner's insight, I am not so much concerned with what Williams is saying in these articles (the 'locutionary' meaning) but rather with what the author is doing (what is its point or 'illocutionary force').[11] The illocutionary force of Williams's work, in focusing on these three institutional processes, is, I believe, to stress the importance of a formalistic approach to the subject. I say so because the importance of these institutional processes is thrown into relief only once the formal doctrine of the separation of powers is invoked. And the importance of this doctrine is fully revealed only by embracing normativism. My point here is that the conservative normativism which constitutes the dominant tradition in public law is bolstered not only by the locutionary meaning of work in public law but also by the illocutionary force of much of this work.

While the main body of work today in the field of public law is of this analytical nature I wish, nevertheless, to focus on some of the more explicitly ideological writing. My objective is to show that the type of debate which was prominent in the inter-war period has continued throughout the post-war period and shapes the way in which we think about public law today.

NORMATIVISM: THE CONSERVATIVE VARIANT

The pre-eminent contemporary writer within the tradition of conservative normativism is Sir William Wade. Wade must essentially be seen as a contemporary disciple of Dicey. 'I yield to no one in admiration of Dicey's brilliant summing up of the spirit of the Constitution in the nineteenth century', he boasted in his Oxford inaugural lecture in 1962, and continued that, while 'many of his ideas can be controverted, the spirit of his work is enduring.'[12] In his work Wade has endeavoured to defend, not only the spirit of Dicey's work but also his ideas.

---

[10] D. G. T. Williams, 'The Donoughmore Report in Retrospect' (1982) 60 *Pub. Admin.* 273; id., 'The Council on Tribunals: the first twenty five years' 1984 *Pub. Law* 79; id., 'Public local inquiries—formal administrative adjudication' (1980) 29 *Int. & Comp. L.Q.* 701.

[11] Q. Skinner, '"Social meaning" and the explanation of social action' in P. Gardiner (ed.), *The Philosophy of History* (Oxford, 1974), 106.

[12] H. W. R. Wade, 'Law, Opinion and Administration' (1962) 78 *L.Q.R.* 188, 189.

In an early essay Wade provided a clear and reflective insight into his view of law.[13] Law, he argued, exists 'to ensure the order which the forces in control of a society desire to impose'.[14] The idea of justice is subsidiary to that of order. 'Justice' is a term susceptible of many meanings and 'in so far as it means "equality", "impartiality" or "uniformity" it has more in common with the political idea of order than with the moral idea which is also implied in the word.'[15] In general, 'it is more important for a rule of law to be certain than for it to be just'.[16] In Wade's opinion, law is 'a condition precedent to life, and stands in relation to philosophy much as pure liberalism stands in relation to politics'.[17] That is, it serves to release energy rather than accumulate it.

Wade's defence of order and legal certainty here has a specific point. He argues that, from the very strength and validity of this view, come the attacks on it.[18] The primary attacks Wade has in mind are those of the American legal realists.[19] To some extent, this movement is viewed as a product of its particular legal culture, since the Supreme Court in the United States 'is in a real sense itself legislative' and 'is normally looked upon as an arm, and an active arm, of the sovereign political body'.[20] But Wade also recognizes that it is connected to the modern tendency 'to more and more governmental interference in regions which used to be thought the preserves of individual enterprise'.[21] The pursuit of certainty thus 'becomes more and more difficult as laws multiply and complicate themselves'.[22] The general message of Wade's essay is that the legal uncertainty—the cases of judicial legislation—are exceptional and 'are growing more and more exceptional as the hitherto uncharted

---

[13] Id., 'The Concept of Legal Certainty. A Preliminary Sketch' (1940–1) 4 *M.L.R.* 183.

[14] Ibid. at p. 185.   [15] Ibid. at p. 187.

[16] Ibid.   [17] Ibid. at p. 188.

[18] Wade invokes T. S. Eliot's views on liberalism in support of his case: '[O]ur danger now is, that the term may come to signify for us only the disorder the fruits of which we inherit, and not the permanent value of the negative element. Out of liberalism itself come philosophies which deny it' *The Idea of a Christian Society*, pp. 12–13; quoted in Wade, 'Law, Opinion and Administration', 188.

[19] Ibid. 189–96. The primary culprit is J. Frank's *Law and the Modern Mind* (New York, 1930), which argues that the desire for certainty is a psychosis; an unhealthy state of mind produced by inhibitions, repressions, and substitutions. On realism in general, see Chap. 6, pp. 129–33.

[20] Wade, 'Law, Opinion and Administration', at 196.

[21] Ibid. at 186.   [22] Ibid. 197.

places of the law are brought more and more systematically under juridical survey'.[23]

In this early essay, Wade provides us with a valuable insight into his normativist approach. The importance of order and the characterization of even the American polity in terms of sovereignty, his adjectival conception of the role of law and the implicit advocacy of a limited role for government, and his defence of judicial decision-making, are all major themes in the normativist style in public law. Wade's general views on the nature of law and government thus have an affinity with those of Dicey. This general perspective permeates his work in public law, where his objective has been to maintain the Diceyan tradition. Wade has, for example, sought to defend Dicey's concept of sovereignty against 'the freethinkers of my own time',[24] and he has strongly supported Dicey's view concerning the importance of 'public opinion' in maintaining the stability of the Constitution.[25] The most persistent theme in Wade's work, however, has been his attempt to reformulate Dicey's concept of the rule of law in the circumstances of modern government. And it is to this issue that we now turn.

'Today', suggested Wade in 1962, 'we have an administrative revolution, precipitated by a social revolution. The welfare state attends to us from the cradle to the grave.' In these circumstances he conceded that we 'can no longer make do with Dicey's theory that wide discretionary power has no place under the rule of law'. He argued that the concept of the rule of law must be reformulated to require that governmental power be exercised in a legal and regular manner.[26] His reformulation is, nevertheless, in accordance with the spirit of Dicey. Wade accepted that the rule of law and the separation of powers are corollaries and argued, contrary to Jennings, that it is not simply a 'principle of political action' but a 'juridical principle'.[27]

---

[23] Wade, 'Law, Opinion and Administration', at 198.
[24] Ibid. 189–90. See id., 'The basis of legal sovereignty' [1955] Camb. L.J. 172; 'Sovereignty and the European Communities' (1972) 88 *L.Q.R.* 1. Amongst the 'freethinkers' we should include Jennings (Chap. 7, p. 168) and Mitchell (below pp. 191–7).
[25] Wade, 'Law, Opinion and Administration', 190; id., *Administrative Law* (Oxford, 6th edn., 1988), 31.
[26] 'Law, Opinion and Administration', 193–4.
[27] Id., ' "Quasi-judicial" and its background' (1949) 10 Camb. L.J. 216 at 225–6.

In his early writing on administrative law, Wade's tone was decidedly pessimistic. He openly expressed doubts, for example, that the concept of natural justice would survive in the administrative state.[28] In his Oxford inaugural lecture, however, his prognosis was more optimistic and he argued, against both the general sceptics[29] and those who promoted the case for administrative courts,[30] that the common law could rise to the occasion. Wade's methodological approach throughout has nevertheless been consistent. Evidently in tune with developments in linguistic philosophy, Wade argued that 'terminology is at the root of the problem'[31] and that many of the difficulties arise from 'the confusion of language abounding in our administrative law'.[32] In 1962, while recognizing the existence of defects in various departments of administrative law, he suggested that the 'materials handed down by previous generations of judges supply all the right raw material' and that:

[T]hese imperfections ought to yield to the normal application of judicial wisdom in the course of time, with the normal amount of help from Parliament. . . . [N]o great outburst of judicial law-making is required. What is required is a more lively appreciation of the materials lying ready to hand in the law reports, and a sense that administrative law is a group of topics which need study and deliberate development.[33]

Here we find Wade following Dicey's direction that the role of the academic lawyer is to arrange laws in their order and explain their meaning.

However, language can be used not only to clarify meaning but also to confer meaning. While Wade recognizes the significance of the social revolution of the twentieth century, the language used to characterize it bears all the hallmarks of nineteenth-century conservatism. Statutes providing powers of planning control are viewed as amounting effectively to 'confiscatory legislation'[34] and modern cases are referred to as landmarks manifesting 'the judicial

---

[28] Id., 'Quasi-judicial', 240: 'How long "natural justice" will survive must for the time being remain an open question.' See also, id., 'The Twilight of Natural Justice' (1951) 67 L.Q.R. 103, 109: 'Will it not be a grievous loss if the "natural justice" of the common law is thrown overboard at the time when it may be of most service?'
[29] See, e.g. P. Devlin, Chap. 7, p. 180.
[30] i.e., Robson, Jennings, and Willis (Chap. 7, n. 172) and Mitchell (below p. 192).
[31] 'Twilight' 109.
[32] 'Quasi-judicial' 218.
[33] 'Law, Opinion and Administration', 198–9.   [34] Ibid. 191.

resistance to statutes which attempt to confer arbitrary power'.[35] The exercise of statutory powers is classified in terms of 'misplaced philanthropy' or 'permissible philanthropy'.[36] This rather anachronistic characterization is revealing not only because this idea of philanthropy to relieve the distress of the poor formed an element of common law doctrine[37] but also because it was a prominent aspect of nineteenth century Tory paternalism.[38] In both his search for solutions through linguistic analysis and his own use of language, Wade reveals the hallmarks of conservative normativism.

These insights help us to understand Wade's attempt to rekindle the spirit of Dicey's concept of the rule of law. In the light of the growth of this type of social legislation, the courts must avoid getting caught up in a narrow and stultified form of interpretation and recognize that their primary constitutional duty is to uphold the idea of the rule of law:[39]

Subject as it is to the vast empires of executive power that have been created, the public must be able to rely on the law to ensure that all this power may be used in a way conformable to its ideas of fair dealing and good administration. As liberty is subtracted, justice must be added.

Wade's exhortation in 1962 was that the courts must develop judicial review to ensure that all errors of law are subject to their control. This was most timely. During the 1960s the courts gradually moved to rid themselves of the restrictions based on overly conceptualistic reasoning.[40] Since the 1960s, then, the performance of the courts has generally been to Wade's satisfaction. He also believes that their capacity has been enhanced by the procedural reforms of the 1970s:[41] 'With judicial review in the hands of the regular judges, but funnelled through a specialised division, we have the means of obtaining the best of both worlds.'[42] Consequently, Wade fully shared Lord Diplock's assessment that the progress of administrative law has been 'the greatest achieve-

---

[35] *Administrative Law*, 452.   [36] Ibid. 424–8.

[37] W. Blackstone, *Commentaries on the Laws of England* (1765–9) (London, 15th edn., 1809), vol. 1, p. 359: 'by the common law the poor were to be sustained by parsons, rectors of the church and the parishioners; so that none of them die for default of sustenance.'

[38] E. Halévy, *A History of the English People in the Nineteenth Century*, Vol. 5 (London, 1951), 226–8.

[39] *Administrative Law*, 7.

[40] See Chap. 7, p. 180.   [41] See Chap. 7, pp. 180–1.

[42] Wade, *Constitutional Fundamentals* (London, 1980), 74.

ment of the English courts in my judicial lifetime'.[43] The only significant reservation Wade has about judicial developments concerns the attempts by the courts to adapt the procedural reforms into a dual system of public and private law:[44]

To impose a dichotomy would be to take a step backwards to the bad old days of the forms of action. . . . I remain of the opinion . . . that the right policy was to fit the prerogative remedies into the mechanism of an ordinary action, so that there would be no dichotomy and no dilemma for the litigant.

What we see here is Wade's allegiance to Dicey's view that the rule of law is founded on the supremacy of ordinary law universally applied by the ordinary courts.

Wade's work constitutes a powerful representation of the contemporary form of the conservative variant of the normativist style. Public law provides a set of principles designed to keep government within its legal bounds. Those bounds must be clearly set and Wade thus maintains a strict conception of legality.[45] Echoing Lord Shaw in *R. v. Halliday*,[46] Wade suggests that the courts are the primary guardians of our Diceyan constitutional principles. He recognized that, in performing this role, judges 'must rely on their own judgment sensing what is required by the interplay of forces in the constitution'.[47] But does this not undermine a strict standard of legality and does it not also mean

---

[43] *R v. Inland Revenue Commissioners, ex parte National Federation of Self-Employed and Small Businesses* [1982] 2 AC 237, 285; see Wade, 'Procedure and prerogative in public law' (1985) 101 *L.Q.R.* 180, 181.

[44] Ibid. 181, 189.

[45] See, e.g., Wade, 'Unlawful administrative action—void or voidable' (1967) 83 *L.Q.R.* 499 (Pt. I); (1968) 84 *L.Q.R.* 95 (Pt. II): 'The danger underlying the newly invented conception of a "voidable" administrative act . . . is that it will confuse and weaken the principle of legality by which the courts keep public authorities within the law' (Pt. II at p. 95); 'There is serious damage in making the *ultra vires* principle, or any part of it, discretionary. Administrative inconvenience should not be allowed to distort the law' (Pt. II at p. 115). It is because of this strict conception of legality that Wade also seeks to define prerogative power in restrictive terms: see *Constitutional Fundamentals* (London, 1980), chap. 4; 'Procedure and prerogative', pp. 190–8. Note also that Wade's view of prerogative power parallels Oakeshott who argues that the private relationship of master and servant is to be categorially distinguished from the public relationship of ruler and subject: *On Human Conduct* (Oxford, 1975), Part III.

[46] Chap. 7, p. 163.

[47] *Administrative Law*, 24.

that judges must inevitably become embroiled in partisan politics? Wade provides the following response:[48]

The fact that this involves questions of degree has sometimes led critics to disparage the rule of law, treating it as a merely political phenomenon which reflects one particular philosophy of government. But this is true only in the sense that every system of law must have its own standards for judging questions of abuse of discretionary power . . . [T]he rules of law which our system has devised for this purpose are objective and non-political, expressing indeed a particular judicial attitude but one that can be applied impartially to any kind of legislation irrespective of its political content.

Wade's answer addresses the latter point but the tensions within his conception of legality remain. The reason for this is that, like Dicey, although invoking the rule of law he seeks to blend elements from the ancient and the modern conceptions. In fact, despite references to the importance of the separation of powers (and hence to the modern conception) Wade's work should be viewed primarily as a contemporary defence of the ancient conception of the rule of law.

Wade's work constitutes the clearest modern attempt to defend the dominant tradition of conservative normativism in public law. His general approach has been to preserve the spirit of Dicey's theory in the light of contemporary challenges. Wade, it appears, would join Macaulay in saying of the British constitution that while 'vile abuses cluster thick round every glorious event . . . the proper course is to abate the nuisance without defacing the shine'.[49]

THE VARIETIES OF FUNCTIONALISM

I propose to examine post-war versions of the functionalist style through an evaluation of the work of J. D. B. Mitchell, J. A. G. Griffith, and Patrick McAuslan. By doing so, I hope to show that, although they maintain distinctive approaches, there is a common functionalist core to their work. It may not be entirely coincidental that all three have been associated with the London School of Economics.

[48] *Administrative Law*, 24.
[49] Macaulay, *The Works of Lord Macaulay*, vol. vi (London, 1866), 94, quoted in S. Collini, D. Winch, and J. Burrow, *That Noble Science of Politics* (Cambridge, 1983), 124.

Functionalism: an idealist variant

J. D. B. Mitchell is most closely associated with Edinburgh University,[50] but undertook both undergraduate and postgraduate work at the LSE and taught there between 1949 and 1954. Mitchell's work in public law may be viewed as a form of evolutionary rationalism. He argued that the balance in the constitution which existed in the seventeenth-century settlement had, by the twentieth century, been arrested. Our system—one of dual control of government by the courts and by Parliament—no longer worked because, since the middle of the nineteeenth century, the control of law has steadily ceded ground to control by political means alone. The reason for that was the growth of the positive state. Our constitutional structure, Mitchell suggested, 'was perfected round about 1911, just at the time when the state for which it was invented was about to die'.[51]

Mitchell argued that what was required was a restoration of law. By this he meant essentially 'a mechanism which can duplicate the evolutionary process of the common law in the field of public law'.[52] The primary difficulty in realizing that requirement was that 'the courts have so severed themselves from the administrative process in thought that their methods have become inappropriate in a variety of ways. The instruments of control which are at their disposal are often too blunt to be used, their techniques are such that control is often no more than a control over form and not of substance.'[53] Mitchell felt that, to a large extent, this situation resulted from an unreasonable acceptance of Dicey's formulation of the rule of law, and in particular the idea that it requires the subjection of all, whether officials or otherwise, to the ordinary law of the land. Consequently, he believed that the creation of an effective system of public law 'would probably require the creation of a new system of courts to break the fetters upon those which now exist'.[54]

[50] He held the Chair of Constitutional Law from 1954 to 1968 and the Salvesen Chair of European Institutions from 1968 until his death in 1980.
[51] J. D. B. Mitchell, 'Why European Institutions?' in L. J. Brinkhorst and J. D. B. Mitchell, *European Law and Institutions* (Edinburgh, 1969), 35. And see also Mitchell, 'The Flexible Constitution' 1960 *Public Law* 332 at p. 334.
[52] Id., *Constitutional Law* (Edinburgh, 2nd edn., 1968), 62   [53] Ibid. 57.
[54] Id., 'The causes and effects of the absence of a system of public law in the United Kingdom' 1965 *Public Law* 95 at p. 118.

In common with the normativist approach, Mitchell recognized the importance of judicial control in maintaining a balanced constitution. But there the similarity stops. Because, unlike the normativists, Mitchell located the main barrier to effective development in the common law method itself.[55] Public law, Mitchell argued, is 'too often regarded as a series of unfortunate exceptions to the desirable generality or universality of the rules of private law, and is not seen as a rational system with its own justification, and perhaps its own philosophy'.[56] Only through a separate jurisdiction could this develop: 'a degree of separation is essential if an appropriately coherent philosophy and jurisprudence are to be evolved, and, above all, distinctive procedures are only likely to be produced in such circumstances'.[57]

One reason why Mitchell can be distinguished from the normativists is that, in the context of public law, he rejected their attempts to draw a strict line between law and policy or law and administration.[58] One of Mitchell's favourite quotations was the maxim of Portalis, *'Juger l'administration, c'est aussi administrer'*. Consequently, he felt that any court with a public law jurisdiction must have a proper awareness of administrative necessities and for this a distinctive recruitment was essential. In turn this suggested a dual system of courts. Mitchell thus proposed a separate administrative jurisdiction which would be 'settled in the Privy Council (and I emphasise that I do not mean the Judicial Committee of the Privy Council) . . . [B]y locating it there it would be easiest to secure the mixed composition of lawyers, administrators and others which is essential.'[59]

But, again in contrast with the normativists, Mitchell does not see the problem of law as being simply founded on the problem of control: 'Not only is the machinery of government outstripping the

---

[55] Mitchell's approach here seems reminiscent of the distinction which Robson made between the importance of the judicial spirit in the processes of government and the existence of a court structure: see Robson, *Justice and Administrative Law*, esp. chaps. 1 and 5.   [56] Mitchell, 'Causes and effects', 96.

[57] Id., 'The constitutional implications of judicial control of the administration in the United Kingdom' [1967] *Camb. L.J.* 46 at p. 48.

[58] See, e.g., Mitchell, 'The Flexible Constitution' 1960 *Public Law* 332 at p. 349. Cf. Wade, 'Quasi-judicial' at p. 223: 'There is a vital difference between "policy" and "law", and this difference is at the root of much legal and constitutional doctrine.'

[59] Mitchell, 'Constitutional implications', 54–5. See also id., 'The Flexible Constitution', at pp. 343–4.

law, it is to the same or greater extent being hampered by an inappropriate law.'[60] That is, it is not simply a problem of government *beyond* law but also one of effective government restricted *by* law. The recognition of these complementary perspectives reflects Mitchell's conception of the relationship between the individual and the state. 'This machinery of government', he writes, 'is not something beyond us and against us: it is a machinery working to achieve our collective needs. We as citizens have as much interest in its efficiency as in its fairness. . . . Increasingly the protection of our individual interests is bought at a cost to our collective interests which is too high.'[61]

Mitchell's general message, however, should not be read as being simply about law. It is primarily a message about the state of our constitution. Constitutional thought must keep in tune with social development. With the growth in government since the nineteenth century, the law has proved itself incapable of meeting the demands of a modern state. As a result, we have come to rely excessively upon parliamentary redress as a method of control. This has operated to the detriment of *both* control systems.

The dogma of parliamentary omnicompetence has led to too great a concentration on parliamentary controls.[62] 'Ministerial responsibility . . . once enlarged freedom, yet later prevented the evolution of other desirable institutions, and has been clung to when it had become a sham.'[63] This has stultified the emergence of a true system of administrative law. But it has also operated to the detriment of parliament; in refusing to recognize the distinction between administration and politics in our control structures, Members of Parliament 'can shelter in the pursuit of detail' and avoid the primary task of 'making up their mind on policy'.[64]

[60] Id., 'The state of public law in the United Kingdom' [1966] 15 *I.C.L.Q.* 133 at p. 148.
[61] Ibid. 148–9. Mitchell elaborates on this relationship further in his *Constitutional Law* (Edinburgh, 2nd edn., 1968), at p. 3: 'State power and individual liberty cannot be separated. Each reacts upon the other. Neither can be regarded in isolation, and the rights and obligations of the state on the one hand and of the individual on the other should not be regarded as essentially opposed to each other. Indeed, the rights of the state are in a sense nothing but the communal rights of the individuals who make up the state.'
[62] Mitchell, 'Flexible Constitution', 346.
[63] Id., 'Why European Institutions?', 34. See also id., 'Reflections on Law and Orders' 1958 *Juridical Review* 19 at p. 26.
[64] Id., 'Constitutional implications', 53.

For Mitchell the great problem of the British constitution is that 'for far too long we have lived in an isolated world of constitutional self-righteousness'[65] and that the supposed virtue of the constitution—its flexibility—has not been realized, essentially because of the constraints imposed by the habits of thought which here I call conservative normativism. The remedy for these past failures must be the establishment of a separate public law jurisdiction; only in this manner can 'the "Rule of Law" be made a reality'.[66] Here we see Mitchell's rationalist and humanist outlook shining through: 'There is no reason why rational constructive thought should not be brought to bear on government, nor why the evolution of governmental structures should be entirely random.'[67]

Mitchell's views on administrative law achieved no greater support or had no greater success than Robson's. During the 1960s Mitchell was particularly concerned to rebuff suggestions that the Ombudsman technique could usefully be adapted to the British system and aid the quest for administrative justice. 'The problem', suggested Mitchell, 'is not of finding solutions in cases of occasional administrative bungling, it is of finding a means of development of a proper corpus of law to deal with the machinery of the modern state.'[68] He argued that:[69]

A half-measure, albeit in the right direction, can be more dangerous than immobility in the present congested state of government, since the glow of self-satisfaction resulting from the consideration of such merits as the half-measure may have, destroys an appreciation of its limitations, and at the same time the half-measure provides a perfect excuse for continuing inertia.

This campaign against that 'administrative palliative',[70] 'paper mouse'[71] and embodiment of the failure of law to respond to the challenges of modern government failed. The Ombudsman tech-

---

[65] Id., 'Why European Institutions?', 36. See also id., 'Administrative Law and Policy Effectiveness' in Griffith (ed.), *From Policy to Administration. Essays in Honour of William A. Robson* (London, 1976), at pp. 193–5.
[66] Mitchell, *Constitutional Law*, 62.
[67] Id., 'Why European Institutions?', 49.
[68] Id., 'Flexible Constitution', 343. See also id., 'The irrelevance of the Ombudsman proposals' in D. C. Rowat (ed.), *The Ombudsman* (London, 1965), 95.
[69] Mitchell, 'The Ombudsman Fallacy' 1962 *Public Law* 24.
[70] Id., 'Causes and effects', 109.
[71] Id., 'A Paper Mouse' 1966 *SLT (News)* 65.

nique was established in Britain in 1967 and has multiplied since. Finally, we can see a clear rejection of Mitchell's project with the refusal of the Government in 1969 to accept the Law Commission's proposal that a Royal Commision be established to review the entire subject of administrative law.

Mitchell undoubtedly had profound personal reasons for embracing the European ideal.[72] But it seems almost certainly in part because of pessimism about the possibilities of municipal reform that in 1968 he resigned his Chair in Constitutional Law to accept the newly established Salvesen Chair in European Institutions. Britain's entry into the European Community in 1972 has had a profound impact on our system of government. A great deal of new legislation over a broad range of issues has been enacted and many of our administrative systems have been radically transformed in order to comply with Community obligations. But, in one sense, such changes are superstructural. From the perspective of public law what is important is not so much that the tide of European Community law is flowing 'into the estuaries and up the rivers'.[73] It is not simply the *extent* of Community law's encroachment that is significant but rather its *philosophy* and its *style*. Community law signals the injection into British law of a corpus of law drawn from a European civilian tradition.

Mitchell was perhaps the first lawyer in this country to see this clearly. His switch to Europe could therefore be seen, not as an abandonment of his public law project, but as a development of it. He argued, for example, that 'the distinction between public and private law, and between the British and continental systems, is a philosophic one, or at least a jurisprudential one. Private law remains a jurisprudence of rights; public law one of interests. It is concerned predominantly with the balancing of public and private interests.'[74] What is evident here is not just the articulation of distinct philosophical foundations of private and public law but also the equation of British and continental legal systems with those two philosophies.

In this sense, it could be argued that Mitchell's project is now coming to fruition. The formalism and rationalism of continental

---

[72] See id., 'A Testimony' (1969) published in Bates *et al.* (eds.), *In Memoriam JDB Mitchell* (1983), at p. xvii.
[73] *Bulmer* v. *Bollinger* [1974] 1 Ch 401, 418 (per Lord Denning).
[74] Mitchell, 'Administrative Law and Policy Effectiveness', 179.

jurisprudence must, if the current pace of development of the Community continues, have a profound impact on British public law. We have already seen some important aspects of these developments on basic ideas in public law.[75] Judicial developments notwithstanding, it could be argued that we still face major legal challenges. The courts may have adjusted their conceptual language but this cannot disguise the lack of an intellectual and institutional infrastructure. Public law lacks the systemic qualities—the institutional structures and basic cultural attitudes—to be able to absorb and integrate the new jurisprudence effectively and we cannot develop a state tradition overnight. This is precisely what Mitchell was warning against during the 1960s. In 1968, for example, he argued 'that there is emerging a new legal order of European public law' and that this means 'that such terms as "Administrative/ constitutional" must in this larger context be re-interpreted'.[76]

But what of the most basic legal question raised by accession to the EC? How can the principle of the supremacy of Community law be reconciled with the doctrine of Parliamentary sovereignty? Mitchell himself had led the domestic debate on the issue. As early as 1960 he was arguing that the idea of parliamentary sovereignty 'was a doctrine suited to particular conditions. It does not follow that it is suited to all conditions. Nor is it so ancient or sacred that it should be regarded as beyond examination in the light of its expanding practical consequences.'[77] With our entry into the European Community Mitchell took the view that this basic legal principle of the British constitution had been substantially modified since we had acceded to a new legal order.[78] In recent years we have seen that, despite the strengthening of this view of Community

---

[75] The conceptual distinction between public and private law which has recently been adopted by the courts may, for example, have been influenced by European developments. What is more clear is that the concepts of proportionality and legitimate expectation almost certainly have. See Wade, *Constitutional Fundamentals* (1980), 74–5; *Council on Civil Service Unions* v. *Minister for the Civil Service* [1985] A.C. 374; C. F. Forsyth, 'The provenance and protection of legitimate expectations', [1988] 47 *Camb. L.J.* 238 at pp. 241–5.

[76] Mitchell, 'Why European Institutions?', 41.

[77] Id., 'Flexible Constitution', at p. 348.

[78] Id., 'The sovereignty of parliament and community law: the stumbling block that isn't there' 1979 *Int. Affairs* 33; 'What happened to the constitution on 1st January 1973?' 1980 *Cambrian Law Rev.* 69; Mitchell, Kuipers, and Gall, 'Constitutional Aspects of the Treaty and Legislation Relating to British Membership' (1972) 9 *Common Market Law Review* 134.

law,[79] our courts have had great difficulty in accepting this as orthodoxy[80] and it was not until 1991 that the courts directly confronted the question and clearly enforced the principle of the primacy of Community law.[81]

In general, Mitchell lamented the fact that 'lawyers, political scientists and administrators no longer talk to each other in terms which they can all understand'.[82] So far as lawyers are concerned, the problem is that, 'perhaps because of the shape of our law' and because we have not learnt to think in terms of public law, we have reconciled ourselves to being lawyers in the narrowest sense.[83] For lawyers the challenge is 'to lift their eyes to the hills and this way regain their rightful place in the world, but above all, they must learn to be artists not tradesmen'.[84] Mitchell's work thus stands largely as an eloquent critique of the limitations of our dominant tradition of conservative normativism.

Functionalism: an empiricist variant

J. A. G. Griffith most clearly personifies the sense of continuity in the functionalist style in the twentieth century. Virtually all of Griffith's career has been spent at the LSE. He was taught by Jennings and was, for many years, a colleague of Robson.[85] However, while in certain respects Mitchell can be viewed as working through some of the rationalist dimensions to Robson's arguments on public law, Griffith's approach is rather different. A much stronger sense of pragmatism pervades his work, which seems, in part at least, the product of a greater degree of pessimism about the possibilities of progressive legal change.

Griffith adopts an approach based on strict sociological positivism. In 1979, when reflecting on the tradition within which he had

[79] This has been achieved in stages. First, through the ECJ's rejection of the dualist theory and adoption of monism in *Costa* v. *ENEL* (1964) ECR 585. Secondly, through the recognition of the capacity of Community law to create rights enforceable by individuals in national courts; the principle of direct effect: see *Marshall* v. *Southampton and South West Hants Area Health Authority* (1976) 2 All ER 584. Thirdly, because of the principle of supremacy of community law: *Simmenthal* (1978) ECR 629.

[80] See, e.g., *Duke* v. *GEC Reliance Ltd* [1988] 1 All ER 626.

[81] *Factortame Ltd* v. *Secretary of State for Transport (No. 2)* [1991] 1 All ER 70.

[82] Mitchell, 'Government and Public Law in Scotland' in J. A. Andrews, *Welsh Studies in Public Law* (Cardiff, 1970), at p. 85.

[83] Mitchell, 'Why European Institutions?', 42.   [84] Ibid.

[85] Griffith edited Robson's *festschrift*: Griffith (ed.), *From Policy to Administration: Essays in Honour of William A. Robson* (London, 1976).

worked, he suggested: 'Our line was based on Comte and led to Durkheim and, for me, to Léon Duguit.'[86] And when deliberating specifically on the issue of order in society he stated:[87]

Societies are by nature authoritarian. Governments even more so. By saying that societies are naturally authoritarian I mean that we are all placed in that 'wearisome condition of humanity' . . . of being both individual and social animals and that this sets up conflicts from which we can never be set free.

Griffith contends that, however it may be disguised, government is essentially about power and legislators exist to represent and promote particular interests in a conflictual society.[88] Consequently, it is only by stripping away the façade of constitutional doctrine that the true character of government can be revealed. Griffith suggests, for example, that the nineteenth-century form of 'liberal democracy' which Dicey sought to sanctify rested on an old order founded on a peculiar faith in authority. And this foundation could not survive the cataclysm of the 1914–18 war.[89]

On the question of law, Griffith adopts a form of positivism derived from Bentham and Austin in which all that is encompassed in the idea of law can be explained in terms of fact.[90] Rather than speaking of human rights, Griffith proposes that we should recognize simply that individuals and groups make claims on society. By doing so, we ensure that we do not evade the real issue, which is that 'law is not and cannot be a substitute for politics'.[91] The 'Rule of Law' may be desirable, and not particularly contentious, he implies, if it means that there should be adequate machinery for ensuring that public authorities do not exceed their legal powers. 'But when it is extended to mean more than that, it is a fantasy invented by Liberals of the old school in the late nineteenth century and patented by the Tories to throw a protective sanctity around certain legal and political institutions and principles which they wish to preserve at any cost.'[92] For Griffith, 'law is not a moral concept . . . laws are merely statements of a power

[86] Id., 'The Political Constitution' (1979) 42 *MLR* 1, 6.
[87] Ibid. at pp. 2–3. See also 'Judges in Politics: England' (1968) 3 *Govt & Oppos.* 485, 498.
[88] 'The Political Constitution', 12, 16.
[89] Ibid. 3–5. Cf. Dicey, chap. 7 at p. 162.
[90] For Bentham and Austin's views see Chap. 1, pp. 19–22.
[91] Griffith, 'The Political Constitution', 16, 17.   [92] Ibid. 15.

relationship and nothing more . . . the constitution is no more and no less than what happens.'[93]

This positivist perspective permeates Griffith's more specific writing on public law. He did not, for example, support the Robson–Mitchell line on the need for a separate administrative jurisdiction, primarily on the ground that this would result in an appointed court supplanting the powers of accountable Ministers and local authorities.[94] Further, he felt that the function of the courts should be limited to 'excess of jurisdiction, breach of the rules of natural justice, bad faith, and the absence of any evidence to support the exercise of the powers'.[95] When they stray beyond this, especially in the review of discretionary powers, the attitude of the courts 'has . . . been so variable that it is difficult to discover what powers they will exercise and in what direction'.[96] This theme underlies much of his writing on the courts. Where Wade sees the courts boldly developing principles of judicial review, Griffith sees little other than the courts usurping discretionary power—a form of 'judicial lawlessness'.[97] Griffith's approach is an exercise in 'continous de-mystification': 'Knocking the judicial bench is as proper a political activity as knocking the front bench; both are powerful and can affect our activities.'[98] It is from this perspective that Griffith undertook a basic study of the politics of the judiciary.[99]

Unlike Mitchell, then, Griffith is not concerned with restoring any notion of 'balance' to the constitution. In fact, given his view that 'conflict is at the heart of modern society', he would reject any

---

[93] Ibid. 19. This view of the British constitution as fact has been a consistent theme in Griffith's writing since the 1960s: see, e.g., [1963] *Public Law* 401–2.

[94] R. Glass and J. A. G. Griffith, 'The context of administrative procedures' in *Report of the Committee on Administrative Tribunals and Enquiries*. Minutes of Evidence, 21st Day, paras. 15–16 (1956) (the Franks Report).

[95] Ibid., para. 67; Griffith, 'Constitutional and Administrative Law' in P. Archer and A. Martin (eds.), *More Law Reform Now* (Chichester, 1983), 49, 56.

[96] Ibid., para.12.

[97] Griffith, 'Administrative discretion and the courts—the better part of valour?' (1955) 18 *M.L.R.* 159, 163. Note that Hewart's theme of 'administrative lawlessness' (see Chap. 7, p. 164) is counterposed by Griffith's idea of 'judicial lawlessness' just as Dicey's theme of 'class legislation' was transformed by Laski into a concern over 'class adjudication' (see Chap. 7 p. 172).

[98] Griffith, 'Administrative Law and the Judges', D. N. Pritt Memorial Lecture (London, 1978), 21.

[99] Id., *The Politics of the Judiciary* (London: 4th edn., 1991).

such metaphor.[100] Griffith's view on the issue of constitutional balances echoes the writing of Robson who, in 1948, proclaimed:[101]

I have little sympathy with those who declare . . . that the balance of the constitution is upset . . . because the Executive is called upon to play a much greater part than it did 50 or 100 years ago. There is no ideal pattern which can serve as a permanent model of constitutional development. The true balance of a polity is to be tested by the extent to which it succeeds in meeting *all* the needs of the people who live under it. . . . If a constitution is able to provide broadly satisfactory results over the whole field of contemporary demand . . . then we can say it is in a state of balance. To reserve that word for a particular set of relationships between the legislature, the executive and the judiciary which happened to emerge in the seventeenth century and which suited the conditions of the eighteenth and early nineteenth century is to display symptoms of chronic nostalgia which are unlikely to be of any help in solving the problems of our own time. These problems demand new ideas, new institutions and new relationships.

The roots of this view are, however, deeply buried in British political thought. As we have seen this view was expressed in a more pithy form by Bentham.[102]

Griffith believes that reforms should be guided by detailed empirical study[103] and be motivated by the aims of strengthening the democratic aspects of the constitution and the mechanisms of political accountability. He considers that 'political decisions should be taken by politicians. In a society like ours this means people who are removable. . . . [O]ur existing institutions, especially the House of Commons, need strengthening. And we need to force governments out of secrecy and into the open.'[104] To the extent that these political and legal mechanisms might be inadequate to deal with the range of problems in a modern

[100] Id., 'The Political Constitution', 1–2.
[101] W. A. Robson, *Public Administration Today* (London, 1948), 16–17. (This is the text of Robson's inaugural lecture on assuming the Chair of Public Administration at LSE.)
[102] See Chap. 1, p. 19.
[103] Griffith is one of the few public lawyers to have engaged in major empirical study. See Griffith, *Central Departments and Local Authorities* (London, 1966); id., *Parliamentary Scrutiny of Government Bills* (London, 1974).
[104] Id., 'The Political Constitution', 17. On the strengthening of parliamentary mechanisms see: id., 'Constitutional and Administrative Law', 52; id., 'Standing Committees in the House of Commons' in S. A. Walkland and M. Ryle, *The Commons in the Seventies* (London, 1977) chap. 5.

administrative state Griffith suggests, following Durkheim and
Duguit, that the way forward is through the promotion of a public
service ethos.[105]

Functionalism: a contemporary perspective

The work of Patrick McAuslan, the successor to Griffith's Chair
in Public Law at the LSE, is also firmly rooted in the functionalist
style. In 1948 William Robson, referring to Maine's dictum about
the movement of progressive societies being from status to contract,
suggested that in 'the twentieth century we are moving from
contract to public administration'.[106] This theme influenced much
of McAuslan's early writing. Writing in the early 1970s of post-war
developments in planning processes, for example, McAuslan
states:[107]

[P]lanning has emerged in the twentieth century as individuals and their
functions within society have grown so numerous and the organisation and
government of societies have become so complex that more regulation,
control and guidance was needed to maintain social equilibrium and
advance change and development than could be provided by the law as it
developed. Just as equity was needed to outflank the fossilisation of law
from the fourteenth century onwards, and statute law was used for the
same purpose in respect of equity and common law from the early
nineteenth century onwards . . . so planning is needed to outflank the
fossilisation of law, legal attitudes and values in the twentieth century to
enable governments to respond to new challenges. . . .

McAuslan's argument here is that law and planning are engaged
in very similar tasks and that, provided lawyers can move away
from their emphasis on property rights and the protection of
property owners and can focus on 'the rights of people qua people,
and the creation of procedures to assist them to participate in
planning',[108] lawyers and planners could together develop the

[105] 'The professionalism of local government officers is the greatest single force
which enables local authorities to carry out, with much efficiency, the considerable
tasks entrusted to them. And pride in a profession is a better insurance of high-class
performance than more material incentives' Griffith, *Central Departments and
Local Authorities* (London, 1966), 534. On Durkheim and Duguit see Chap. 6,
pp. 110, 112.
[106] Robson, *Public Administration Today*, 3.
[107] McAuslan, 'The Plan, the Planners and the Lawyers' 1971 *Pub. Law* 247,
274.
[108] Ibid. 275.

procedures needed to enable government to respond effectively to new challenges. This is reminiscent of the evolutionary rationalism of Mitchell. But while Mitchell's rationalism took an institutional form—of establishing a new system of courts—McAuslan's is expressed in a more general cultural manner of an appeal to lawyers to change their values and attitudes and develop an appropriate culture of public law.

In 'Planning law's contribution to the problems of an urban society' McAuslan elaborates on the failures of law to rise to this challenge. The complexity and formality of law are identified as contributing factors but the private property orientation is presented as the main problem: 'The stress on property pervades the whole planning process and distorts the vision of both lawyers and planners.'[109] So while Wade identifies statutes which amount to 'confiscatory legislation' as a critical issue in public law, for McAuslan that attitude simply epitomizes the nature of the problem. But McAuslan is also concerned with the increased discretionary powers of planners and administrators. Here, his argument is that the property orientation of the law has diverted attention from the role which law could play in 'creating opportunities for more meaningful public debate on alternative policy choices' and of subjecting to examination 'the values and ideologies of . . . the planners'.[110] 'What is needed', concludes McAuslan, 'are lawyers educated to realise that the law has long standing connections with human rights and civil liberties, and that a system of planning founded on those principles might make a better contribution to the solution of urban problems than one founded, as now, on property.'[111]

From this early 1970s optimism, however, McAuslan gradually adopts a more radical and empiricist tone, which perhaps reflects his growing pessimism about the probability of law and lawyers rising to this challenge. So, while *The Ideologies of Planning Law*[112] is in essence no more than a comprehensive statement of earlier expressed views, the tone is more strident and perhaps less hopeful. In this book, he states his thesis in straightforward terms. Law is 'a major contributory factor to the continuing disarray of planning'. This is because, far from being a neutral medium, it incorporates three competing ideologies:[113]

[109] (1974) 37 *M.L.R.* 134, 152.   [110] Ibid.
[111] Ibid.   [112] (Oxford, 1980).   [113] Ibid. 2.

Firstly, that the law exists and should be used to protect private property and its institutions; . . . [s]econdly, the law exists and should be used to advance the public interest; [t]hirdly, the law exists and should be used to advance the cause of public participation against both the orthodox public administration approach to the public interest and the common law approach of the overriding importance of private property . . .

Through a detailed examination of law and practice, McAuslan tracks the influence of these ideologies and concludes that the first two are the dominant ideologies and that, although there are from time to time clashes between them, there is none the less a fundamental community of interest between the proponents of these ideologies. He argues that this 'community of interest is basically a shared understanding that the existing governmental and social structures, the existing balance of property relations . . . must be maintained and preserved against too swift or radical an attempt to alter it'.[114]

McAuslan argues that what is needed 'is a commitment to work, via the creation of new legislation, new institutions, new procedures, towards new decision-making processes which will have as their aim more open government, more searching debates on major policy issues, decisions bringing about positive discrimination in the allocation of resources in favour of deprived persons and groups in the community, and an institutional framework which allows those groups power, subject to appropriate safeguards, to determine their own future.'[115] The path may not be easy but it is necessary:[116]

For lawyers and others openly to espouse such a democracy in the likely future climate of society and government will take courage and faith . . . [B]ut the alternative (continued acceptance and reliance on traditional models of public administration and management which appear less and less capable of fair operation for the powerless and the property-less) will too easily end up as defence of, and support for, the erosion of civil liberties of the more traditional kind in the interests of the stability of the state and the maintenance of the rule of law. There are, alas, too many examples of too many lawyers opting for this latter position to be certain that the same will not happen in the United Kingdom . . . and this places a heavy burden of responsibility on those lawyers who opt for the challenging task of making a reality of participatory democracy.

[114] Ibid. 213.   [115] Ibid. 272.   [116] Ibid. 274.

In his Chorley Lecture of 1982 McAuslan applies this theoretical framework to the general field of administrative law. He begins by examining the institutional structures of the post-war welfare state, and suggests that courts have been peripheral in shaping these structures and that, as a result, collective grievance-handling agencies (Commissioners and Commissions of various types, consumer councils, and law and advice centres) have grown up in response to felt needs. One important aspect of these agencies is that they are 'relatively harmless' and that 'where they appeared to be too effective, funds could be withdrawn, personnel changed or . . . their reports and recommendations ignored'.[117] He also argues that administrative lawyers, because of their 'concentration on tribunals and inquiries', have been insufficiently concerned with the structures and processes of the welfare state. Consequently, and here we find the basic theme of the lecture, administrative lawyers are 'ill-equipped to deal with, or make sense of, the major clashes of policy and ideology taking place within our system of administrative law'.[118]

This issue, McAuslan suggests, has come to a head as a result of public expenditure restrictions since the mid-1970s. Many of the disputes that previously were handled by the administrative system came to be fought out in the courts. But these were politically contentious issues and the courts have been unable or unwilling to handle them satisfactorily. The reason for this is the belief on the part of the judiciary that 'it can be all reduced to a matter of individual rights versus the bureaucracy'.[119] McAuslan argues that 'this reduction is in fact part and parcel of their general preference— their ideological preference—for the individual as opposed to the collective' and that this 'makes it very difficult for judges to hold an even balance between the competing ideologies of collective consumption and privatisation'.[120] After examining the cases he concludes that judicial decisions 'may have been presented in legal terms and in legal language but they were an expression of judicial policy . . . to restrict the scope of the processes of collective consumption'.[121] Finally, he argues that 'the time is ripe for a relook, a rethink and a rewrite on the evolution of our modern system of administrative law and its relationship to the state,

[117] McAuslan, 'Administrative law, collective consumption and judicial policy' (1983) 46 *M.L.R.* 1, 7.
[118] Ibid. 2.   [119] Ibid. 8.   [120] Ibid. 11.   [121] Ibid. 18.

policy-making and resource allocation within the state including policy-making by the judges'.[122]

We see here the recurrence of familiar themes. The distorted effect of formalism on administrative lawyers is present; thus, the dominant focus on tribunals and inquiries operates to the detriment of a concern for general administrative processes. The lack of detailed legal regulation of the institutions of the welfare state reflects the pervasive influence of the public interest ideology. And the individualistic biases of the judiciary can be equated with the private property ideology. But are we beginning to lose sight of an alternative based on participatory democracy? And in presenting disputes in terms of collective consumption/public interest/planning versus privatization/individualism/ private property does not McAuslan come down strongly in favour of the former?

Functionalist thought

Despite their distinctive approaches these three public lawyers can be seen to reflect variants of the functionalist style. All try to reorientate public law away from the concern with control and rights and towards function and effectiveness. In Mitchell and the earlier writing of McAuslan we can see that their work is clearly rooted in an evolutionary conception of progress. This leads Mitchell to advocate the restoration of law through the development of a system of public law and the fragments of this line can be seen in McAuslan's advocacy of a fundamental value re-orientation by public lawyers. Griffith, however, places his faith in the strengthening of mechanisms of political accountability within a traditional set of constitutional arrangements. Such reforms, together with the inculcation of a public service ethos through professional development, he suggests, are the best protections against bureaucratic power. McAuslan seems to accept much of this analysis but probably takes a more jaundiced view of professions and (at least in his work on planning) specifically advocates the development of participatory structures to check official power. But Griffith and McAuslan adopt similar conceptions of law. They reflect the traditional functionalist distrust of abstractions and do not accord law the status of a concept: law is merely an instrument for achieving particular objectives; legal decisions are thus to be

---

[122] Ibid. 20.

evaluated in terms of outcomes; and those who make such decisions must be held to account for their politics and their prejudices.

THE EMERGENCE OF THE LIBERAL VARIANT OF NORMATIVISM

Liberalism as a political ideology has undoubtedly exerted an influence on the development of public law in the twentieth century. But liberalism in public law thought has generally operated within the shadow of the conservative variant of normativism. In recent years, however, the rationalistic and more doctrinaire liberal form of normativism has become increasingly more influential and has gradually emerged from the shadows. This growth in the authority of liberalism as a theoretical framework for analysing public law seems to be directly related to the spread in dissatisfaction with our existing constitutional arrangements.

The emergence of the liberal variant of normativism is linked to the analysis of rights within the British constitution. The movement has been closely bound to attempts to provide for the entrenchment of individual rights in British law. This analysis has been articulated most clearly by Anthony Lester. Lester has argued that, during the post-war period, there has been a progressive disaffection with the ability of traditional arrangements to sustain liberty. He suggests that since the 1950s the latent defects in the constitution have become ever more apparent. The key indicators of stress are identified as follows: the status of Northern Ireland within the United Kingdom, where 50 years of one party rule has, since 1972, been replaced with direct rule with emergency legislation; the 'clash between colour and citizenship' which arose as a result of immigration from the Commonwealth since the 1960s and in which clash the idea of colour prevailed; the lack of a common core of civil rights throughout the United Kingdom; the failure of attempts to modernize the constitution, through such provisions as devolution, because of the failure to examine constitutional questions in a fundamental and rational manner; and, contrary to the Diceyan principle of rule by ordinary law, the fact that public authorities continue to enjoy special immunities.[123]

[123] A. Lester, 'The Constitution: Decline and Renewal' in J. Jowell and D. Oliver (eds.), *The Changing Constitution* (Oxford, 2nd edn., 1989), chap. 13.

The roots of these problems, Lester argues, lie in our 'constitutional arrangements which had been settled by the Victorians and rationalized by A. V. Dicey into deceptively lucid theorems'.[124] As a result, despite the fact that the 'peculiar genius of the British constitution is supposed to consist in its flexibility and capacity for evolutionary change . . . the most striking characteristic . . . has been its failure to adapt to the changed needs of the nation'.[125] The solution advocated by Lester is that of a new constitutional settlement requiring a written constitution incorporating an entrenched Bill of Rights.

The main handle for promoting reforms based on this liberal normativist analysis has been the European Convention on Human Rights which Britain signed in 1950 and which was ratified by Parliament in 1951. After 1951 pressure was mounted to permit the right of individual petition to the European Court of Human Rights. Since Westminster had used the European Convention as the model for codes of rights in most of the Commonwealth countries gaining independence since the 1950s, it was argued that British citizens should also possess such enforceable rights. When individual petition was eventually granted in 1965, the reform movement switched its energies to that of seeking the incorporation of the Convention into domestic law.[126]

Constitutional reform has therefore been the benchmark of this liberal variant of normativism. But the liberal normativist programme consists not only of an explicit political programme for constitutional reform. This programme has also taken an implicit form through the work of public lawyers who have exploited the similarities in the normativist style in public law and constructed a radical re-interpretation of our tradition in a liberal rather than a conservative guise.

The jurisprudential foundations of this programme have been laid mainly by Ronald Dworkin who, during the last 20 years, has developed a normative theory of law based on liberal, rationalist premises.[127] This theory has been explicated in the context of

[124] Ibid. 346–7.   [125] Ibid. 368.
[126] See, e.g., Lester, *Democracy and Individual Rights* (London, 1968); L. Scarman, *English Law—the New Dimension* (London, 1974); M. Zander, *A Bill of Rights?* (London, 3rd edn., 1985).
[127] See *Taking Rights Seriously* (Cambridge, Mass., 1977); *A Matter of Principle* (Cambridge, Mass., and London, 1985); *Law's Empire* (Cambridge, Mass., 1986).

public law by T. R. S. Allan,[128] Anthony Lester,[129] and Jeffrey Jowell.[130] Their approach has been to argue that public law, in order to evolve, needs to rid itself of the shackles of conservative normativism, in which the authority of the judiciary is a product of their status as carriers of traditional wisdom. The courts, they contend, can renew their authority only by embracing liberal normativism in the form of rational principles of judicial review. Whereas the conservatives see the development of public law in the systematization of procedural developments in judicial review the liberals see it essentially in the creation of a rational jurisprudence of judicial review. Where the functionalists see only policy and politics the liberal normativists see principles of institutional morality.

These liberal normativists first seek to attack the legal positivism which permeates the language of public law. They thus challenge not only such distinctions as the legality and merits of action, or between process and substance, but also the idea of the separation of powers. Jowell has, for example, argued that:[131]

Modern administrative law is still involved in myth-making; much of it . . . in an effort to sustain that same old myth of the separation of powers. . . . Today's commentators and judges go to extraordinary lengths to demonstrate that the judiciary does not in practice interfere with the executive task of governing. It is said, therefore, that administrative law deals only with process and not substance. That is clearly wrong. It is said that the standards of judicial review differ from those imposed by direct appeals on law. That too avoids the truth. It is said that judicial review pays no heed to the merits of decisions. Even that proposition is highly dubious.

---

[128] Allan, 'Legislative Supremacy and the Rule of Law: Democracy and Constitutionalism' [1985] *Camb. L.J.* 111; id., 'Pragmatism and Theory in Public Law' [1988] 104 *L.Q.R.* 422; id., 'Dicey and Dworkin: the Rule of Law as Integrity' (1988) 8 *O.J.L.S.* 266; 'Constitutional Rights and Common Law' (1991) 11 *O.J.L.S.* 453.

[129] Jowell and Lester, 'Beyond *Wednesbury*: substantive principles of administrative law' 1987 *Public Law* 368; Jowell and Lester, 'Proportionality: neither novel nor dangerous' in Jowell and Oliver (eds.), *New Directions in Judicial Review* (London, 1988).

[130] In addition to those cited ibid. in n. 129 see Jowell, 'The Rule of Law Today' in Jowell and Oliver (eds.), *The Changing Constitution*; id., 'Courts and Administration in Britain: Standards, Principles and Rights' (1988) *Israel L.R.* 409.

[131] 'Courts and Administration', 415. See also Allan, 'Pragmatism and Theory', 423–4.

The second aspect of their critical attack is on judicial logic of justification. The primary illustrative target of this attack is the criteria of judicial review laid down by Lord Greene MR in the *Wednesbury* case.[132] Jowell and Lester have argued that the *Wednesbury* principle of unreasonableness is inadequate, is unrealistic and is confusing; 'the incantation of the word "unreasonable" simply does not provide sufficient justification for judicial intervention'.[133] In a later essay, they maintain that 'the legitimacy and integrity of the judicial process is in the long run damaged by vague and obscure reasoning. *Wednesbury* camouflage at best invites attack on the ground of inadequate justification and at worst invites suspicion on the ground of political motivation'.[134] Allan reinforces these claims, contending that 'recent examples of judicial theorising appear ad hoc and unconvincing; but they should be understood as a consequence of the poorly constructed basis of administrative law'.[135]

The liberal normativists argue that principles rather than rules are the building blocks of the legal order. They seek to distinguish between principles and rules and also between principles and policies. Principles, they contend, are rational and they also embody rights. The task of explicating these rational principles is undertaken mainly by Jowell and Lester who seek to unpack the *Wednesbury* criteria and discover principles of proportionality, legal certainty, consistency, and respect for fundamental human rights.[136] Allan's task has been to reinterpret the traditions of the common law in the language of rights. He argues that the 'failure of the courts to develop a clear and coherent doctrine [of the rule of law] is the consequence of Dicey's own failure to present his theory in clear juristic terms'.[137] He suggests that the 'rule of law, as a juristic principle, . . . embodies the liberal and individualistic bias of the common law in favour of the citizen'.[138] And, in a later essay, he develops his views on the common law as a vehicle within the context of public law for protecting rights.[139]

---

[132] *Associated Provincial Picture Houses v. Wednesbury Corporation* [1948] 1 K.B. 223.
[133] 'Beyond *Wednesbury*', 371–2.
[134] 'Proportionality', 68.   [135] 'Pragmatism and Theory'. 429.
[136] 'Beyond *Wednesbury*', 374–81.
[137] 'Legislative Supremacy', 115.
[138] Ibid. 119.   [139] 'Constitutional Rights'.

This liberal normativist project must be seen as a sophisticated attack on the dominant tradition of conservative normativism. It argues that, 'in the absence of principle, legal control depends on judicial instinct alone, employed in the manipulation of an undefined discretion'.[140] It therefore seeks to reinterpret the idea of the rule of law as 'integrity'.[141] Liberal normativist lawyers have thus sought to reinterpret our dominant tradition in a rationalistic light and have tried to explicate a corpus of rights inherent in the common law. In effect, they are seeking to reinvent our traditions, by supplanting the ancient conception of the rule of law with a modern conception.[142]

It is worthy of note that in this venture they are beginning to obtain some support on the judicial bench.[143] One should not, however, underestimate the scale of the project. Our anti-rationalist traditions are not confined to the work of the judiciary; they permeate our entire political culture. The form of our statutes, for example, are just as much a product of this tradition as are the style of judgments. Liberal normativists may be correct in stating that 'public law . . . cannot gain in coherence without better constitutional theory'.[144] But we must not assume that liberal normativism is simply bringing a dimension to our legal culture that hitherto has been neglected. Their implicit programme of injecting rationalist liberal theory into public law should be viewed, like their explicit political programme for constitutional reform founded on the need for an entrenched system of rights, as being essentially an exercise in political reform.

[140] Allan, 'Pragmatism and Theory', 431.
[141] See esp. R. Dworkin, *A Matter of Principle*, chap. 1; id., *Law's Empire*, chap. 7. We might note that the former essay, 'Political Judges and the Rule of Law' takes Griffith's empiricist view of judicial decision-making as its stalking horse.
[142] It is worthy of note that a distinctively Scottish dimension to the liberal normativist project can be seen in recent attempts to argue that the Treaty of Union constitutes judicially enforceable fundamental law. See, e.g., M. Upton, 'Marriage Vows of the Elephant: the Constitution of 1707' (1989) 105 L.Q.R. 79.
[143] The leader of the judicial movement is Lord Browne-Wilkinson, whose dissenting judgment in the Court of Appeal in the case of *Wheeler* v. *Leicester City Council* [1985] A.C. 1054, at 1063, has become the clarion call for liberal normativism. On Browne-Wilkinson LJ's dissent see: Allan, 'Pragmatism and Theory', 437; Jowell, 'Courts and Administration', 421; Jowell and Lester, 'Beyond Wednesbury', 373–4. See also, Lord Browne-Wilkinson, 'The Infiltration of a Bill of Rights' [1992] *Public Law* (forthcoming).
[144] Allan, 'Dworkin and Dicey', 276–7.

9

The Triumph of Liberal Normativism?

THE styles of conservative normativism and functionalism both express extreme scepticism about the ability to fashion a constitutional order on the foundation of individual rights. Conservatives in general reject rights-talk because such language is fundamentalist and thus fails to recognize the conditionality of its claims. They argue that, when the language of rights is intensively utilized, it tends to destroy the intricate heritage of understandings which sustains a society.[1] Oakeshott, for example, argues that abstract principles are incapable of determining actions. Such principles are cribs of practical knowledge and hence are contingent and indeterminate.[2]

Socialists have also been sceptical, primarily because of the empiricist and pragmatic strains in British socialist thought. As a result of the empiricist strain, statements of legal principle tend to be viewed as 'metaphysical nonsense'. Because of their pragmatic outlook every dispute is viewed as a unique situation which requires a creative act; consequently they are highly reluctant to promote a rights-based culture since the effect would be to increase the power of upper-class, conservative, male judges.[3] Socialists were therefore largely content to maintain the traditional constitutional arrangements and pursue 'the parliamentary road to socialism'. Aneurin Bevan reflected this view in suggesting that the absence of a written constitution gives the British constitution 'a revolutionary quality, and enables us to entertain the hope of bringing about

---

[1] K. Minogue, 'What is Wrong with Rights', in C. Harlow (ed.), *Public Law and Politics* (London, 1986), chap. 11.

[2] M. Oakeshott, *On Human Conduct* (Oxford, 1975), 173–4.

[3] J. A. G. Griffith, 'The Political Constitution' (1979) 42 *M.L.R.* 1, esp. at 12–20; id., 'Whose Bill of Rights?' *New Statesman* 14 Nov. 1975.

social transformations, without the agony and prolonged crises experienced by less fortunate nations'.[4]

Despite the rootedness of these views in conservative and socialist thought, during the last two decades both Conservatives and Socialists have had cause to re-assess their views. This has led many to embrace liberal normativism.

CONSERVATIVES AND LIBERAL NORMATIVISM

The primary impetus which caused Conservatives to reassess their position on the question of rights was the dominance of Labour rule in the 1960s and 1970s and, in particular, the articulation of a belief that the Labour Party was 'the natural party of government'. Evidence of such concern can be seen in two pamphlets published by the Conservative Political Centre in which Quintin Hogg and Sir Keith Joseph advocated the adoption of a Bill of Rights.[5] In 1969 Hogg argued that, although formerly he had subscribed to the traditional legal view that it was remedies and not rights which were crucial to the protection of liberties, he now felt that new institutional mechanisms were required. Today, he continued, the problem is not simply that of keeping civil servants or Ministers in check. Rather, it is the more embrasive one of the 'arbitrary rule of the modern Parliament itself'.[6] This argument was reinforced by Joseph's view in 1975 that a Bill of Rights was needed to save the rule of law. Joseph, however, put the case explicitly in a liberal framework with Hayekian undertones: 'The rule of law begins with the individual, because individuals are real, whereas society is an abstraction. . . . Cut down legislation and save the law.'[7]

Concerns of this nature were expressed by a number of Conservatives over this period. What they had in mind was the breakdown of law and order manifested by such incidents as the Clay Cross affair, the threat to freedom of the press by Labour trades union legislation and the destruction of independent business by Socialist tax policy.[8] The concern reached full flowering in 1976

---

[4] A. Bevan, *In Place of Fear* (London, 1952), 100.
[5] Q. Hogg, *New Charter* (London, 1969); Sir K. Joseph, *Freedom Under Law* (London, 1975).
[6] Hogg, *New Charter*, 12.
[7] Joseph, *Freedom Under Law*, 6.   [8] Ibid.

when Lord Hailsham (as Hogg had once more become) expounded his thesis on 'elective dictatorship'.[9] Our system, which has always been an elective dictatorship in theory, has been tolerable in practice, Hailsham argued, because the component parts operated to control one another. But with the rise of the party system those checks have disappeared: 'the sovereignty of Parliament has increasingly become, in practice, the sovereignty of the Commons, and the sovereignty of the Commons has increasingly become the sovereignty of the government which . . . controls the party whips, the party machine and the civil service'.[10] Hailsham advocated the re-creation of checks and balances by the adoption of a new constitutional structure which would be federal in nature and would incorporate electoral reform, the reform of the second chamber and the entrenchment of a Bill of Rights.

These concerns have also been reflected in academic work. In 1962 Professor Wade had struck an optimistic note on the ability of the courts to rise to the challenges of the modern administrative state. But, rather shrewdly, he hedged his bet:[11]

If the pessimists should prove to be true prophets, we would have to consider whether Parliament ought to come to the rescue with a general statute in the nature of a Bill of Rights. . . . I am sure we should be slow to abandon Dicey's principle that our fundamental rights are derived not from constitutional documents but from the decisions of courts in ordinary cases. Yet there might still be a case for taking out an insurance policy with Parliament, just in case fear should be well founded. I am not thinking of a declaration of the rights of man, and certainly not of anything restrictive of Parliamentary sovereignty, even if that were possible. I am thinking rather of an Act dealing with practical points and encouraging the courts to uphold the principles of an enlightened administrative code.

By the end of the 1970s, however, Wade fully recognized the case for constitutional reform and had embraced both Lord Hailsham's analysis and prescription.[12] The shift in Wade's thought between 1962 and 1980 thus seems to imitate the shift in Dicey's views between 1884 and 1914; in the twilight of their careers they both

---

[9] Lord Hailsham 'Elective dictatorship' (The Richard Dimbleby Lecture, 1976) *The Listener* 21 Oct. 1976, p. 496; see also, Lord Hailsham, *The Dilemma of Democracy* (London, 1977).

[10] Id., 'Elective dictatorship', p. 497.

[11] H. W. R. Wade, 'Law, Opinion and Administration' (1962) 78 *L.Q.R.* 188, p. 204.

[12] Wade, *Constitutional Fundamentals* (London, 1980).

moved from conservative normativism to embrace the doctrinal protections of liberal normativism. This shift in Wade's thought can even be seen in his views on the fundamental legal principle of sovereignty. Commenting on the *Factortame* decision he said:[12a]

> The Parliament of 1972 has evidently succeeded in binding its successors, due to the necessity of honouring the Treaty. The House of Lords said not a word about this constitutional revolution. But the perspectives opened up are interesting. What about the European Convention on Human Rights, which is also buttressed by a treaty? If it were to be incorporated into our law by Act of Parliament (as should have been done long ago . . .), could the Act entrench it by some formula similar to that in the European Communities Act? The argument here is weaker, since the European Convention, unlike the Treaty of Rome, imposes no obligation to enact, still less to entrench, its provisions. But *Factortame* shows how international law, in the shape of treaty obligations, may help to overthrow the dogmas of constitutional law, and how smoothly the courts may discard fundamental doctrine without appearing to notice.

Through this shrug of the shoulders, the contemporary defender of Dicey's theory cast off this 'dogma' and went in search of new agendas.

In general terms, by 1980 the view seems to have been well rooted in conservative thought that the prescriptive constitution had come to the end of its useful life and that it was necessary to consider fundamental constitutional reform. The apparent paradox thus arose that, in order to preserve the values which are rooted in conservative thought, conservatives felt obliged to embrace rational principles—the precise system of thought which conservatives eschew.[13]

Socialists and Liberal Normativism

If the 1970s was the decade of Conservative conversion to rational principles in legal thought, the 1980s was the decade of Socialist conversion to liberal values. If the Conservative concern of the 1970s was the hegemony of Labour, the Socialist concern of the 1980s was the agenda of Thatcherism. During the 1980s the

---

[12a] Wade, 'What has happened to the Sovereignty of Parliament?' (1991) 107 *L.Q.R.* 1, p. 4. For *Factortame* see Chap. 8, n. 81.

[13] See N. Johnson, 'Constitutional Reform: Some Dilemmas for a Conservative Philosophy' in Z. Layton-Henry, *Conservative Party Politics* (London, 1980). See generally Johnson, *In Search of the Constitution* (London, 1977).

Conservative Party adopted the rhetoric of Hayek's economic liberalism but not his liberal constitutionalism. Their argument on this point was that liberty is threatened by the collectivist state and that, in order radically to restructure the State and to restore liberty, the full legal authority of the State must be used.

The Conservative agenda led many socialists to mount a defence of the welfare state and its structures and to attack the methods of the Conservative government as being founded on authoritarian centralism. It also caused them to reconsider constitutional issues. Perhaps the most influential academic contribution to this discussion was E. P. Thompson's examination of the importance of the idea of the rule of law. In 1975 Thompson, a social historian who works in a Marxist tradition, published a major study of the Black Acts of 1723.[14] His basic aim was to show how law had been used as a repressive force by Whig governments in defence of property rights. In a powerful conclusion, however, he criticized the view that law should be seen simply as an instrument of the ruling class. Law, he argued, could also be viewed as an ideological tool for legitimizing class rule. But, he continued, since this ideological function depended on the acceptance of the credibility of law as a system of justice law could, in turn, impose restrictions and limits on the ruling class. From this specific study he sought to draw more general conclusions:[15]

I am insisting only upon the obvious point, which some modern Marxists have overlooked, that there is a difference between arbitrary power and the rule of law. We ought to expose the shams and inequities which may be concealed beneath this law. But the rule of law itself, the imposing of effective inhibitions upon power and the defence of the citizen from power's all-intrusive claims, seems to me to be an unqualified human good. To deny or belittle this good is, in this dangerous century when the resources and pretensions of power continue to enlarge, a desperate error of intellectual abstraction.

As the final sentence of the quotation suggests, Thompson's conclusions in *Whigs and Hunters* should not just be read as an historical assessment. During the period of the late 1970s Thompson's political essays were charting the strengthening of the police, security, and secrecy mechanisms within the State, the weakening of the protections afforded by the law, and the lack of parliamentary

---

[14] E. P. Thompson, *Whigs and Hunters* (Harmondsworth, 1975).
[15] Ibid. 266.

control over these developments.[16] In these essays he invoked an abstract notion of the rule of law in defence of civil liberties. Thompson's views on the rule of law have been the subject of much debate on the left.[17]

The functionalist style in public law, however, is not easily adaptable to these defensive purposes. This is essentially because underpinning the functionalist style is a belief in the progressive nature of history. When the State comes to be viewed as a force of reaction, there is little in the functionalist style to assist in the defence of the welfare state. If the constitution is 'what happens' and if the law is to be viewed simply as an instrument of governmental power there is little tension within legal discourse to sanction restraint. If, additionally, the judiciary are recommended to keep their noses out of politics there may not be much in the way of institutional constraint; one may be forced to rely on an unelected second Chamber or the power of the bureaucracy as a 'dynamic conservative'[18] force.

These strains are reflected in functionalist writing in the 1980s. In 1985, for example, John Griffith, after decades of critical writing on judicial intervention in political questions in public law, came forward with his first proposal for assisting the judges in undertaking such tasks. In his Harry Street Lecture, after critically examining judicial performance in the *GCHQ*,[19] *Guardian Newspapers*,[20] and *Bromley*[21] cases, Griffith concluded with a call for 'the appointment of a public officer whose responsibility it would be to act as an advocate-general, to present such evidence as he considered necessary in the public interest, and generally to draw the attention of the court to those matters affecting the public interest which he considered the court should take into account'.[22]

---

[16] Thompson, *Writing By Candlelight* (London, 1980).

[17] See, e.g., P. Anderson, *Arguments within English Marxism* (London, 1980) esp. 197–207; B. Fine, *Democracy and the Rule of Law* (London, 1984); C. Sypnowitch, *The Concept of Socialist Law* (Oxford, 1990); M. J. Horwitz, 'The Rule of Law: An Unqualified Human Good?' (1977) 86 *Yale L.J.* 561; A. Merrett, 'The Nature and Function of Law: A Criticism of E. P. Thompson's *Whigs and Hunters*' (1980) 7 *Brit. J. of Law & Soc.* 195.

[18] See D. Schon, *Beyond the Stable State* (New York, 1971), chap. 2.

[19] *Council of Civil Service Unions* v. *Minister for the Civil Service* [1985] 1 AC 374.

[20] *Secretary of State for Defence* v. *Guardian Newspapers* [1984] 3 WLR 986.

[21] *Bromley LBC* v. *Greater London Council* [1983] 1 AC 768.

[22] Griffith, 'Judicial Decision-Making in Public Law' 1985 *Pub. Law* 564, 582.

This was, of course, accompanied by a plea that judges should not extend their jurisdiction and that the object was simply to enable them to be informed about the significance of the decisions which they are in fact making. But this constructive approach might, nevertheless, be viewed as an indication of the strains on the functionalist approach in the 1980s.

The work of Patrick McAuslan is even more revealing. In choosing 'Public Law and Public Choice' as the title for his inaugural lecture on acceding to Griffith's Chair at LSE in 1987 he appeared to be directly tackling the challenges which the Thatcher phenomenon posed for the functionalist style.[23] As we have seen,[24] public choice theory, of which Hayek is a key intellectual inspiration, contends that government failure is potentially as pervasive a phenomenon as market failure. Public choice theory seemed to provide much of the intellectual underpinning for the Conservative government's agenda. It was thus in the spirit of 'John Griffith's pioneering work on the interface between public law and politics' that McAuslan approached this theme.[25]

But McAuslan does not in fact squarely face the challenge of public choice theory. Despite his call in 1982 for 'a relook, a rethink and a rewrite on the evolution of our modern system of administrative law',[26] developments in the 1980s do not cause him either to analyse why public choice theory has become fashionable or to re-examine his conceptual structure of public law. This is surprising because there is a degree of similarity, in symptom at least, between the public choice theorist's attack on government bureaucracy and McAuslan's criticisms of 'traditional models of public administration and management'.[27] But he does not examine the similarities and differences. Instead, public choice theory is simply fitted into the role which the 'private property ideology'[28] and 'individualism'[29] played in his earlier work; and, as such, it is treated essentially as the target to attack. The attack mainly takes the form of criticizing public choice theory for the use of such pejorative terms as 'log-rolling', 'vote-trading', and 'rent-seeking' in

---

[23] P. McAuslan, 'Public Law and Public Choice' (1988) 51 *M.L.R.* 681.
[24] Chap. 5, pp. 97–9.
[25] McAuslan, 'Public Care and Public Choice', 682.
[26] Chap. 8, p. 204.   [27] Chap. 8, p. 203.
[28] *The Ideologies of Planning Law*. See Chap. 8, pp. 202–3.
[29] 'Administrative law, collective consumption and judicial policy', see Chap. 8, p. 204.

order to explain political and administrative behaviour. But what is of particular interest is the fact that, not only is the attack launched from the standpoint of the 'public interest ideology', but that McAuslan seems to claim that this perspective has a degree of neutrality:[30]

> For the Welfare Statists there *is* something which we call 'the public interest' which exists over and above the politicians and public servants who manage the Welfare State; to 'advance the public interest' is to adopt policies and practices which advance the good of all citizens directly or indirectly. To ensure that that public interest is advanced, we have constructed an enormous administrative superstructure in which lawyers have played an important role: we have argued for public participation and constructed systems of public participation in the planning and housing fields; we have established, through the mechanism of judicial review, a considerable extension of natural justice . . . By developing the idea of relevant and irrelevant considerations in decision-making, we implicitly accept that decision-makers are motivated by factors other than self-interest . . . Enormous resources have been devoted to trying to create and support a more responsive local government, a more accountable central government, a more checkable public bureaucracy. . . . All this is based on the fundamental principle that the 'public interest' does exist and can be better advanced through better political and administrative mechanisms.

The tone adopted here (not least in his use of the plural pronoun) is very different from that of his earlier work. In response to the reorganization of the planning system on market-orientated lines in the 1980s, McAuslan conceded that, for 'the old-fashioned democrat, the evolution of the planning system in the 20–25 years from 1958 . . . was in some respects a model of how government ought to be carried on . . . to ensure that the public interest was given effect to'.[31] This is a rather different emphasis to that in *The Ideologies of Planning Law*. Further, in praising developments in judicial review[32] and in highlighting the importance of the formal institutions that administrative lawyers traditionally focus upon,[33]

---

[30] 'Public Law and Public Choice', 688.

[31] Ibid. 691.

[32] 'Public lawyers have praised the onward march of judicial review since *Ridge* v. *Baldwin* was decided 25 years ago; we consider that government is now more under law than it was . . .', ibid. 693.

[33] 'There is a clear challenge here for public lawyers; where is the place in this new world for our fundamental principles—openness, fairness, and impartiality—and their institutional manifestations—public inquiries, appeals, and other formalised systems of redress of grievances?', ibid. 699.

McAuslan significantly re-orientates his position from that in his Chorley Lecture.

In fact, McAuslan seems to be seeking to wrap the cloak of neutrality around his public interest ideology so as to be able to claim a consensual vantage point *within* public law for the purpose of criticizing Government reforms of the 1980s. This failure of 'faith'[34] is probably attributable to the achievements of the Thatcher governments. Elsewhere, McAuslan argued that the practices of the Thatcher governments had led to a crisis in the constitution, which he identified in terms of 'the increasing use of governmental power and law for partisan ends, the increasingly aggressive manner in which this power is exercised, and the increasingly casual way in which the legal framework for and legal controls on the exercise of power are being treated'.[35] Furthermore, in turning to constitutional principles to attack such practices, McAuslan also seems willing to embrace Diceyan normativism.[36]

The attempt to construct a neutral and hegemonic position for public law around the principles of the Franks Report in administrative law and Dicey's principles in constitutional law does not, however, seem particularly convincing. McAuslan himself seemed to recognize this in 1985 when arguing that functionalists 'have to recapture the high ground . . . and begin the process of reconstituting a constitutional law of the United Kingdom which can provide a better and more enduring framework for the containment of overweening Executive power and authoritarian trends in government'.[37] It is perhaps symptomatic of the general disorientation of the functionalist style in the 1980s that McAuslan became a founder signatory of Charter 88, a document in the liberal normativist style, calling for a written constitution incorporating a Bill of Rights.

---

[34] *The Ideologies of Planning Law.* See Chap. 8, p. 203.
[35] P. McAuslan and J. F. McEldowney, 'Legitimacy and the Constitution: the dissonance between theory and practice' in McAuslan and McEldowney (eds.), *Law, Legitimacy and the Constitution* (London, 1985), 1, 7.
[36] Ibid. McAuslan refers to the idea of 'limited government' implicit in Dicey's work as being the fundamental principle of the constitution (p. 8) and states, when presenting his critique: 'If this model bears a resemblance to the model Dicey offered us 100 years ago, it is none the worse for that . . .' (p. 38).
[37] McAuslan, 'Dicey and his influence on public law' 1985 *Pub. Law* 721, 723.

THE MOVEMENT FOR CONSTITUTIONAL REFORM

Conservatives, who traditionally possess a rather pessimistic view of human nature together with a certain degree of scepticism about rationalist possibilities, seem gradually to be coming to see that perhaps they should temper their scepticism in order to protect against their pessimism. They seem increasingly prepared to embrace rationalist constitutional reform in order to protect traditional liberties against the dangers of democracy, rather in the spirit of Locke's attempt in his *Second Treatise of Civil Government*[38] to bring about a restoration of the ancient constitution. The conservatives' rationalist response seems to be born of a lingering appeal to pre-urban and pre-industrial values in a world in which faith in the immutable order of society has been forever lost.

By way of contrast, socialists, who possessed a great deal of optimism about human nature together with a degree of cynicism about the motives of rationalist constitutionalists, are realizing that human beings are capable of 'less than they hoped for and more than they feared'.[39] They are coming to realize that 'a legislative dogma, a legislative instrument, and a legislative tendency'[40] may not be enough. The functionalists in public law, it has been argued, have been unable adequately to articulate their concerns in the 1980s precisely because they have eschewed

serious consideration of law as a system or social institution. They are more at home with a catalogue of injustices than with a theory of justice, with the bias and distortions of the legal process than with the nature and functions of law, with the politics of the judiciary than with the role of legal traditions, techniques and values.[41]

They can now see more clearly how public institutions can be made to work for private interests and that the activities of a virtuous citizenry may not be sufficient in the face of private power. The functionalist style was a product of the opening up of a new age founded on growing interdependencies based on an urban, industrial society. Their contemporary difficulties seem, in part at

[38] J. Locke, *Two Treatises of Government* (1690) (P. Laslett (ed.), Cambridge, 1960).
[39] J. T. Kloppenberg, *Uncertain Victory*, 415.
[40] Dicey, *Law and Opinion*, p. 302.
[41] E. Kamenka, 'Demythologizing the law', *Times Lit. Suppt.* 1 May 1981, pp. 475, 476.

least, to emanate from the crisis of political order in a post-industrial society.

Can, then, a consensus be constructed around the liberal normativist constitutional project? The evidence for this thesis is to be found most graphically in the fact that Sir William Wade, Anthony Lester, and Patrick McAuslan were all founder signatories to Charter 88. An initiative born of an alliance between the 'libertarian left' and the 'democratic centre', Charter 88 is a political campaign to force the pace of constitutional reform.[42] The movement argues that the British system of 'club government', founded on benign paternalism, national consensus, and the conventions of compromise and tolerance, has disintegrated and that parliamentarians are ineffective guardians of liberty in the contemporary world. The system of parliamentary government, it suggests, has run its course. Charter 88 calls for fundamental constitutional reform, including the reform of Parliament and the creation of an electoral system based on proportional representation. Its centrepiece is the idea of a written constitution incorporating a Bill of Rights. Its primary concern is therefore with constitutional law: 'No country can be considered free in which the government is above the law. No democracy can be considered safe whose freedoms are not encoded in a basic constitution.'[43]

Charter 88 can be viewed as a specific response to a broadly held feeling of dissatisfaction with existing constitutional arrangements.[44] Nevertheless, there exist major obstacles to the achievement of its aims, although if we are to accept Marquand's thesis,[45] the stakes are very high. However, I am not directly concerned here to assess the movement's chances of political success. Rather, since I am primarily concerned with thought, I wish to examine its coherence. We know what Charter 88 stands against, but do we know positively what it stands for?

The first thing to note is that Charter 88 is not a particularly well-

[42] See *New Statesman & Society*, 2 Dec. 1988.
[43] Ibid.
[44] See, e.g., Campaign for a Scottish Assembly, *The Claim of Right for Scotland* (Edinburgh, 1987); D. Marquand, *The Unprincipled Society* (London, 1988); Institute for Public Policy Research, *The Constitution of the United Kingdom* (London, 1991).
[45] See Chap. 1, p. 26–7.

written document. Of its ten point manifesto, no less than three range over the issue of executive power and the rule of law:

We call . . . for a new constitutional settlement which would: . . .
[2] Subject executive powers . . . to the rule of law; . . .
[6] Place . . . all agencies of the state under the rule of law; . . .
[8] Provide legal remedies for all abuses of power by the state . . .

This reads very much like a crude version of Diceyan normativism. Other proposals are, of course, made. An 'equitable distribution of power' between local, regional, and national government is recommended [point 9]; although we are not told whether it is devolution or federalism that is being touted.[46] Proportional representation is suggested as a model of electoral reform [point 4]. This might alleviate the problem of government by the largest minority and—together with reform of the upper house [point 5]—open up the space for a genuine differentiation of parliamentary and executive power. But this seems to be regarded as a necessary but not sufficient condition of reform.

At the core of the Charter, however, lies the idea of entrenched rights. The primary focus of the Charter is on a Bill of Rights [point 1] and 'a written constitution anchored in the idea of universal citizenship' [point 10]. Here rests not only the essence of the Charter but also its principal point of tension. Charter 88 refers explicitly to *civil* rights—peaceful assembly, freedoms of association and expression, the right to privacy and the like [point 1]. But it also refers, somewhat elliptically, to the idea of 'universal citizenship' [point 10]. But what is to be included in such citizenship rights?

This is of fundamental importance because today the *principle* of civil and political rights (and there will always be disputes about application) is relatively uncontested. The contemporary challenge concerns social and economic entitlements: employment, health, education, and social security. Indeed, in the post-industrial era of the 1980s in which growth occurs without a significant proportion of the population being at all involved, some would argue that the issue of socio-economic citizenship rights has become *the* political question.

---

[46] Cf. Report to the Scottish People by the Scottish Constitutional Convention, *Towards Scotland's Parliament* (Edinburgh, 1990) which proposes an asymmetric federal solution to the position of Scotland within the United Kingdom.

On this issue the Charter provides no answers. If its objective is simply to establish a mechanism for the better protection and enforcement of civil rights then we are back to the old arguments about whether the judiciary are better able than Parliament to protect liberties. Can a judiciary rooted in the culture of the ancient constitution respond to the challenges of a modern Bill of Rights? (Of course, the Chartists wish to see a 'reformed' judiciary [point 7], but we are not told what this means or how it will be achieved.) If, however, the Charter is seeking to promote a particular view on socio-economic citizenship rights then this should have been explicitly declared. While the issue remains ambiguous the Chartists fall prey to the criticism that 'the Bill of Rights is the intellectual equivalent of the latest computer, a toy which promises to do whatever the heart desires'.[47]

The repetitions, ambiguities, and omissions[48] render Charter 88 fundamentally flawed as a statement of principle. Signatories presumably are expected to breathe coherence into it by filling its gaps or resolving its uncertainties by reference to their own values. And it is this that casts doubt on its credibility. Is there a genuine consensus amongst the founder signatories? What, for example, might we assume in common about the views of Ralph Miliband and Sir William Wade on the nature of the state?[49] Between Anthony Lester and Patrick McAuslan's conceptions of law?[50] Between G. A. Cohen and Robert Skidelsky's philosophy of history?[51] Between the views of Tom Nairn and Lord Scarman on

---

[47] Minogue, 'What is Wrong with Rights', 224.

[48] The one glaring omission in Charter 88 is that the document contains no statement of the proposed role of the monarchy in this new constitutional settlement. One of the Charter's founder signatories has recently argued that, since the monarchy has become a symbol of our national self-identity, if we are serious about modernizing our political institutions we must radically reform the constitutional role of the monarchy. See T. Nairn, *The Enchanted Glass. Britain and its Monarchy* (London, 1988).

[49] Miliband is the foremost contemporary disciple of the version of Marxism which Laski embraced in his later years. See, R. Miliband, *Parliamentary Socialism* (London, 1961); id., *The State in Capitalist Society* (London, 1969); id., *Marxism and Politics* (Oxford, 1978); id., *Capitalist Democracy in Britain* (Oxford, 1982). For Wade's views see Chap. 8, pp. 184–90.

[50] See Chap. 8, pp. 207–9 and 205–6 respectively.

[51] See G. A. Cohen, *Karl Marx's Theory of History: A Defence* (Oxford, 1978); R. Skidelsky, *Politicians and the Slump: the Labour Government of 1929–31* (London, 1967); id., *John Maynard Keynes* (London, 1983).

the break-up of Britain?[52] Between Duncan Campbell and Lord Zuckerman's views about free access to defence information?[53] This has all the makings of an entertaining parlour game. But it also highlights a serious issue. Some have found such contrasts reassuring: 'When the inheritors of Calvin and Rome agree, then something really has changed in the British order of things.'[54] But is it not also possible that Charter 88 constitutes a spurious agreement founded on vacuity?

ONE STEP FORWARD, TWO STEPS BACKWARDS?

Despite the impressive list of signatories, Charter 88 should not be viewed as marking the intellectual triumph of liberal normativism. It does stand, however, as a symbol of the intellectual crisis facing the functionalist style. In order to understand the challenges facing public law today we should therefore consider the nature of this crisis. Symptoms of this crisis can, I believe, be identified through recent philosophical debate and recent political developments.

Philosophy and liberal democracy

The philosophical dimension to the crisis can most concisely be viewed by examining the contemporary relationship between pragmatism and liberal political philosophy. These two philosophical positions, I have suggested, have exerted a significant influence over the two styles that have permeated public law thought.[55]

When John Rawls wrote *A Theory of Justice* in 1971 he seemed to treat the idea of justice as a moral rather than a political concept. Politics, Rawls argued, exhibited the 'imperfections' of practical life and should be subordinated to the principles of 'pure procedural justice'.[56] In 1985, however, Rawls shifted his position and argued that 'justice as fairness' is a political rather than a moral

---

[52] See Nairn, *The Break-Up of Britain: Crisis and Neo-Nationalism* (London, 2nd edn., 1981); L. Scarman, *English Law—The New Dimension* (London, 1975), 63–8 ('The Regional Challenge').

[53] See D. Campbell, *WarPlan UK. The Truth about Civil Defence in Britain* (London, 1982). Campbell was also a defendant in the ABC security secrets trial in the 1970s. Lord Zuckerman was Chief Scientific Adviser to the Ministry of Defence between 1960 and 1966.

[54] A. Barnett, *New Statesman & Society*, 2 Dec. 1988.

[55] See Chap. 5, pp. 84–101; Chap. 6, pp. 121–33.

[56] *A Theory of Justice* (Oxford, 1972), 88. On Rawls see Chap. 5, pp. 93–6.

conception.[57] As a result of this shift his theory seemed to lose its universalistic quality and could be reformulated to apply to the 'basic structure' of a 'modern constitutional democracy'.[58] He thus argued that support for his two principles of justice can be found in an 'overlapping consensus, that is, by a consensus that includes all the opposing philosophical and religious doctrines likely to persist and gain adherents in a more or less just constitutional democratic society'.[59] Rawls's reformulated theory is thus targeted directly to the political concerns of contemporary advanced societies.

What is most significant about this development for our purposes is that, in this reformulated version, Rawls's theory has recently received support from Richard Rorty.[60] Rorty, perhaps the most influential of the contemporary pragmatists, argued that, in the light of this later essay, Rawls can now be rescued from Kantianism and re-interpreted in a Hegelian and Deweyan light: 'Rawls is not attempting a transcendental deduction of American liberalism or supplying philosophical foundations for democratic institutions, but [is] simply trying to systematize the principles and intuitions typical of American liberals.'[61] By interpreting Rawls in this manner, Rorty claimed to deflect criticisms that 'the social theory of the liberal state rests on false philosophical presuppositions'[62] and went on to argue, as the title of his essay suggests, that liberal democracy does not require any philosophical justification.

Such philosophical work is of interest to us because in certain respects it can be seen to parallel the recent attempt in Britain to achieve a consensus around the principles of liberal constitutionalism. Rorty's defence of Rawls and liberal democracy has not, however, gone unchallenged. Richard Bernstein has contested Rorty's position mainly on the ground that 'it diverts us from the pragmatically important issues that need to be confronted'.[63] He first notes certain striking features of Rorty's defence:[64]

There is scarcely any mention of such themes as the 'original position', 'the veil of ignorance' . . . or Rawls's understanding of rationality and rational

---

[57] Rawls, 'Justice as Fairness: Political not Metaphysical' (1985) 14 *Philosophy and Public Affairs* 223.   [58] Ibid. at p. 224.   [59] Ibid. at pp. 225–6.

[60] R. Rorty, 'The Priority of Democracy to Philosphy' in A. Malachowski (ed.), *Reading Rorty* (Oxford, 1990), 279.

[61] Ibid. at p. 289.   [62] Ibid. at p. 293.

[63] R. Bernstein, 'One Step Forward, Two Steps Backward. Richard Rorty on Liberal Democracy and Philosophy' (1987) 15 *Political Theory* 538 at p. 546.

[64] Ibid. at pp. 545–6.

226   *The Triumph of Liberal Normativism?*

choice. Nor does Rorty pay attention to Rawls's detailed critique of utilitarianism or other versions of liberalism. What is even more surprising is that Rorty never even mentions what—on any interpretation of Rawls— is the heart of his theory, that is, the successive formulations and defense of the two principles of justice. Throughout Rorty simply speaks globally about 'liberal democracy' without ever unpacking what it involves or doing justice to the enormous historical controversy about what liberal democracy is or ought to be.

In addition to criticizing Rorty's vague appeal to liberal democracy on the ground that that term embraces many diverse and even incompatible positions, Bernstein also reprimands Rorty for retreating into 'an essentialist mode of speech when he speaks of "liberal democracy" or "political freedom"'[65]—precisely because Rorty has done so much to argue against such essentialism.[66]

While Rorty recognizes that there are differences within liberalism, he emphasizes that these are political and not philosophical differences. Although this statement can be taken as an important reminder that we should not expect more of philosophy than it can deliver, Bernstein argues that it obscures more than it reveals since Rorty 'does not clarify what constitutes "the political" or how one is to evaluate critically competing political *arguments*'.[67] Rorty thus seems to be relying on common moral and political intuitions as the source of justification for liberal democracy and here Bernstein argues he tends to downplay 'the disparity between the "ideals" of liberty and equality that liberals profess and the actual state of affairs in so-called liberal societies'.[68] Bernstein concludes that Rorty's present position is 'little more than an ideological *apologia* for an old-fashioned version of cold war liberalism dressed up in fashionable "post-modern" discourse. This is surely one step forward, two steps backward.'[69]

These philosophical debates are interesting because they show first how some pragmatists have come to embrace liberal democracy and secondly the nature of the criticisms that have been launched

[65] R. Bernstein, 'One Step Forward, Two Steps Backward. Richard Rorty on Liberal Democracy and Philosophy' (1987) 15 *Political Theory* 538 at p. 547.
[66] See Rorty, *Philosophy and the Mirror of Nature* (Princeton, 1979); id., *Consequences of Pragmatism* (Minneapolis, 1982).
[67] Bernstein, 'One Step Forward, Two Steps Backward', at p. 547.
[68] Ibid., at p. 552.
[69] Ibid., at p. 556. For Rorty's response see 'Thugs and Theorists. A Reply to Bernstein' (1987) 15 *Political Theory* 564.

against them in doing so. In this respect there are certain parallels in public law thought, both in the advocacy by certain functionalists of liberal constitutionalism and of the criticisms that may be made of the attempt to derive a consensus from this fact. In order to throw further light on the issue we should also consider the nature of the political developments which have shaped thinking on these matters.

Social democracy and politics

Throughout most of the post-war period social democratic reformism has been viewed largely in terms of the State's function in siphoning off the proceeds of economic growth and then using these resources to improve the position of the most disadvantaged members of society. This 'mechanical' model of the role of the State could be viewed in terms of Keynesian macro-economic management strategies and, since no one was to be made worse-off, it did not depend on a strong sense of civic virtue or altruism on the part of citizens. This mechanical approach went hand-in-hand with the establishment of a centralized, managerial, professionally dominated state.

This organizational model of the state has, however, been subject to severe strains in recent decades. A major source of this strain has been the decline in the capacity of society to maintain economic growth at the rate required to meet growing needs through this mechanism. Consequently, in order to maintain social democratic reforms it seems necessary to appeal more explicitly to a moral foundation for the just society. However, owing to the pace of social changes and in part also because of the dominance of the mechanical reform model, the resources to which an appeal might be made in seeking a moral foundation—altruism and a sense of community—have been depleted. This problem seems to have been compounded since, as a result of shifts in the nature of the economy, we seem to have entered an industrial phase in which the old orthodoxy has been called into question. Economic growth now seems to be taking place without a significant portion of the population being at all involved. While the size of this 'economically inactive' group—which some have called an 'underclass'—is a subject of dispute, there is little doubt that it raises a serious political issue. These changes are of great importance and cannot be properly examined here.[70] Their effect on politics, however, is potentially very great. Ralf Dahrendorf, for example, has argued that, as a result of such changes, the social basis of modern politics has shifted. He claims that class politics is being displaced by issue politics and that this raises greater problems in mobilizing different groups of people in different situations in support of particular policies. The formation of political coalitions is likely to become increasingly complex.[71] In these circumstances Dahrendorf also suggests that a new social compact—a new contract of citizenship— needs to be forged.

Dahrendorf's essay is interesting because it provides us with a political explanation both for the shifts in authority of the various styles of public law thought and for the attempt to construct a coalition rooted in constitutionalism. But both the philosophical debates and the political developments indicate that the building of such a coalition is an extremely hazardous exercise.

The triumph of liberal normativism?

This brief examination of recent philosophical debates and political developments tends to confirm the impression that documents such as Charter 88 constitute a 'statement of political conflict pretending to be a resolution of it'.[72] The challenge of liberal normativism is far from being decisive. At the level of legal practice the liberal normativist objective—of trying to reinvent the traditions of the common law in a rationalistic light and of substituting a modern for the ancient conception of the rule of law as the foundation of our constitutional tradition—remains far from being realized. At level of political thought their programme for constitutional reform has achieved a degree of intellectual consensus only by fudging the issues. At this level, the ambiguity is most clearly expressed in the tension between negative and positive conceptions of liberty. As we have seen this tension, between classical liberalism and New Liberalism, goes to the heart of the

---

[70] For illustrations of this now voluminous literature see: J. Habermas, *Legitimation Crisis* (Boston, 1975); F. Hirsch, *The Social Limits to Growth* (London, 1976); C. Offe, *Contradictions of the Welfare State* (J. Keane (ed.), London, 1984); M. J. Piore and C. F. Sabel, *The Second Industrial Divide* (New York, 1984).

[71] R. Dahrendorf, 'Citizenship and the modern social conflict' in R. Holme and M. Elliott (eds.), *1688–1988. Time for a New Constitution* (London, 1988), chap. 7.

[72] Griffith, The Political Constitution', p. 14.

tension between the two styles of public law thought which form the polarities of our split legal consciousness.[73]

The consideration of these issues is, nevertheless, revealing. We seemed to have reached a more fluid stage in which the dominant political ideologies cannot so easily be equated with particular styles of public law thought. Furthermore, recent developments also seem to be indicative of a crisis within the functionalist style. The reasons for this are, I believe, evident in the issues we have examined. During the 'mechanical' era of social democracy the positivistic and utilitarian dimensions of the functionalist style achieved prominence. While social rights, such as a right to health or housing, were articulated and given expression in this period they often did not take a positive legal form. The functionalist style could therefore only be fully appreciated when viewed sociologically. Unfortunately, certain functionalists, retreating into a form of legal positivism, themselves became blind to this fact.

The effect of recent change has required a reassessment of this style of public law thought. The nature of the changes seem indicative of a shift in language from the Fabian strain rooted in efficiency to the New Liberal strain based on a more explicit normative foundation. As the language of the times has shifted from felt needs to that of citizenship rights, and from the notion of the social health of the nation to that of the dignity of the person, so too must the language of functionalism. It is in part because of a failure to recognize this that functionalists, faced with contemporary challenges, have in confusion apparently embraced liberal normativism. And it is because of the doubts about the ability of liberal normativism to produce an adequate language to express and respond to contemporary challenges that I suggest that recent trends amount to taking one step forward and two steps backwards.

[73] See Chap. 6, pp. 121–2.

10

Public Law in the Face of the Future

THIS book opened with the suggestion that public law is currently in a rather unsatisfactory state. We are now in a position to appreciate why this might be the case. I have tried to show, first, that public law discourse is bifurcated. There are two basic styles of thought in public law, which I have labelled normativism and functionalism. Between adherents of these two styles there is virtually no agreement over the contours and boundaries of the subject. Although writers may use similar concepts—such as sovereignty, liberty, democracy, and law—the meanings which such concepts convey tend to be rather different. This is hardly surprising since these concepts perform different roles within competing models of public law. I have, secondly, endeavoured to demonstrate that the roots of these competing styles are to be found in theories of politics and society. There is no neutral language of public law. We can understand what a writer is saying only if we understand the political tradition within which the writer works.

These insights have not been widely acknowledged. In part, this is because of the subject. The presentation to the world of an objectivist, even absolutist, view of the subject (what Bagehot would call a 'dignified' view) is necessary, it seems, in order to retain faith in the ideals of our political and legal system. Law, after all, exists to uphold the values of our political traditions, not to subvert them. We must, it seems (in Burke's words), maintain 'the decent drapery of life'. The projection of this objectivist view of the subject has been reinforced by the acceptance of legal positivism as the orthodox mode of legal thought. Legal positivism severs the concepts of public law from their roots and thus impedes our appreciation of their meaning. This objectivist approach may be understandable in the world of practice. But the reintegration of meaning—by connecting the languages of public law with traditions of political thought—has not even been carried out in legal theory. This, it would appear, is because mainstream jurisprudence is, at a basic level, constructed on the adoption of the idea of law as an autonomous subject. Other perspectives tend to be marginalized.

It has been a basic theme of this book, however, that in order to *understand* public law we should adopt the sort of perspective here presented. Many may argue that there are important reasons for affirming the myths of the subject. These myths may, for example, enable us to retain allegiance to general ideals while our political system responds in complex ways to diffuse pressures. Nevertheless, there are serious dangers if, by adopting this orientation, we erect barriers to understanding. In particular, we should not forget that the myths promoted by the objectivist view of the subject can be manipulated for self-serving or exploitative purposes. There is, however, a more pressing reason for adopting the perspective employed in this book. Today, the myths themselves have become too tarnished to be able to win over and retain faith in the political system. Even those who do not accept the scholarly role of examining the darker regions of the subject, now need to examine the foundations of public law.

THE CRISIS IN PUBLIC LAW THOUGHT

The perspective adopted in this book is one which advocates a theoretical approach to the subject. This theoretical approach to public law tries to extend our understanding of the subject by making clear something which, although dimly apprehended, is obscure. It is an exercise in moving from a position of knowing something indistinctly to one in which our knowledge is more explicit and systematic. I have suggested that a theoretical approach must be interpretative, empirical, critical, and historical: interpretative in the sense that knowledge should be related to human purposes and to the meanings we impart to situations; empirical in the sense that such knowledge must be rooted in an appreciation of government and the functions law is expected to perform in respect of those functions; critical in that the range of explanations should be subjected to rational scrutiny; and, finally, that such exercises should be undertaken with a degree of historical sensitivity. I have tried to draw out these various facets of this theoretical approach in the exercise of explicating the two main styles of public law thought. I should now examine more directly the contemporary crisis in public law thought.

The dominant tradition in public law thought is found in the conservative variant of normativism. This is an anti-rationalist tradition rooted in the primacy of practical knowledge. The inheritance of this tradition can be seen all around us. Most obviously, it is to be seen in the common law method with its distaste for system and its adherence to precedent. Within this tradition, law was felt to be a subject quite unsuited to university study; after liberal education at the ancient universities gentlemen were expected to acquire their knowledge of law through apprenticeship. The tradition, however, is also seen clearly expressed in the unwritten British constitution. With us, the constitution 'is not an independently generated beginning from which [government] can spring; it is nothing more than an abstract of somebody's knowledge of how to [govern]; it is the stepchild, not the parent of the activity.'[1] The constitution is based on practical knowledge—practices, understandings, and conventions—concerning the business of ruling. This practical knowledge is rooted in political experience and is passed down within the ruling class from generation to generation.[2] Children born within this class were educated within this tradition from the moment of birth; a process given its clearest institutional expression in the values and traditions of the major public schools.

This tradition of public law denies the distinctiveness of public law; to recognize it would be to undermine the universality of the common law and to accept the special character of the institutions of the state. Historically, this lack of system appeared to possess certain merits. Heterogeneity and the existence of anomalies, for example, tend to ensure the maintenance of options and might therefore enable us to respond effectively as new challenges arise. This tradition could not, however, respond constructively to its two

---

[1] M. Oakeshott, *Rationalism in Politics*, 119 (The words 'government' and 'govern' have been substituted for 'cooking' and 'cook': cf. Chap. 5, pp. 68–9.

[2] Cf. ibid. 30: '[S]o impractical is a *purely* rationalist politics, that a new man, lately risen to power, will often be found throwing away his book and relying upon his general experience of the world as, for example, a business man or a trade union official. This experience is certainly a more trustworthy guide than the book . . . but it is not a knowledge of the political traditions of his society, which, in the most favourable circumstances, takes two or three generations to acquire.'

most basic challenges; viz., the rise of democracy and the growth in government. From rather different perspectives and time-frames we have seen both Maine and Marquand identify the latter half of the nineteenth century as being a critical period for this tradition of conservative normativism. Maine identifies democracy as 'the blackest omen' for the successful survival of the tradition.[3] Maine was, it seems, essentially correct, as Dicey implicitly acknowledged towards the end of his career. Nevertheless, although a new political and governmental system has emerged during this century, we have clung on to conservative normativism at the level of thought. And it is precisely this issue that Marquand was alluding to when, from a contemporary viewpoint, he argued that the survival of this tradition since the late nineteenth century has provided a major obstacle to successful social and economic adjustment.[4]

The tradition of conservative normativism has thus lived on as the dominant tradition in public law thought throughout the twentieth century, even though the political environment has been transformed. We have fastened on to such ideas as sovereignty, the universal rule of ordinary law, and a conception of the rule of law which places the judiciary beyond reproach and have tried to re-order the world through this ideological grid. On occasion, this can be seen starkly, as when, in debates over European Community relations, words like 'federalism' come to be treated with the same sort of disdain which, a century earlier, Dicey reserved for *droit administratif*. But, of course, this dominant tradition has had an impact beyond the world of ideas. One important consequence has been that, since much of the modern political-administrative system could not be accommodated in legal thought, law ceded its control and regulatory functions in respect of this evolving system to other mechanisms.

While we have endured throughout much of this century with this situation, the form of accommodation which was fashioned has become increasingly awkward, particularly as the pace of change has quickened. Conventional understandings concerning the practice of government, which have arisen through administrative and professional networks, have gradually lost their authority. Our quandary has perhaps best been expressed by Oakeshott who

---

[3] See Chap. 7, p. 142.   [4] See Chap. 1, pp. 26–7.

argues that moral ideas are a 'sediment' and that the 'predicament of our time is that the Rationalists have been at work so long on their project of drawing off the liquid in which our moral ideals were suspended (and pouring it away as worthless) that we are left only with the dry and gritty residue which chokes us as we try to take it down.'[5] Another way in which this problem has been expressed within the conservative tradition is to suggest that the 'rate of social and technical change has depreciated the value of the wisdom of our ancestors' and that 'the appeal to the past for guidance in the matter of constitutional change often turns out to be mere romanticism, an appeal to conditions and experiences which have vanished for good'.[6] As conventional restraints have disintegrated, conservatives have turned to law; if we may no longer trust politicians then our faith should be placed in judges. But the problem here is that, as a result of retaining the conception of law embodied in the common law tradition, not only has law been displaced as an expression of the constitutive order of society but that, as the liberal normativists have argued,[7] it lacks the clear normative structure required to establish conditions of justice.

In recent times, the limitations of this informal and unsystematic regime of government have been acutely felt. One reason for this has been that, as a result of the growing influence of European law on our system of government, the attempt at the meshing of legal orders has revealed the drawbacks of our traditional approach. Another is caused by the strains which have arisen as a result of fundamental economic changes which have been taking place.[8] One consequence of such change has been to place government under pressure to reassess its role, and generally to reduce the scale of public sector activity and reorder its priorities. This in turn has led to increasingly systematic review of government programmes, the formalization of public policy objectives and, to maintain this impetus, the strengthening of accountability mechanisms; all of which work against the grain of the dominant tradition.

We have thus reached a critical stage in the development of our system of government. The language of our constitutional discourse

---

[5] *Rationalism in Politics*, 36.

[6] N. Johnson, 'Constitutional Reform: Some Dilemmas for a Conservative Philosophy' in Z. Layton-Henry (ed.), *Conservative Party Politics* (London, 1980), 126 at pp. 128–9.

[7] See Chap. 8, pp. 206–10.   [8] See Chap. 9, pp. 227–8.

is now moribund. The dominant tradition of conservative normativism has failed to meet the requirements of our times and can no
longer be defended at an intellectual level.

For much of this century the challenge to that dominant tradition
has come from work within the functionalist style. As a movement
for reform, the functionalists argued that conservative normativism
was rooted in an earlier era and that, with the emergence of the
positive state, a new style of law was required. Our tradition of
universal customary law was incapable of rising to that challenge;
what was needed was the development of a system of public law.
This required not only a new jurisprudence but also new
institutional structures to deal constructively with the juristic tasks
of modern society. This argument, which is associated most closely
with Robson in relation to his submissions to the Donoughmore
and Franks Committees and Mitchell in challenging ombudsmen
mechanisms, failed to generate support.[9] Not only was the
argument concerning the need for a separate system of public law
decisively rejected but, by ensuring that administrative bodies
emerged in an unsystematic fashion and restricted their role to
grievance-handling in the narrowest sense, the normativists effectively prevented the evolution of a jurisprudence of administrative
law. Functionalism thereafter became a dissenting tradition rooted
in critical analysis.

In recent years, however, the functionalist style, even as an
explanatory and critical approach, seems to have lost much of its
power. This stems mainly from the fact that, as the possibilities for
fundamental reform diminished, the empiricist and legal positivist
aspects of the functionalist style came to predominate. Furthermore,
this empiricist approach went hand-in-hand with a largely uncritical
view of the nature of the British constitution. The reason for this
was that the challenge for many socialists was not to reform the
constitution but to transform society. And for that purpose, the
existing instruments of state power were adequate, particularly

---

[9] See Chap. 7, pp. 178, 179; Chap. 8, pp. 194–5. Mitchell's continued advocacy
is indicated by an entry in Richard Crossman's diary for 3 Dec. 1966: 'Last night I
went to Oxford to a great conference at All Souls'. Richard Wilberforce and Justice
Salmon had about forty lawyers there with some civil servants, including Lady
Sharp, to discuss administrative law. Some professor suggested introducing the
French system of administrative law and fortunately everybody said it was
nonsense', R. H. S. Crossman, *Diaries of a Cabinet Minister*, vol. 2 (London, 1976),
76. The unfortunate professor was, of course, Mitchell. See 1987 *Public Law* 485.

since the constitution incorporated few formal restraints on the
exercise of the majority power of the House of Commons. The
instrumental view of law within this vision of the parliamentary
road to socialism is well illustrated by the thoughts of Sir Stafford
Cripps on the question of whether socialism can be achieved by
constitutional methods. During the 1930s Cripps wrote that:[10]

The first requisite in bringing about a peaceful revolution is to obtain a
Parliamentary majority of adequate size to carry all necessary measures
through the House of Commons . . . Given such a majority, success or
failure will be proved in the first full Parliamentary term. Unless during
the first five years so great a change has been accomplished as to deprive
capitalism of its power, it is unlikely that a Socialist Party will be able to
maintain its position of control without adopting some exceptional means
such as the prolongation of the life of Parliament for a further term without
election. Whether such action would be possible would depend entirely
upon the temper of the country . . .
    From the moment when the Government takes control rapid and
effective action must be possible in every sphere of the national life. . . . The
Government's first step will be to call Parliament together at the earliest
moment and place before it an Emergency Powers Bill to be passed
through all its stages on the first day. This Bill will be wide enough in its
terms to allow all that will be immediately necessary to be done by
ministerial orders. These orders must be incapable of challenge in the
Courts or in any way except in the House of Commons.

    There seems little concern in this approach about using the
sovereign power of the state to its full, or vesting broad discretionary
power in executive bodies, or severely restricting mechanisms of
accountability for executive action to scrutiny through Parliament.
The approach seems to be based on a faith that the House of
Commons, as an expression of democratic will, is able to transform
society. This faith in both the processes and the outcomes of
parliamentary socialism has been severely shaken since the 1930s.
The achievements of the bureaucratic state have been much less,
and the problems of maintaining control and accountability much
greater, than the early thinkers anticipated. The empiricist variant
of the functionalist style, however, provides little that might enable
us fruitfully to examine the problems. The functionalist style, in
becoming wedded to an empiricist view of law and in generally

[10] S. Cripps, 'Can Socialism come by Constitutional Methods?' in C. Addison *et
al.*, *Problems of a Socialist Government* (London, 1933), 35 at pp. 38–9, 42–2.

clinging on to an evolutionary conception of progress, seems unsuited to the task of providing an adequate interpretation of the challenges with which we are faced.

It is precisely because of this crisis in authority of the dominant tradition—and the failure of the dissenting tradition to capture the high ground—that has led to the emergence of the liberal normativist project. In its explicit form this is a movement for constitutional reform, the objective of which is to establish formal institutional checks on the exercise of state power in order to protect individual liberty. There is, however, also an implicit programme within the liberal normativist project. This programme seeks to re-invent our constitutional history by re-interpreting our traditions in a rationalist manner. The tensions within Dicey's thought[11] are thus skewed towards modernism. A modern conception of the rule of law is promoted as best expressing our constitutional tradition and, as a result, a subtle change in the balance in the relationship between the sovereignty of Parliament and the rule of law is effected. This can clearly be seen in the following passage from T. R. S. Allan:[12]

Properly formulated as a constitutional principle, the rule of law operates to govern the interpretation of parliamentary intent: it provides the legitimate vehicle for the application of the statutory wording to the particular circumstances of the case in hand. *Some* such vehicle is demanded by the nature of the legislative process: the intrinsic ambiguity of language and the inherent incompleteness of parliamentary intent alike require *some* background values or preconceptions to be supplied. It seems obvious that those values and preconceptions should reflect, as fairly as possible, those traditional and liberal principles which the judges perceive as fundamental to the legal order.

Conservative normativism views the rule of law as an expression of a tradition of behaviour. Functionalists tend to view it as a guide to political action. With liberal normativism, however, the rule of law has assumed the status of a juridical principle. The watchword of this principle is that of 'integrity'.[13] Integrity, we are told, 'demands fidelity not just to rules but to the theories of fairness and justice which these rules presuppose'.[14]

---

[11] See Chap. 7, pp. 146–53.　　　　[12] 'Legislative supremacy', 139.
[13] See T. R. S. Allan, 'Dicey and Dworkin: the Rule of Law as Integrity'. Jowell and Lester also embrace this idea: see 'Beyond *Wednesbury*', 382.
[14] Allan, 'Dicey and Dworkin', 267.

In the last chapter, I argued that, as a political movement for reform, the ideas of liberal normativism could not be said to have triumphed. While there appeared to be a growing consensus around such documents as Charter 88, this apparent consensus was pitched at such a level of generality that it served simply to mask fundamental differences of outlook. Here, however, we must directly consider the legal theory of liberal normativism. In so doing we should consider the work of Ronald Dworkin, the primary theorist of the liberal normativist style in public law.

Dworkin's theory, which emerged from a proceduralist approach to law which flourished in post-war American jurisprudence,[15] can be understood as an attack on legal positivism. Dworkin argues, contrary to the positivists, that principles and not rules are the fundamental building blocks of a legal order. These principles are not just norms of a higher level of generality than rules. Rather they are higher order items which govern the meaning and application of rules. Even if we accept this basic proposition, Dworkin's argument raises a number of important questions. What is the nature of these principles? From which source do they derive their authority? How do they function to render determinate decisions?

We may best address these questions by considering the positivist account of the role of rules. Rules generally come into existence by enactment. They tend to apply in an all-or-nothing manner; if the situation falls within the jurisdiction of the rule then the rule governs the outcome. Rules, nevertheless, are occasionally indeterminate. Such indeterminacy arises in part because of the indeterminacy inherent in the ordinary use of language. But it is also a product of the fact that we have a limited understanding of all possible future occurrences and consequently the question of whether or not the rule applies to a given situation may be ambiguous. In Hart's words, we live under the twin handicaps of 'our relative ignorance of fact' and 'our relative indeterminacy of aim'.[16]

In arguing that principles and not rules are the basic building blocks of legal order, Dworkin challenges the attempt to construct an autonomous structure of law founded on a hierarchy of rules

[15] See, L. L. Fuller, *The Morality of Law* (New Haven, rev. edn., 1969); H. Hart and A. Sacks, *The Legal Process: Basic Problems in the Making and Application of Law* (Mimeo: Cambridge, Mass., 1958). Although never commercially published, these materials have been highly influential in shaping post-war legal thought in the United States.

[16] H. L. A. Hart, *The Concept of Law*, 125.

whose authority rests on enactment. Dworkin argues, by contrast, that the origin of legal principles lies 'not in a particular decision of some legislature or court, but in a sense of appropriateness developed . . . over time'.[17] He suggests, furthermore, that principles do not apply in an all-or-nothing fashion to situations; in any situation a number of principles may be relevant and the function of the adjudicator will be to assess the weight of these competing principles in that particular context. Essentially, the judge should study the entire legal enterprise to see what rights it contains, what general principles it reflects, and decide in particular disputes which result would produce the best elaboration of those basic principles embedded within the law.

This obviously requires a Herculean effort on the part of the judge. But even if we accept what Dworkin says about the importance of principles in relation to rules, we still need to consider whether there is any possibility of reaching determinate decisions by reference to such principles. That is, since principles are fluid and depend on a 'sense of appropriateness' for their origin and weight, could not any number of normative theories be elaborated to express the nature of the legal enterprise? Indeed, if my views on public law are expressed within the framework of Dworkin's theory, then this is precisely what I have been arguing, since the styles of public law thought express different theories of law. But Dworkin does not accept this view. He presents a 'rights thesis' which holds that, in every legal dispute coming before the courts, there is a right answer to the issue. How might this be so? The key to Dworkin's position lies in the recognition that the truth of his rights thesis is dependent on the truth of a political theory as providing the key to understanding our legal and political institutions and traditions. Dworkin himself recognizes this and argues for the truth of a particular version of liberalism based on a conception of equal concern and respect for all people.[18]

I have sketched Dworkin's views because they elaborate the foundations on which the liberal normativist project is constructed. When thus revealed, we can identify one obvious weakness. Dworkin argues that the truth of the rights thesis depends on a particular version of liberalism as providing the best interpretation of our constitutional tradition. What is clear, however, is that, from

---

[17] R. Dworkin, *Taking Rights Seriously* (Cambridge, Mass., 1977), 40.
[18] Dworkin, *A Matter of Principle* (Cambridge, Mass., 1985), chap. 8.

my perspective, the theory fails on grounds of historical fact. Our dominant tradition has not been one of liberal normativism but of conservative normativism; it has been argued in this book that it is the anti-rationalist structure of conservative thought which makes sense of our constitutional arrangements and traditions. But can we argue, nevertheless, that today we should embrace liberal normativism as the best elaboration of contemporary political values?

In addressing this question we need to evaluate the interpretative, empirical, and critical power of liberal normativism. This requires us to examine further the theory of interpretation which Dworkin employs in making this claim and also to re-examine our maps of the landscape. We begin with the empirical dimension.

MAPPING THE LANDSCAPE

The dominant styles of public law thought are, as we have seen, rooted in the political ideologies which the nineteenth century bequeathed to the twentieth. It may not therefore be surprising to discover that the visions of law, society, and government which are expressed in these styles are also rooted in this period. With industrialization and urbanization, the authority of the old order was rapidly eroded and functional interdependencies began to replace the traditional forms of social cohesion. The normativist and functionalist styles in public law can be understood to reflect basic stances which were adopted in relation to the social and economic changes which were taking place.

The functionalist style is fashioned to respond positively to these changes, and generally views these developments as being inspired by the application of a scientific approach to public affairs. This style reflects the view that the state, through the use of law, has the key role in regulating these growing interdependencies. The normativist style, however, is rooted in the largely pre-urban and pre-industrial values of a past high culture of law which was based on a vision of limited government. The functionalist style looks positively to the future and to the creative power of legislation while the normativist style, expressing uneasiness about the cultural implications of democracy, looks to the past and to the common law tradition. The normativist style invokes a conception of law which is founded on customary legal values and which assumes an intrinsic link between legality and morality. The functionalist tends to equate law with the outcome of a contest of social interests; metaphysics and mystery are replaced by functional necessities.

In their ideal typical forms, we might argue that neither style is adequately grounded. We should not embrace the romantic yearnings of conservative normativists for some ancient, immutable order. But neither can we equate moral progress with the growth in the size of the public sector. We should not look at a constitution either as a straightforward guarantor of justice or as a mere instrument of sovereign will. If we are to advance our understanding of public law, we must learn from the limitations imposed by these styles. We can not maintain the 'ought' of the Diceyan era in the face of the realities of modern government. But neither can we eliminate the 'ought' from our understanding of law and deal only with the 'is'. The tension between 'is' and 'ought' is an inescapable part of our condition. In normativism the 'ought' is over-theorized and not integrated with practice and functionalism, although rooted in practice, is not adequately theorized. We should look to practice to correct theory. And we should turn to theory to inform practice. We need to think more creatively about this tension than we have done until now.

In mapping the territory of public law, our theories must be rooted in the practices of government and, in particular, should be sensitive to the impact which social and economic changes have wrought on our systems of government and law. We might also maintain an open mind about the overall effects of modernization on society; history should be detached from purpose.

When we turn to the subject, what do we find? The answer, it would appear, is that we unearth vast heaps of arcane rules which are extremely technical and specialized, are highly context-specific, and tend to be constructed in a manner that requires a detailed understanding of the environment before one can begin to understand the meaning of the rules. The empirical world of public law is best symbolized, not by some slim constitutive document, but rather by the loose-leaf encyclopedias on such subjects as housing, planning, social welfare, health and safety, and the regulation of competition. These are weighty, dense, rapidly changing compendia of the rules, orders, and guidance relating to particular social fields. This, in fact, is our experience of modern law in general.

This feature of law was evident even during the formative period of debate between normativism and functionalism. During the 1920s, for example, C. T. Carr pointed out that the mass of delegated legislation then being produced was of the order of five times greater than primary legislation. In his words, 'the child now dwarfs the parent'.[19] Even in the 1880s Maitland was able to show that if you 'pick up a modern volume of the reports of the Queen's Bench division, you will find that about half the cases reported have to do with the rules of administrative law'.[20] Since those times, the rapid growth of the mass of the material of public law has continued to the present day.[21]

During this century we have witnessed an explosion of positive law. We are now 'choking on statutes'.[22] While we recognize this at an empirical level, however, we have not adequately addressed the question at a theoretical level. A century ago Maitland indicated the problem. He suggested that, if administrative law is neglected, 'you will frame a false and antiquated notion of our constitution'. But, in the process of so doing, he continued, you will also form a distorted conception of law.[23] Today, it would appear, public law is a hopelessly fragmented subject with little in terms of an authoritative structure.

The contemporary challenge is to develop a perspective through which the empirical reality of modern public law is adequately reflected in our attempts to theorize law. We have already examined the limitations of conservative normativism and empiricist functionalism. What of liberal normativism?

[19] C. T. Carr, *Delegated Legislation. Three Lectures* (Cambridge, 1921), 2.

[20] F. W. Maitland, *The Constitutional History of England* (Cambridge, 1908), 505.

[21] In recent decades there have been on average around 2,000 statutory instruments promulgated each year, filling between 6,000–8,000 pages of text, and this does not include the growing volume of European secondary legislation. This is about twice the volume of statutory instruments promulgated at the turn of the century. In addition, the Royal Commission on Legal Services estimated that 'the total number of cases heard by tribunals in 1978 was six times the number of contested civil cases that were disposed of at trial before the High Court and county courts'. *Report of the Royal Commission on Legal Services* (1980) Cmnd. 7448 para. 15.1. See W. H. Greenleaf, *The British Political Tradition, Vol. III, Pt. II. A Much Governed Nation* (London, 1987), 557–8, 599–600; M. Galanter, 'Law Abounding: Legalisation Around the North Atlantic' (1992) 55 *M.L.R.* 1.

[22] See G. Gilmore, *The Ages of American Law* (New Haven, 1977), 95; G. Calabresi, *A Common Law for the Age of Statutes* (Cambridge, Mass., 1982), chap. 1; H. Friendly, 'The Gap in Law-Making—Judges Who Can't and Legislators Who Won't' (1963) 63 *Colum. L. Rev.* 787.

[23] Maitland, *The Constitutional History of England*, at p. 505.

My argument here is that liberal normativism fails to provide us with an adequate theory of public law. It fails on both empirical and interpretative grounds. These two dimensions of failure are linked but I shall reserve until later my specific criticisms of liberal normativism as an interpretative theory. As a 'map' of the landscape, however, liberal normativism provides us with a highly distorted guide. The reason for this is that liberal normativism draws the main contours of its map before having ever surveyed the ground. Thus, its conception of the individual, the state and the law are put in place prior to the survey. Liberal normativism is built on a model of the rational subject and value-laden conceptions of law and government. This normativist approach, which can be clearly seen in the dualisms of normativism,[24] fails to confront directly the empirical reality of law. The dualisms of normativism are constructed a priori so as to identify the positive state as a degenerate form of government and modern regulatory law as a debased form of law. The fact that a fundamental transformation in social scale has occurred this century and that this might, for example, have produced a different kind of political community—one in which we might need to recast the relationship between the individual and the state—is not squarely faced.

REVITALIZING THE FUNCTIONALIST STYLE

We have come to the conclusion that the main contemporary styles of public law thought all fail to provide an adequate explanation of our experience of the modern phenomenon of law. One dimension in which these contemporary styles all fail is in providing an account of the relationship between law and society which matches our experience. The conceptualism of the normativist style distorts any attempt to examine the social significance of law while the instrumental or behavioural orientation of the functionalist style fails adequately to account for our understanding of the normative character of law.

We therefore need to develop a style of public law thought which is able to reflect more adequately the relationships between law and society. This style must recognize the normativity of law; that is, the fact of the ought. But it must also be able to assimilate the idea

---

[24] See Chap. 5, Fig. 1, p. 103.

of the positivity of law. Law is a human creation which seeks to perform certain social functions. As a human creation it must clearly be recognized that law is capable of being altered, and that the primary means of doing so is through the process of legislation. Any conception of law must therefore be capable of adequately accommodating legislation as a constituent element of law.

Reflection on such matters takes us back to a concern which was addressed at the start of this book, when we examined the attempt in the eighteenth century to develop a 'science of legislation'. That exercise, which was directed to the discovery of principles of practical guidance in the business of government, may not have succeeded. But there are important lessons which can be learned from that endeavour. The project taught us that any attempt to seek an understanding of law could not be restricted to the search for a classification of constitutional forms. And I think it was also on sound ground in assuming that the answer was not to be found in ideal models. These lessons count against normativist approaches to public law. The retreat during the nineteenth century to an attempt to construct a science of law based on a formal, analytical method, and one which marginalizes the importance of legislation, has had a critical influence on the development of public law thought during this century. Today it constitutes a major barrier to the understanding of public law. While the normativist style has been reinvigorated in recent years through a rationalistic reinterpretation, its appeal to an ideal model founded on the autonomy of law also poses major difficulties.

In seeking a style appropriate for our times we should turn to the functionalist approach. The functionalist style in public law more readily accords with contemporary experience of law. It also more closely connects with our legal traditions.[25] The functionalists are

[25] My argument here is that the functionalist style is more in accordance with our traditions than is the liberal variant of normativism. We may, for example, discern closer connections between the work of Oakeshott and pragmatism than between Oakeshott and liberalism. This is particularly so if we deemphasize the Kantian elements in Oakeshott's work. It is, for example, unclear how Oakeshott comes to identify morality with a non-purposive or non-instrumental practice or, more specifically, how he comes to incorporate an intrinsic moral quality (*jus*) into the concept of law (*lex*) (see Chap. 5, pp. 73–4). This seems to follow simply from his acceptance of Kant's distinction between moral and prudential conduct. The overall thrust of Oakeshott's work, however, is undoubtedly Hegelian.
The attempt to understand Oakeshott in the tradition of pragmatism has been made by Richard Rorty. See R. Rorty, *Philosophy and the Mirror of Nature*

undoubtedly correct in arguing that many of our problems stem from the fact that public law thought in Britain is still rooted in a world which no longer exists. And there is a great deal in the functionalist style which retains its relevance and vitality today. The main problem with the functionalist style is that in recent years it has become wedded to an empiricist outlook, to legal positivism, and to an instrumentalist view of law. This approach has its value as critique. But it does not provide much assistance with the task of reconstruction. One further important lesson of the Enlightenment project was that a theory of government and law had to be rooted in a theory of society. The theory provided by the sociological positivism that tends to underpin functionalism is not up to the task.[26]

In attempting to revitalize the functionalist style the central issue to address must be the question of law.[27] We might begin by rejecting the techniques and assumptions of legal positivism, since there is little hope of understanding law if we seek to sever text from context and assume that the force of law lies in enactment. Secondly, the normativity of law should be openly recognized. This means that the instrumentalist conception of law, which has been a prominent feature of much recent writing in the functionalist style, should be rejected. Although law should be viewed as normative, the nature of the normativity of law is itself problematic. Once the positivity (or revisability) of law is generally accepted then law cannot seek its validity in higher norms of divine origin. That is, law cannot be separated out of society. But if law is viewed as providing a normative foundation of society then we cannot simply say that law is determined by society.

These difficulties have been glimpsed within the tradition of functionalist thought in public law. The point is recognized most clearly in Laski's sophisticated conception of law in which law is

---

(Princeton, 1979), 389–94 and id., 'Postmodernist Bourgeois Liberalism' (1983) 80 *J. of Philosophy* 383. In the latter Rorty divides contemporary political theorists into three camps: Kantians (e.g. Rawls and Dworkin); Hegelians (e.g. MacIntyre); and Hegelians who wish to preserve liberal institutions but not on a Kantian basis. Into this last group Rorty places himself, along with Dewey and Oakeshott. For a critical evaluation see P. Franco, *The Political Philosophy of Michael Oakeshott* (New Haven, 1990), 16, 65–6, 232–3.

[26] See Chap. 6, pp. 112–13.

[27] See Chap. 9, pp. 214–9, where the lack of a legal theory was identified as a weakness in the functionalist style.

based not in command but experience and 'emerges as the evaluation of the interests by the interweaving of interests'.[28] What this really means, however, as Laski readily concedes, is scarcely transparent. What is needed is some way of addressing these difficulties more systematically. Can we develop a legal theory to underpin a revitalized functionalist style in public law?

PUBLIC LAW AND LEGAL THEORY

Contemporary jurisprudence takes as one of its central tasks that of trying to clarify the question of what law is. This orientation may, however, lead us to misunderstand the role of jurisprudence. It may, for example, cause some to believe that jurisprudence must orientate itself away from the contingent in favour of the necessary; that it should shun the particular in favour of the universal. However, any attempt to search for the essence of law is, I believe, mistaken. When we examine legal theories, our objective should not be to accept or reject a particular theory as an expression of a universal truth. Instead, we should ask ourselves what vision of law the theory is seeking to clarify. That is, to engage in legal theory is to become immersed in an attempt to theorize about a specific and contingent set of practices. Legal theorists should be understood as seeking to express particular styles *within* legal thought.

From this perspective, legal theory helps us to render explicit the styles of public law thought. For example, we might read John Austin's non-normative account of law alongside an American realist view of the judicial process as providing a theoretical elaboration of the empiricist variant of the functionalist style.[29] And in seeking a theoretical underpinning for the dominant tradition of conservative normativism we might turn to H. L. A. Hart's normative theory of legal positivism.[30] Hart's theory seeks to provide a foundation for the authority of law by establishing its autonomy as a distinct subject, separate from politics or morality. His idea of the rule of recognition, that basic rule which provides a criterion of identity of the legal system, can be interpreted as providing a structure which is compatible both with the idea of

---

[28] See Chap. 7, pp. 170–1.
[29] On Austin see Chap. 1, pp. 20–1; on American realism see Chap. 6, pp. 129–33; on empiricist variant of functionalism see Chap. 8, pp. 197–201.
[30] H. L. A. Hart, *The Concept of Law.* See Chap. 5, pp. 78–80.

legal sovereignty and the recognition of the courts' role as purveyors of the artificial reason of the common law.[31]

As we have seen, Dworkin can be understood as providing a legal theory of the liberal normativist style. I have already argued that the liberal variant of normativism provides neither the best interpretation of our tradition of public law (which is rooted in conservative normativism); nor does it adequately reflect the contemporary reality of law. But Dworkin's exercise is nevertheless illuminating. He does, for example, provide us with an explicit interpretative theory and, by undertaking an evaluation of his theory of interpretation, we might more clearly identify the road of progress. There are two critical aspects of this theory on which attention should be focused: his treatment of hermeneutics; and his view of law as a social phenomenon. I shall argue that, through an appreciation of the deficiencies of Dworkin's theory in relation to these two issues, we can identify both a theory and a programme for a revitalized functionalist style.

The important point to note about Dworkin's theory of interpretation of legal practices is that he seeks to go further than providing a range of competing interpretations and aspires to establish liberalism as providing the *best* interpretation of legal practice. How can these rival interpretations be ranked? Dworkin's answer is to argue for that interpretation which reveals the practice in its best light. But does this not simply beg the question? As Dworkin accepts, we cannot determine the 'best' interpretation without making assumptions about human identity and the character of modern society. Liberal theories, like others, are constructed on certain understandings about these matters. But, as we have also seen, those views of human nature and the human condition have been subjected to telling criticism.[32] These issues remain the subject of controversy.

On interpretative theory in general Dworkin is altogether too flirtatious. He recognizes that different theories or traditions of interpretation are rooted in different theories of politics. But he also recognizes that 'a theory of [politics] may depend on a theory of interpretation as much as vice versa'.[33] Dworkin thus recognizes

---

[31] Ibid., chaps. VI, VII.
[32] See Chap. 5, pp. 94–6, 99–101.
[33] R. Dworkin, *A Matter of Principle* (Cambridge, Mass., 1985), 153.

that these two kinds of theories are mutually reinforcing and contends that:[34]

My point is exactly that the connection is reciprocal, so that anyone called upon to defend a particular approach to interpretation would be forced to rely on more general aspects of a theory of [politics], whether he realises it or not. And this may be true even though the opposite is, to some extent, true as well.

Here, it seems, Dworkin has put his finger on the major issue. If the two theories are in a relationship of complete reciprocal dependence this will inevitably lead to a vicious circularity. This point is recognized by Dworkin's critics who argue that he seeks to extricate himself from this circularity essentially by seeking to suppress the issue he began by squarely identifying.[35] Thus, while we should adopt an interpretative approach, we must also openly embrace circularity and reflexivity. This can provide the starting point for a legal theory of the functionalist style.

Before addressing the issue of that legal theory, however, we might first turn to Dworkin's appreciation of law as a social phenomenon. In Chapter 3 I argued that, in adopting an interpretative approach, we should reject a method which incorporates a predisposition to favour a professionally prescribed view of the subject. In *Law's Empire* Dworkin apparently confronts this argument directly. He points out that '[s]ome critics will be anxious to say at this point that our project is not only partial . . . but wrong, that we will misunderstand legal process if we pay special attention to lawyers' doctrinal arguments about what the law is'.[36] But then he continues:[37]

They [the critics] say these arguments obscure . . . the important social function of law as ideological force and witness. A proper understanding of law as a social phenomenon demands, these critics say, a more scientific or sociological or historical approach that pays no or little attention to jurisprudential puzzles over the correct characterization of legal argument. We should pursue, they think, very different questions like these: How far, and in what way, are judges influenced by class consciousness or economic circumstance? Did the judicial decisions of nineteenth century America

---

[34] R. Dworkin, *A Matter of Principle* (Cambridge, Mass., 1985), 154.
[35] N. Simmonds, 'Imperial visions and mundane practices' 1987 *Camb L.J.* 465, p. 476 (n. 21).
[36] Dworkin, *Law's Empire* (London, 1986), 12.   [37] Ibid. 12–13.

play an important part in forming the distinctive American version of capitalism? Or were those decisions only mirrors reflecting change and conflict, but neither promoting the one nor resolving it?

Dworkin's response to the views presented in Chapter 3 is to suggest that the complexity, function, and consequence of law as a social phenomenon depends on a special feature of its structure. He argues that, unlike many other social phenomena, legal practice consists in arguing about propositions of law. Further, he suggests that this argumentative aspect of legal practice can be examined from either an internal or external point of view. The internal aspect is concerned with the soundness of arguments which are presented within the practice whereas the external point of view, that of the sociologist or historian, considers such questions as why certain patterns of legal argument develop in certain periods rather than others. Dworkin considers that both aspects are essential. We need a social theory of law, but it must be jurisprudential because, for example, 'the historian cannot understand law as an argument-ative social practice, even enough to reject it as deceptive, until he has a participant's understanding, until he has his own sense of what counts as a good or bad argument within that practice'.[38]

This seems to be a powerful argument. The main problem with it is that, despite taking an interpretative approach to legal practices Dworkin, rather surprisingly, refuses to take an interpretative approach to social practices. Further, in employing a distinction between the internal and external point of view, he effectively adopts a positivist approach to history and sociology; hermeneutics is, after all, based on the idea that the study of social life involves the study of meanings and interpretations and not the study of causes. No explanation is provided for this adoption of a causal approach in matters of history or sociology but an interpretative approach in relation to law. It is difficult to see how it might be justified since the manner in which social context is shaped must exert a profound influence on the meanings which we attach to the idea of law. Dworkin's attempt to develop an interpretative approach distinct from social context thus seems best understood as an attempt a priori to inject a specific—normativist—conception of law into his theory. Dworkin's theory should be seen as a legal theory of liberal normativism.

[38] Ibid. 14.

In conclusion, it is suggested that an interpretative attitude is one which takes an interpretative approach not simply to law but also to matters of history and politics. Such an approach is rooted in the belief, which we may identify in post-empiricist political theory, that social science is not an experimental science in search of a law, but an interpretative one in search of meaning. Certainly, this approach opens up the field to a wide range of meanings and increases the complexity and contingency of our interpretations. It also suggests that reflexivity must be an element in our understanding of law. But if we really wish to advance our understanding of public law then these relationships must be openly explored.

The Widening Gyre

In developing a legal theory of the revitalized functionalist style I have suggested that we need to address the question of circularity and reciprocal dependence in the interpretation of legal practice. In order to assist us we might turn to the work of Niklas Luhmann. Luhmann is a German social theorist who, since the 1960s, has been developing a distinctive theory of social systems. As part of this exercise he has produced a sociological theory of law which, perhaps because of his initial training as a lawyer, is illuminating.[39] His starting point is that of the complexity and contingency of the contemporary world. The complexity of the world requires us to choose; to make decisions between options. The contingent nature of these decisions means that certain expectations will be disappointed. It also means that we are required to take risks. From the perspective of Luhmann's theory, society should be understood as a social system which tries to maintain some degree of constancy in this over-complex and contingent environment.

The complexity of society, like any system, is regulated by its structure; that is, by the pre-selection of possible environmental conditions which the system can accommodate. Structural questions therefore provide the key to system-environment relations. There are in society a range of structural mechanisms in operation, including cognitive structures (knowledge) and media of communication (truth, power, money). From our point of view, however, law is of particular significance; law can be viewed as a structure

[39] N. Luhmann, *A Sociological Theory of Law* (London, 1985).

which defines the boundaries and selection types of the societal system.

In order to understand the idea of law Luhmann suggests that we must reflect on the way in which human behaviour, social institutions, and the mind conjoin to form law. First, there is the *temporal* dimension. Human beings, through action and experience, generate expectations about the world. These expectations are structural since only a small proportion of the possible is probable (i.e. expectable). In considering the idea of expectation we should distinguish between cognitive and normative expectation. Expectations are cognitive when, in the case of disappointment, that expectation is adjusted to reality; learning then takes place. In the case of normative expectations the opposite applies; one does not adjust expectations when someone acts contrary to them. If, on walking along the street, I habitually bump into lamp-posts, as a result of an expectation that they will move out of my way, I am soon likely to learn and adjust my expectations of the behaviour of lamp-posts. If, on the other hand, I expect officials to treat citizens with equal respect regardless of the colour of their skin, I am unlikely to adjust my expectation even if I regularly encounter officials who act contrary to it. Secondly, there is the *social* dimension. Certain expectations are institutionalized. With institutionalization of behavioural expectation a degree of consensus is enforced. Thirdly, and finally, there is the *material* dimension. Since we do not have direct access to the consciousness of others we achieve an inter-subjective synthesis of a variety of experiences through the medium of meaning.

For Luhmann, law is to be viewed as a congruence of aspects from each of the three dimensions. Whenever that congruence exists law exists. Law may therefore be defined as congruent generalization of behavioural normative expectation. The more complete the congruence among these three dimensions, the greater the inclusiveness and complexity of law. We may think of law as the institutionalization of behavioural expectations through the medium of meaning.

From this perspective, we can begin to appreciate the character of modern law. In simple societies, for example, a synthesis between action and experience can be achieved in the acceptance of a natural world order. Greater evolution from this simple state is possible only by shifting the level of congruency formation. With

252 *Public Law in the Face of the Future*

this evolutionary impetus (which arises largely because of the surplus production of possibilities), the dependency of law on concretely fixed meanings decreases, the differentiation between cognitive and normative expectations increases, and law segregates itself from daily life. Law is no longer secreted in events but instead in the norm that serves as the basis for legal evaluation of events. Law therefore becomes more abstract and meaning is less rooted in a precise context. There is, consequentially, a greater dependency on particular machinery for the selection of valid law.

Modern law, then, is a more complex and contingent form of law. It is characterized primarily by the positivity of law and by the consciousness of law's contingency. Law is seen not only to be made by decision (that is, selected) but is also valid by decision (that is, contingent and alterable). This recognition of law's positivity results in a significant increase in its complexity. As a result of a temporal differentiation of law (in which law is valid today but not necessarily tomorrow), law has to be institutionalized as being alterable over time. But this institutionalization has to be effected without impairing law's normative function.

The positivity of law is a recognition of the statutory nature of law. Law becomes an instrument of the planned change of reality. But this view must be distinguished from that of legal positivism. Legislative decision-making cannot be treated as the explanatory origin of the meaning of norms; there are always further origins. Law does not originate in the will of the legislator. The function of legislation is simply that of the selection from, and giving symbolic dignity to, certain norms as binding law. Legal positivism thus does not provide an answer to the question of law. But, as we have seen, with the emergence of positive law, law can no longer be anchored in a belief in a true worldly order with a fixed moral base. Here, then, we have the central problem of a general theory of law: wherein, precisely, does the identity of law lie?

For Luhmann the answer is that law can no longer be conceived of in ontological terms but can only be considered functionally. Modern law has become a mechanism for guiding and distributing opportunities and for resolving dysfunctional problems which occur as a result of the rapid increase in functional systems differentiation. This conception of modern law raises certain difficulties. Since justice as an ethical principle is now placed outside law, the question of the legitimacy of law is raised. Further, once the positivity of law is accepted, we are unable to appeal to any residual moral values which constitute a natural legal minimum of norms in order to justify the legal order. Luhmann in fact suggests that we can no longer treat law morally but must view it sociologically.

When we view law in this light the key question becomes: how does law stabilize itself? In order to address this question we might reflect on the character of modern law. In modern times, as law has attempted to stabilize society at the requisite level of complexity, law has become increasingly abstract. Abstraction enables law to provide for a greater range of possibilities at the level of expectations. Expectations can be linked to various levels of abstraction; persons, roles, programmes, and values may, for example, be taken to represent increasing levels of generalization. If law must be raised to a higher level of indifference, we would expect norms to be orientated at higher levels: away from persons towards roles; or away from role-determined norms to programmatic norms and value-orientated (e.g. ideological) norms. With the increasing complexity of society, there has in general been a shift to higher levels of generalization. Law is not typically rooted at the level of persons. Much of the common law and our criminal law is based on roles and this is reflected through conditional (if/then) programmes. But during this century, we have seen the emergence on a large scale of purposive programmes; programmes which focus on the objective of furthering the general welfare.

This development has a number of consequences. First, increased generalization of law leads to an increased differentiation of law and morality. Law is not rooted in morality. This results in what may be called a moral trivialization of law. Secondly, law cannot be taken to rest on history. Positive law faces the future, not the past. The past thus loses its authority. While the authority of the common law depends on how old it is and how far back it stretches, that of legislation rests on how recently it has been enacted. Positive law is no longer valid through unalterability. Rather its validity is now based on its function. And this validity is interpreted in the light of the future. Thirdly, modern law also loses its socializing, educational, and edifying functions. That is, law traditionally had a cultural role in society which now is no longer rooted in the reality of law. Modern law is not suitable for committing to memory or for cultural enlightenment. Indeed, modern law is so complex that no individual can any longer know it; it is not even rational for any individual to attempt the task. Modern law is suitable only for the purpose of reference in the search for solutions to specific problems. Luhmann thus argues that 'the stability and validity of the law no longer rests upon a higher and more stable order, but instead upon a principle of variation: it is the very alterability of law that is the foundation for its stability and its validity'.[40] At a theoretical level the problem is that 'contemporary legal thought in its emotional anchorages and dogmaticity of its rationality still lives to a great extent in the perspective of ideas provided by past high cultures. Transitions to positivisms which already taken off at the practical, political and procedural levels is still on the agenda at an intellectual level.'[41]

These developments have, however, placed major burdens on the legal system. As Luhmann says 'the clamping of the legal system with an ever more complex society could be maintained, because the clamping of law was not carried through'.[42] That is, contrary to most juridical claims (such as Dworkin's) there is a very low inter-dependence of positive law. From a sociological perspective this poses a problem primarily because this lack of inter-dependence affects law's regenerative capacity. In the early 1970s Luhmann argued that neither jurists nor sociologists had yet developed an adequate concept of positive law and he suggested that we are only at the stage of moralizing the inadequacy of attempts to date. What was needed, he argued, were *legal* norms of norm-making. In adopting this formulation what Luhmann was recognizing was the self-referential nature of modern law. He suggested that this reflexive idea of meaning, which had already been developed in the sociological theory of social systems, could be applied to law. A good example of what he seems to have had in mind can be seen through the work of Lon Fuller. In *The Morality of Law* Fuller argued that certain procedural purposes must be honoured before a legal system could be said to be in operation. He argued that legal norms must fulfill eight desiderata. They must be: general, publicly promulgated, sufficiently prospective, intelligible, free of contradiction, sufficiently constant, congruently administered, and must not require the impossible.[43] Fuller called these moral precepts. But if

---

[40] Luhmann, *The Differentiation of Society* (New York, 1982), 94.
[41] *A Sociological Theory of Law*, p. 269.   [42] Ibid. 255.
[43] Fuller, *The Morality of Law* (New Haven, rev. edn., 1969), chap. II.

we were to reinterpret these as functional precepts within Luhmann's framework, then we might get closer to the idea of legal reflexivity.

By the 1980s, however, when Luhmann wrote new conclusions to a revised edition of *A Sociological Theory of Law*, he had developed his ideas on reflexivity more fully in relation to the theory of autopoiesis. Autopoiesis (derived from Greek and meaning 'self-reproducing') is a theory of self-referential systems which has developed from biology, through cybernetics and social systems, and is applied by Luhmann to law. Its utility for Luhmann lies in the fact that it enables him to produce a sociological theory of the unity of the legal system. The legal theory of autopoiesis posits the legal system as normatively closed but cognitively open.[44] Normative closure means that the system produces and delimits the operational unity of its elements (i.e. legally relevant decisions and events) through the operation of its elements. It is in this sense that we may talk of the unity of the system.

Some have seen legal autopoiesis as a new formalism. Although there are aspects of Luhmann's work on autopoiesis which might be construed in this light—and it should be said that Luhmann is less than lucid on this point—it is important not to misconstrue what is being claimed. We must appreciate that the claims to law's autonomy can be understood only in the context of the normative/ cognitive (or system/environment) relationship. The legal system is a cognitively open system; it remains orientated to its environment not simply despite its closedness, but rather because of its closedness. Closure does not mean the absence of an environment; nor does it mean complete determination by itself (in the old sense of legal formality). A system can reproduce itself only in an environment. If it were not continually irritated, stimulated, disturbed, and faced with changes in the environment (i.e. learning), it would soon terminate its own operations and lose its autopoietic character. Rather, the point is that, although the system is compelled to select aspects of its environment, legal facts are not imported from the outside in a straightforward causal sense but are *constructed* within the law by the operations of the legal system. We may say that every operation in law, all juristic processing of

---

[44] This type of formulation is well known in systems theory. It is traceable to W. R. Ashby's famous definition of a cybernetic system as one 'open to energy but closed to information and control'. Also physicists talk of the universe as being thermodynamically open but mechanically closed.

information, uses normative and cognitive orientations simultaneously. There is an intrinsic link; but differentiation occurs because these orientations serve different functions. The cognitive quality demonstrates the system's openness to its environment. The normative quality emphasizes the unity of law as a recursive system. The system can in this way discriminate according to its function without exposing its normative reproduction to the environment; it can transfer normative validity from element to element only by its own action.

Luhmann's work provides us with an interesting theory of law and legal development and it could perhaps be of assistance in developing a legal theory of a revitalized functionalist style. His is, for example, an interpretative theory of law which is firmly anchored in our contemporary experience of law. From Luhmann's perspective, normativist legal theories are simply rooted in the past. Conservative normativism clings to the values and traditions of the common law in a world now based on the positivity of law. The limitations of liberal normativist theories are also exposed. Like Luhmann, Hayek bases his theory of law in evolution and with an eye on law's regenerative capacity. But, unlike Luhmann, he builds into his theory a specific ideological view of law rooted in common law development. Hayek thus rejects the basic claims which Luhmann makes about the positivity of modern law. Finally, Dworkin's theory does not seem to take on board the fact that there is a very low inter-dependence of positive law; his is a theory still rooted in a past high culture of law. Furthermore, unlike Dworkin, Luhmann's legal theory of autopoiesis directly challenges the taboo of circularity in legal thinking. For Luhmann, circularity is not a flaw which ought to be avoided; law in fact consists of a multitude of circular processes associated with normative closure.[45]

In addition to these critical insights, Luhmann's theory may be of positive assistance in the development of a legal theory of the functionalist style. Like functionalism in public law, his theory openly confronts the positivity of modern law and recognizes that modern law can only be looked at functionally. The advantage of his theory is that it overcomes the tendency of the functionalist style

---

[45] Luhmann 'The Third Question: The Creative Use of Paradoxes in Law and Legal History' (1988) 15 *J. of Law & Soc.* 153; G. Teubner ' "And God Laughed . . ." ' Indeterminacy, Self-Reference and Paradox in Law', in C. Joerges and D. M. Trubek (eds.), *Critical Legal Thought: An American–German Debate* (Baden-Baden, 1989).

to become dominated by an empiricist, legal positivist orientation. Instead, Luhmann provides us with an interpretative theory rooted in experience. His approach helps us to overcome the limitations of viewing the law-society relationship in terms of some mechanistic conveyor belt for transforming social and economic interests into legal decisions and actions. The turn to self-referential systems shifts the focus from control to autonomy. In conditions of complexity, the issue is no longer simply that of knowing how to control systems but rather that of understanding how the legal system can manage its own reproduction within an environment which is not in itself attuned to the precepts of the system.

FACING THE FUTURE

Writing around the turn of the century Maitland suggested that:[46]

For the presentation . . . of unfamiliar truth we have need of all the metaphors that we can command, and any source of new and apt metaphors is a source of new knowledge. I am . . . very far from denying that every advance of biological science . . . will supply the historian and the political theorist with new thoughts, and with new phrases which will make old thoughts truer. I can conceive that a century hence political events will be currently described in a language which I could not understand, so full will it be of terms from biology or, for this also is possible, from some science of which no one has yet laid the first stone.

Does legal autopoiesis fulfil Maitland's predictions? Despite the insights provided by Luhmann's work we should, for a number of reasons, proceed with caution. First, it has often been recognized that systems theory has a tendency to produce sophisticated conceptual frameworks which are disproportionate to their operational utility.[47] Secondly, the relationship between Luhmann's early functionalist work and his later autopoietic turn has not convincingly been addressed. Thirdly, while there has been some attempt to develop further the implications of Luhmann's work for our

---

[46] Maitland, 'The Body Politic' in H. A. L. Fisher (ed.), *The Collected Papers of Frederic William Maitland* (Cambridge, 1911), vol. III, 285 at p. 289.

[47] See T. McCarthy, 'Complexity and Democracy, or The Seducements of Systems Theory' (1985) 35 *New German Critique* 27.

understanding of law, this work has remained at the level of theory.[48]

The critical issue, it would appear, is to ensure that we keep the role of theory in perspective. In terms of the metaphor of the map which has been adopted in this book, the value of the map (or theory) is revealed by how well you get around using it. Theories are not to be evaluated in terms of their innate sophistication. The mark of a good theory is not so much that it produces solutions to perplexing questions but rather whether it provides a fruitful programme for further work. In adopting a general perspective conditioned by systems theory, can we identify such a programme?

One strength of the general approach advocated by theorists such as Luhmann is that it requires us to confront the contemporary realities of public law and, in rejecting legal positivism, to address the question of how law responds to the challenge of providing a normative framework capable of structuring and conditioning the performance of the political-administrative system. This has been the critical question facing public law this century. The transformation in the scale of government over the last one hundred years has had a major impact on our legal systems. The movement of law with the emergence of the welfare-regulatory state has been characterized in a number of ways: we may speak of a general movement from prevention to promotion; of constitutive to regulative rules; of formal to substantive legal rationality; of conditional programmes to purposive programmes; or, more generally, of the socialization of law. However it is precisely characterized, the general issue which looms is that of the impact which the instrumentalization of law for regulatory purposes has had on the normative structure of law.[49]

These questions have recently been the subject of debate, both in continental Europe and in the United States.[50] Such discussions

---

[48] Luhmann's legal theory of autopoiesis has recently been developed in a programme organized by Gunther Teubner. See G. Teubner (ed.), *Autopoietic Law: A New Approach to Law and Society* (Berlin, 1988); A. Febbrajo and G. Teubner (eds.), *State, Law, Economy as Autopoietic Systems: Regulation and Autonomy in a New Perspective* (Milan, forthcoming). Those with French may also consult, M. van der Kerchove and F. Ost, *Le système juridique entre ordre et désordre* (Paris, 1988): see N. Duxbury (1990) 53 *M.L.R.* 836.

[49] For an informative discussion see Teubner (ed.), *Dilemmas of Law in the Welfare State* (Berlin, 1986).

[50] See, e.g., Galanter, 'Legality and its Discontents: A Preliminary Assessment of Current Theories of Legalization and Delegalization' in E. Blankenburg, E. Klausa,

have generally been shaped by the perception of regulatory failures within the welfare state and a widespread recognition, over the last decade or so, of the need for fundamental restructuring of state programmes. Within the frame of this discussion, we can understand the contribution which Luhmann's theory of autopoiesis can make in terms of the interplay between normative closure and cognitive openness. Luhmann's theory suggests that only a limited scope exists for the combination of normative and cognitive expectations and that this provides an explanation of the problems facing regulatory law. Legal autopoiesis implies limits to the variability of legal functions. The autopoietic closure imposes restrictions on the political instrumentalization of law. For Luhmann, law's autonomy becomes threatened if the legal coding is in danger of being replaced by criteria of economic utility or political expediency.

This is an interesting and important debate from which there is much that can be learned. But in order to progress there is a need to root the insights derived from such debates in our own, somewhat peculiar, experience of public law. The legacy of our political and legal culture, as reflected through the dominance of the conservative normativist style of public law, has been the displacement of positive law as an active regulatory mechanism over great areas of operation of the political-administrative system. Law has performed a purely facilitative role in respect of many important spheres of the political-administrative system. It has functioned to establish flexible frameworks and left regulatory patterns to emerge through administrative and political networks, often mediated by the work of professional associations. As a result, we have failed to think juridically about many of the basic questions concerning the shaping, implementing, and reviewing of government programmes.

We have retained in consciousness a common law conception of law which is rooted at a low level of congruency formation, despite

and H. Rottleuthner (eds.), *Alternative Rechtsformen und Alternativen zum Recht* (Opladen, 1980); R. Stewart, 'The Discontents of Legalism: Interest Group Relations in Administrative Regulation' 1985 *Wisc. L. Rev.* 655; Teubner, 'Substantive and Reflexive Elements in Modern Law' (1983) 17 *Law & Soc. Rev.* 239; E. Blankenburg, 'The Poverty of Evolutionism: A Critique of Teubner's Case for "Reflexive Law"' (1984) 18 *Law & Soc. Rev.* 273; Teubner, 'Autopoiesis in Law and Society: A Rejoinder to Blankenburg' (1984) 18 *Law & Soc. Rev.* 291; Teubner, 'Juridification—Concepts, Aspects, Limits, Solutions' in id. (ed.), *Juridification of Social Spheres* (Berlin, 1987); H. Rottleuthner, 'The Limits of Law—The Myth of the Regulatory Crisis' (1989) 17 *Int. J. of Soc. of Law* 273.

the functional need for abstraction. We have clung on to the idea of a singular and universal concept of law, despite the pressures for differentiation. We could perhaps live with this concept of law in the nineteenth century when the functions of the state were relatively limited and legislation was primarily made for, and directed to, lawyers. With the emergence of the positive state, however, there has been an explosion of statute law-making and much of this legislation has come to be made for, and directed to, others; accountants, bankers, chemists, doctors, economists, farmers, engineers, grocers, and the like.[51] This change presented a major challenge, raising basic questions both about the style, intelligibility, and purpose of legislation and the manner in which disputes over the implementation of such legislation might be resolved. But because of conservative normativism and the conception of legality it embodied, we have been unable to develop an adequate juridical response and have come to rely on the conventional, the particular, and the mediative.

In recent years, however, we have been required to face this issue afresh. The pressures imposed by the increasing pace of social, economic, and technological change have become too great for our dominant political and legal culture to accommodate. The gathering dissolution in the authority of the culture informing the conservative normativist style presents a major challenge for legal thought. The recent governmental strategy of seeking to secure economy, efficiency, and effectiveness throughout the public sector provides a good illustration of the problem. The strategy has, for example, directly confronted our traditional government structures and has led to major changes in the organizational frameworks of government. It has placed major strains on conventional practices by requiring public objectives to be formally and precisely specified. And it has also led to the recognition of the need to institutionalize systematic mechanisms of review.

This strategy is an initiative of major significance. It has, however, been driven and fashioned almost entirely by a political–economic impetus and with virtually no legal or constitutional consciousness. A few illustrations seem in order. The executive agencies being carved from the body of central departments might result in the creation of more effective managerial units, but there is

---

[51] This point is made by J. D. B. Mitchell, 'Reflections on Law and Orders' 1958 *Juridical Review* 19 at p. 25.

little evidence that the impact on notions of ministerial responsibility and civil service anonymity, let alone broader concerns about public accountability, have been adequately addressed.[52] Even if we accept the view that the privatization of public utilities will produce more efficient and responsive services,[53] these privatization processes were fashioned without any regard to constitutional considerations,[54] and, contrary to initial claims, the regulatory structures which have emerged are of inordinate complexity.[55] The fundamental restructuring in the relationships between central and local government during the 1980s has been achieved only by severely straining—and in certain spheres destroying—the conventional networks; and only after a highly unsuccessful attempt to invoke law as a primary mechanism of control.[56]

Such examples could be multiplied. But the general point is that recent developments in government have once again placed the larger issues of public law on the political agenda. Indeed, since there can be no going back to the old arrangements, the challenge presented by these developments seems to be here to stay. Furthermore, the rapidly extending influence of European Community law on our programmes and structures of government serves to reinforce this challenge, particularly since the institutions and culture of this 'new legal order' are drawn from civilian systems which are founded on the distinction between public and private

[52] See, Prime Minister's Efficiency Unit, *Improving Management in Government: the Next Steps* (1988) (Ibbs Report); Eighth Report from the Treasury and Civil Service Committee, Session 1987–88, *Civil Service Management Reform: The Next Steps*, HC 494; *Civil Service Management Reform: The Next Steps. The Government Reply to the Eighth Report*, Cm. 524 (1988); R. Baldwin, 'The Next Steps: Ministerial Responsibility and Government by Agency' (1988) 51 *Mod. L. Rev.* 622; G. Drewry, 'Forward from FMI: "The Next Steps"' 1988 *Public Law* 505.

[53] Note, however, that research has failed to show that such a change in organizational form has resulted in enhanced organizational performance. See, A. Dunsire, K. Hartley, and D. Parker, 'Organisational Status and Performance: Summary of the Findings' (1991) 69 *Public Admin.* 21.

[54] In France, by contrast, the Conseil Constitutionel has held that the sale of state assets for less than their market value would be unconstitutional. See C. Graham and T. Prosser, *Privatizing Public Enterprises: Constitutions, the State and Regulation in Comparative Perspective* (Oxford, 1991), chap. 3.

[55] B. Sas, 'Regulation of the Privatised Electricity Supply Industry' (1990) 53 *M.L.R.* 485.

[56] M. Loughlin, 'Law, Ideologies, and the Political–Administrative System' (1989) 16 *J. of Law & Soc.* 21; 'Innovative Financing in Local Government: The Limits of Legal Instrumentalism' 1990 *Public Law* 372 (Pt. I); 1991 *Public Law* 568 (Pt. II).

262 Public Law in the Face of the Future

law. Finally, both these trends, in combination with a growing sense of politically expressed dissatisfaction with the existing arrangements of government, may cause us to reflect on the adequacy of existing constitutional structures.

The ordering of these issues—specific government initiatives, European developments, general constitutional concerns—is deliberate. From the functionalist perspective, attempts to discover a solution to the issues facing public law in fundamental constitutional reform or in the adoption of a Bill of Rights is altogether too facile. Reforms proposed at this level, which have been the subject of much pamphleteering recently,[57] throw up more heat than light. They leave too many issues of primary importance unresolved. We should think carefully about the question to which we think the introduction of a Charter of Rights provides an answer. Whatever it might be, it is not the question of public law.

In confronting these important issues concerning the relationship between government and law, the functional logic of modern law must be accepted. This means that any contribution which public law may provide to the development of effective and accountable structures of government should be based on a sociological orientation. Studies need to be rooted in a socially constructed field and, from that perspective, should investigate the interplay of cognitive and normative considerations. The normative structure of law should be recognized. But, unlike the normativist approach, the question of law's normative structure is itself an object of inquiry.

This last point can best be illustrated by reference to the analysis of some recent cases in the field of central–local government relations. Take, for example, *Bromley L.B.C.* v. *Greater London Council*, in which the House of Lords struck down the GLC's attempt to reduce public transport fares by 25 per cent.[58] Jowell and Lester have argued that Lord Diplock's speech in that case could have been rendered more rigorous if it had been framed in the

---

[57] See, e.g., R. Dworkin, *A Bill of Rights for Britain* (London, 1990); K. Ewing, *A Bill of Rights for Britain?* (London, Institute of Empolyment Rights, 1990); A. Lester et al., *A British Bill of Rights* (London, Institute of Public Policy Research, Consultation Paper No. 1, 1990); K. D. Ewing and C. A. Gearty, *Democracy or a Bill of Rights* (London, Society of Labour Lawyers, 1991); Institute for Public Policy Research, *The Constitution of the United Kingdom* (London, 1991); F. Vibert (ed.), *Britain's Constitutional Future* (London, Institute of Economic Affairs, 1991) Liberty, *A People's Charter: Liberty's Bill of Rights* (London, 1991).

[58] [1983] 1 AC 768.

language of proportionality.[59] From a functionalist perspective, however, this analysis does not take us much further. It does not help us to resolve the crucial question of what should be the appropriate standard of review.[60] And it certainly does not assist in addressing the fact that Lord Diplock's approach contained an entirely inadequate attempt at cost–benefit analysis, was based on a misunderstanding of the way in which the government grant system worked, and created a great deal of havoc in the local government system.[61] A second illustration can be found in *Nottinghamshire C.C. v. Secretary of State for the Environment*, a case in which the House of Lords rejected a challenge to the way in which the Secretary of State had constructed the expenditure targets of certain local authorities.[62] One commentator has suggested that the case shows the Law Lords 'displaying a fine understanding of the legislative, political and constitutional contexts in which judicial review operates'.[63] From a functionalist perspective, which is not itself easy to explain since it is not impossible even to understand the nature of the local authorities' grievances from the judgments in this case, I would suggest that the case actually shows the House of Lords displaying complete bewilderment with the material with which it was presented and simply signalling that local authorities should not expect the courts to resolve their legal grievances in matters of grant allocation.[64] Finally, we might note that in the decision of the House of Lords upon the issue of the legality of local authority involvement in the swaps market, the leading speech manifests a misunderstanding of the way in which the swaps market actually operates.[65]

---

[59] Jowell and Lester, 'Beyond *Wednesbury*' 1987 *Public Law* 368, pp. 381–2; 'Proportionality' in Jowell and Oliver (eds.), *New Directions in Judicial Review*, 51, 62.
[60] See P. P. Craig, *Administrative Law* (London, 2nd edn., 1989), 299–300.
[61] See M. Loughlin, *Local Government in the Modern State* (London, 1986), chap. 3.
[62] *Nottinghamshire CC v. Secretary of State for the Environment* (1986) 2 W.L.R. 1.
[63] S. Lee, 'Understanding Judicial Review as a Game of Chess' (1986) 102 *L.Q.R.* 493, 496.
[64] See Loughlin, 'Law, Ideologies, and the Political–Administrative System' (1989) 16 *J. of Law & Soc.* 21, 30–1.
[65] *Hazell v. Hammersmith L.B.C.* (1991) 2 W.L.R. 372. M. Loughlin, 'Innovative Financing in Local Government: The Limits of Legal Instrumentalism' 1991 *Public Law* 568 at 590–5.

These illustrations are provided not from some malevolent desire to highlight the shortcomings of the higher judiciary; nor for the purpose of providing a platform for a debate about political bias. The illustrations furnish specific examples of what I have in mind when referring to the limitations of a normativist analysis. Judicial decisions should not be viewed as communications within some hermetically sealed legal world in which the scholarly role is to seek to rationalize all judicial decisions and fit them into a coherent body of doctrine. These disputes arose in the political–administrative system and the decisions taken have significant impacts within that system. The illustrations thus may be taken as good examples of the difficulties which exist in conversing between systems. And in seeking to understand public law, it is suggested that this complex relationship between government and law should provide the focus of our inquiry. Since the examples all concern judicial decisions it should perhaps also be emphasized that, although undoubtedly of importance, the courts should be recognized as providing only one specific institutional focus for addressing questions of law.

It is through this type of analysis that we may begin to identify the distinctiveness of public law. Public law arises from the recognition that modern law has, in Dicey's expression, become 'officialized'.[66] Rather than attempt to adhere to a normativist conception of law and moralize about this development, public lawyers should be seeking to understand the impact which these developments have had on our conceptions of legality and, in particular, to grapple with the cognitive–normative dynamic as it is presented in public law. Public law should adopt as its principal focus the examination of the manner in which the normative structures of law can contribute to the tasks of guidance, control, and evaluation in government. While this exhorts lawyers to grapple with the material and interpretative frameworks of the political and social sciences, it also requires social scientists concerned with matters of government to pay close attention to the importance of normative structures in general and specifically to the issue of the internal complexity of law.

---

[66] Dicey, *Law of the Constitution* (London, 8th edn., 1915), p. xliv.

Bibliography

ACKERMAN, B., *Social Justice in the Liberal State* (New Haven, 1980).

ALLAN, T. R. S., 'Legislative Supremacy and the Rule of Law: Democracy and Constitutionalism' (1985) 44 *Camb. L.J.* 111.

—— 'Dicey and Dworkin: the Rule of Law as Integrity' (1988) 8 *O.J.L.S.* 266.

—— 'Pragmatism and Theory in Public Law' (1988) 104 *L.Q.R.* 422.

—— 'Constitutional Rights and Common Law' (1991) 11 *O.J.L.S.* 453.

ALLEN, C. K., *Law in the Making* (London, 1927).

—— *Bureaucracy Triumphant* (London, 1931).

—— *Democracy and the Individual* (London, 1943).

—— *Law and Orders* (London, 1945).

—— 'Administrative Jurisdiction' 1956 *Public Law* 13.

ANDERSON, P., *Arguments within English Marxism* (London, 1980).

ANSON, W. R., *The Law and Custom of the Constitution* (Oxford, 1886; 4th edn., 1909).

ARNOLD, M., *The Poems of Matthew Arnold* (London, 1905), vol. 2.

AUSTIN, J., *The Province of Jurisprudence Determined* (1832) (H. L. A. Hart (ed.), London, 1954).

BAGEHOT, W., *The English Constitution* (1867) (R. H. S. Crossman (ed.)) (London and Glasgow, 1963).

BALDWIN, R., 'The Next Steps: Ministerial Responsibility and Government by Agency' (1988) 51 *Mod. L. Rev.* 622.

BARKER, E., *Political Thought in England 1848–1914* (London, 1915).

BARKER, R., 'The Fabian State' in B. Pimlott (ed.), *Fabian Essays in Socialist Thought* (London, 1984).

BARNETT, A., *New Statesman & Society*, 2 Dec. 1988.

BARRY, B., 'Hayek on Liberty' in J. Gray and Z. Pelczynski (eds.), *Conceptions of Liberty in Political Philosophy* (London, 1984).

BELL, D., *The End of Ideology: On the Exhaustion of Political Ideas in the Fifties* (New York, 1961).

BENTHAM, J., *The Works of Jeremy Bentham* (J. Bowring (ed.), 1843), vol. III.

——*A Fragment on Government and An Introduction to the Principles of Morals and Legislation* (W. Harrison (ed.)) (Oxford, 1948).

BERKI, R. N., 'Oakeshott's concept of civil association: notes for a critical analysis' (1981) XXIX *Political Studies* 570.

BERLIN, I., *Four Essays on Liberty* (Oxford, 1969).

—— 'Does political theory still exist?' in P. Laslett and W. G. Runciman (eds.), *Philosophy, Politics and Society (Second Series)* (Oxford, 1962).

BERNSTEIN, R. J., *John Dewey* (New York, 1966).
—— *Praxis and Action* (Philadelphia, 1971).
—— *The Restructuring of Social and Political Theory* (Philadelphia, 1976).
—— 'One Step Forward, Two Steps Backward. Richard Rorty on Liberal Democracy and Philosophy' (1987) 15 *Political Theory* 538.
BEVAN, A., *In Place of Fear* (London, 1952).
BIRKS, P., *An Introduction to the Law of Restitution* (Oxford, 1985).
BLACKSTONE, W., *Commentaries on the Laws of England* (1765–9) (London, 15th edn., 1809), 4 vols.
BLANKENBURG, E., 'The Poverty of Evolutionism: A Critique of Teubner's Case for "Reflexive Law"' (1984) 18 *Law & Soc. Rev.* 273.
BLOM-COOPER, L., 'The new face of judicial review: administrative changes in Order 53' 1982 *Public Law* 250.
BOGDANOR, V., *The People and the Party System. The Referendum and Electoral Reform in British Politics* (Cambridge, 1981).
—— 'Constitutional Law and Politics' (1987) 7 *Oxford J. of Legal Studies* 454.
BOURGEOIS, L., *Solidarité* (1896: Paris, 7th edn., 1912).
BRADLEY, A. W., 'Applications for judicial review—the Scottish model' 1987 *Pub. Law* 313.
BRAZIER, R., *Constitutional Practice* (Oxford, 1988).
BRENNAN, G. and BUCHANAN, J. M., *The Reason of Rules. Constitutional Political Economy* (Cambridge, 1985).
BRETON, A., *The Economic Theory of Representative Government* (London, 1974).
BROWNE-WILKINSON, N., 'The Infiltration of a Bill of Rights' 1992 *Public Law* (forthcoming).
BUCHANAN, J. M., *The Limits of Liberty* (Chicago, 1975).
BURKE, E., *Reflections on the Revolution in France* in *Works* (Bohn edn., London, 1897).
BURROW, J. W., *Evolution and Society. A Study in Victorian Social Theory* (Cambridge, 1968).
CALABRESI, G., *A Common Law for the Age of Statutes* (Cambrige, Mass., 1982).
Campaign for a Scottish Assembly, *The Claim of Right for Scotland* (Edinburgh, 1987).
CAMPBELL, D., *WarPlan UK. The Truth about Civil Defence in Britain* (London, 1982).
CARR, C. T., *Delegated Legislation. Three Lectures* (Cambridge, 1921).
CHARLTON, D. G., *Positivist Thought in France during the Second Empire, 1852–70* (Oxford, 1959).
CLARKE, P. F., *Liberals and Social Democrats* (Cambridge, 1978).

COCKS, R. C. J., *Sir Henry Maine: A Study in Victorian Jurisprudence* (Cambridge, 1988).

COHEN, F., 'The Problems of a Functional Jurisprudence' (1937) 1 *M.L.R.* 5.

—— Foreword, 'The Holmes-Cohen Correspondence' (1948) IX *J. of the History of Ideas* 3.

COHEN, G. A., *Karl Marx's Theory of History: A Defence* (Oxford, 1978).

COLLINI, S., *Liberalism and Sociology. L. T. Hobhouse and Political Argument in England 1880–1914* (Cambridge, 1979).

—— 'Hobhouse, Bosanquet and the State: Philosophical Idealism and Political Argument in England 1880–1918' (1976) 72 *Past and Present* 87.

—— WINCH D., and BURROW, J., *That Noble Science of Politics. A Study in Nineteenth Century Intellectual History* (Cambridge, 1983).

COMTE, A., *Introduction to Positive Philosophy* (1830–42) (F. Ferre (ed.)) (Indianapolis, 1946).

CONNOLLY, W. E., *The Terms of Political Discourse* (Oxford, 2nd edn., 1983).

COTTERRELL, R., *The Politics of Jurisprudence* (London, 1989).

COVELL, C., *The Redefinition of Conservatism* (London, 1986).

CRAIG, P. P., *Administrative Law* (London, 2nd edn., 1989).

—— *Public Law and Democracy in the United Kingdom and the United States of America* (Oxford, 1990).

CRANSTON, M., 'Michael Oakeshott's Politics' (1967) 28 *Encounter* 82.

CRICK, B., 'The Sovereignty of Parliament and the Irish Question' in D. Rea (ed.), *Political Co-operation in Divided Societies* (London, 1983), 229.

CRIPPS, S., 'Can Socialism come by Constitutional Methods?' in C. Addison *et al.*, Problems of a Socialist Government (London, 1933).

CROSSMAN, R. H. S., *Diaries of a Cabinet Minister*, vol. 2 (London, 1976).

DAHRENDORF, R., 'Citizenship and the modern social conflict' in R. Holme and M. Elliott (eds.), *1688–1988. Time for a New Constitution* (London, 1988), chap. 7.

DAINTITH, T. C., 'Political Programmes and the Content of the Constitution' in W. Finnie, C. Himsworth, and N. Walker (eds.), *Edinburgh Essays in Public Law* (Edinburgh, 1991).

DANIELS, N. (ed.), *Reading Rawls. Critical Studies of A Theory of Justice* (Oxford, 1975).

DE SMITH, S. A., *The Lawyers and the Constitution* (Inaugural Lecture, London School of Economics, 10 May 1960).

—— *Constitutional and Adminstrative Law* (Harmondsworth, 1971; 6th edn., 1989 by R. Brazier).

DENNING, A., *Freedom Under Law* (London, 1949).

DEVLIN, P., 'The Common Law, Public Policy and the Executive' 1956 *Current Legal Problems* 1.

DEWEY, J., *The Ethics of Democracy* (1888), in *John Dewey. The Early Works, 1882–1898* (Boydston *et al.* (eds.)) (Carbondale, Ill., 1967).

—— *Democracy and Education* (New York, 1916).

—— *The Public and its Problems* (New York, 1927).

—— *The Quest for Certainty* (1929) (New York, 1960).

—— *Liberalism and Social Action* (New York, 1935).

—— 'The need for a recovery of philosophy' in R. J. Bernstein (ed.), *John Dewey: On Experience, Nature and Freedom* (New York, 1960).

—— 'The Logic of Judgments of Practise' (1915) 12 *J. of Philosophy* 505.

—— 'Logical Method and Law' (1924) 10 *Cornell L.Q.* 17.

DICEY, A. V., *Introduction to the Study of the Law of the Constitution* (London, 1885; 8th edn., 1915; 10th edn., 1959 with intro. by E. C. S. Wade).

—— *Lectures on the Relation between Law and Public Opinion in England during the Nineteenth Century* (London, 1905).

—— 'The development of administrative law in England' 31 *L.Q.R.* 148.

DOWNS, A., *An Economic Theory of Democracy* (New York, 1957).

DREWRY, G., 'Forward from FMI: "The Next Steps"' 1988 *Public Law* 505.

DUGUIT, L., *Law in the Modern State* (F. and H. J. Laski (trans.)) (London, 1921).

—— 'Law and the State' (1917) 31 *Harvard Law Rev.* 1.

DUNSIRE, A., HARTLEY, K., and PARKER, D., 'Organisational Status and Performance: Summary of the Findings' (1991) 69 *Public Admin.* 21.

DURKHEIM, E., *The Division of Labour in Society* (G. Simpson (trans.)) (1893: New York, 1964).

—— *Professional Ethics and Civic Morals* (C. Brookfield (trans.)) (London, 1957).

DUXBURY, N., *Patterns of American Jurisprudence* (forthcoming).

—— 'Deconstruction, History and the Uses of Legal Theory' (1990) 41 *N. Ireland L.Q.* 167.

—— Review of M. van der Kerchove and F. Ost, *Le système juridique entre ordre et désordre* (1990) 53 *M.L.R.* 836.

DWORKIN, R., *Taking Rights Seriously* (Camb. Mass., 1977).

—— *A Matter of Principle* (Cambridge, Mass., and London, 1985).

—— *Law's Empire* (London, 1986).

—— *A Bill of Rights for Britain* (London, 1990).

ECCLESHALL, R., 'English Conservatism as Ideology' (1977) XXV *Political Studies* 62.

EMY, H. V., *Liberals, Radicals and Social Politics, 1892–1914* (Cambridge, 1973).

EVANS-PRITCHARD, E. E., *The Sociology of Comte* (Manchester, 1970).

EWING, K., *A Bill of Rights for Britain?* (London, Institute of Employment Rights 1990).

EWING, K. D. and GEARTY, C. A., *Democracy or a Bill of Rights* (London, Society of Labour Lawyers, 1991).

FEBBRAJO, A. and TEUBNER, G. (eds.), *State, Law, Economy as Autopoietic Systems: Regulation and Autonomy in a New Perspective* (Milan, forthcoming).

FENNELL, P., 'Roberts v. Hopwood: the Rule against Socialism' (1986) 13 *J. of Law & Society* 401.

FIGGIS, J. N., *Churches in the Modern State* (London, 1913).

FINE, B., *Democracy and the Rule of Law: Liberal Ideals and Marxist Critiques* (London, 1984).

FINER, S. E., 'The Individual Responsibility of Ministers' (1956) 34 *Public Admin.* 377.

FIRTH, R. (ed.), *Man and Culture: An Evaluation of the Work of Malinowski* (London, 1957).

FISCH, M. H., 'Justice Holmes, the Prediction Theory of Law, and Pragmatism' (1942) 39 *J. of Philosophy* 85.

FORBES, D., 'Scientific Whiggism: Adam Smith and John Millar' (1953–4) 7 *Camb. J.* 643.

—— 'Sceptical whiggism, commerce and liberty' in A. S. Skinner and T. Wilson (eds.), *Essays on Adam Smith* (Oxford, 1976).

FORSYTH, C. F., 'Beyond *O'Reilly* v. *Mackman*: the foundations and nature of procedural exclusivity' (1985) 44 *Camb. L.J.* 415.

—— 'The provenance and protection of legitimate expectations', (1988) 47 *Camb. L.J.* 238.

FRANCO, P., *The Political Philosophy of Michael Oakeshott* (New Haven, 1990).

FRANK, J., *Law and the Modern Mind* (New York, 1930).

FREEDEN, M., *The New Liberalism: An Ideology of Social Reform* (Oxford, 1978).

—— 'Biological and evolutionary roots of the New Liberalism in England' 1976 *Political Theory* 487.

FREEMAN, A. D., 'Truth and Mystification in Legal Scholarship' (1981) 90 *Yale L.J.* 1229.

FRIED, C., 'The Artificial Reason of the Law or: What Lawyers Know' (1981) 60 *Texas L. Rev.* 35.

FRIENDLY, H., 'The Gap in Law-Making—Judges Who Can't and Legislators Who Won't' (1963) 63 *Column. L. Rev.* 787.

FULLER, L. L., *The Morality of Law* (New Haven, 2nd edn., 1969).

—— 'Positivism and Fidelity to Law—A Reply to Professor Hart' (1958) 71 *Harv. L. Rev.* 630.

GADAMER, H-G., *Truth and Method* (New York, 1975).

—— *Reason in the Age of Science* (Cambridge, Mass., 1981).

GALANTER, M., 'Legality and its Discontents: A Preliminary Assessment of Current Theories of Legalization and Delegalization' in E. Blankenburg, E. Klausa, and H. Rottleuthner (eds.), *Alternative Rechtsformen und Alternativen zum Recht* (Opladen, 1980).

—— 'Law Abounding: Legalisation Around the North Atlantic' (1992) 55 *M.L.R.* 1.

GALLIE, W. B., 'Essentially Contested Concepts', vol. 56 *Proceedings of the Aristotelian Society* 167 (1955–6).

GELLNER, E., *Words and Things. A Critical Account of Linguistic Philosophy and A Study in Ideology* (London, 1959).

—— 'The Re-Enchantment Industry, or the Californian Way of Subjectivity' 5 *Philosophy of the Social Sciences* 173 (1975).

GILMORE, G., *The Ages of American Law* (New Haven, 1977).

GILMOUR, I., *Inside Right: A Study of Conservatism* (London, 1977).

GINSBERG, M., *Essays in Sociology and Social Philosophy* (Harmondsworth, 1968).

GLASS, R. and GRIFFITH, J. A. G., 'The context of administrative procedures' in *Report of the Committee on Administrative Tribunals and Enquiries*. Minutes of Evidence (HMSO, 1956).

GLASSER, C., 'Radicals and Refugees: The Foundation of The Modern Law Review and English Legal Scholarship' (1987) 50 *M.L.R.* 688.

GRAHAM, C. and PROSSER, T., *Privatizing Public Enterprises: Constitutions, the State and Regulation in Comparative Perspective* (Oxford, 1991).

GRAY, J., *Hayek on Liberty* (London, 1986).

GRAY, J. C., *The Nature and Sources of the Law* (New York, 1909).

GREEN, T.H., 'Liberal legislation and freedom of contract' (1880) in *Works*, vol. 3, p. 365.

—— *Lectures on the Principles of Political Obligation* (London, 1907).

GREENGARTEN, I. M., *Thomas Hill Green and the Development of Liberal-Democratic Thought* (Toronto, 1981).

GREENLEAF, W. H., *The British Political Tradition. Vol. II. The Ideological Heritage* (London, 1983); *Vol. III, Pt. II. A Much Governed Nation* (London, 1987).

GRIFFITH, J. A. G., *Central Departments and Local Authorities* (London, 1966).

—— *Parliamentary Scrutiny of Government Bills* (London, 1974).

—— *The Politics of the Judiciary* (London: 4th edn., 1991).

—— 'Administrative discretion and the courts—the better part of valour?' (1955) 18 *M.L.R.* 159.

—— Note [1963] *Public Law* 401–2.

—— 'Judges in Politics: England' (1968) 3 *Govt. & Oppos.* 485.

—— 'Whose Bill of Rights?' *New Statesman* 14 Nov. 1975.

—— 'Standing Committees in the House of Commons' in S. A. Walkland and M. Ryle (eds.), *The Commons in the Seventies* (London, 1977), Chap. 5.

—— 'The Political Constitution' (1979) 42 *M.L.R.* 1.

—— 'Administrative Law and the Judges' D. N. Pritt Memorial Lecture (London, 1978).

——'*Justice and Administrative Law Revisited*' in J. A. G. Griffith (ed.), *From Policy to Administration. Essays in Honour of William A. Robson* (London, 1976).

—— 'Constitutional and Administrative Law' in P. Archer and A. Martin (eds.), *More Law Reform Now* (Chichester, 1983).

—— 'Judicial Decision-Making in Public Law' 1985 *Pub. Law* 564.

—— (ed.), *From Policy to Administration: Essays in Honour of William A. Robson* (London, 1976).

GUTMANN, A., 'Communitarian Critics of Liberalism' 1985 *Philosophy and Public Affairs* 308.

H.M. Government, *Civil Service Management Reform: The Next Steps. The Government Reply to the Eighth Report*, Cm. 524 (1988).

HAAKONSSEN, K., *The Science of a Legislator: The Natural Jurisprudence of David Hume and Adam Smith* (Cambridge, 1981).

—— 'John Millar and the Science of a Legislator' (1985) 30(NS) *Juridical Review* 41.

HABERMAS, J., *Legitimation Crisis* (Boston, 1975).

HAILSHAM, *The Dilemma of Democracy* (London, 1977).

—— 'Elective dictatorship' (The Richard Dimbleby Lecture, 1976), *The Listener* 21 Oct. 1976, p. 496.

HALEVY, E., *A History of the English People in the Nineteenth Century* (London, 1961).

HALLAM, H., *Middle Ages* (London, 12th edn., 1818), vol. 2.

HAMSON, C. J., *Executive Discretion and Judicial Control* (London, 1954).

HARDEN, I. and LEWIS, N., *The Noble Lie. The British Constitution and the Rule of Law* (London, 1986).

HARLOW, C. R. and RAWLINGS, R. W., *Law and Administration* (London, 1984).

HART, H. and SACKS, A., *The Legal Process: Basic Problems in the Making and Application of Law* (Mimeo: Cambridge, Mass., 1958).

HART, H. L. A., *The Concept of Law* (Oxford, 1961).

—— 'Definition and Theory in Jurisprudence' (1954) 70 *L.Q.R.* 37.

—— 'Positivism and the Separation of Law and Morals' (1958) 71 *Harv. L. Rev.* 593.

HAWTHORN, G., *Enlightenment and Despair. A History of Social Theory* (Cambridge 2nd edn., 1987).

272 Bibliography

HAYEK, F. A., *The Road to Serfdom* (London, 1944).
—— *The Sensory Order: An Inquiry into the Foundations of Theoretical Psychology* (London, 1952).
—— *The Counter-Revolution of Science* (Glencoe, Ill., 1952).
—— *The Political Ideal of the Rule of Law* (Cairo, 1955).
—— *The Constitution of Liberty* (Chicago, 1960).
—— *Studies in Philosophy, Politics and Economics* (London, 1967).
—— *Law, Legislation and Liberty. Vol. 1 Rules and Order* (London, 1973); *Vol. 2 The Mirage of Social Justice* (London, 1976); *Vol. 3 The Political Order of a Free People* (London, 1979).
—— *Knowledge, Evolution and Society* (London, 1984).
HAYWARD, J. E. S., 'Solidarity: the social history of an idea in nineteenth-century France' (1959) 4 *International Review of Social History* 261.
—— 'The official social philosophy of the French Third Republic: Léon Bourgeois and Solidarism' (1961) 6 *International Review of Social History* 19.
HENNESSY, P., *Whitehall* (London, 1989).
HETHERINGTON, H. J. W., *Life and Letters of Sir Henry Jones* (London, 1924).
HEUSTON, R. F. V., *Essays in Constitutional Law* (London, 1964).
HEWART, G., *The New Despotism* (London, 1929).
HICKS, J. R., 'The Hayek Story' in *Critical Essays in Monetary Theory* (Oxford, 1967).
HIRSCH, F., *The Social Limits to Growth* (London, 1976).
HIRSCHMANN, A. O., *The Passions and the Interests. Political Arguments for Capitalism before its Triumph* (Princeton, 1977).
HOBBES, T., *Leviathan* (1651) (C. B. Macpherson (ed.)) (Harmondsworth, 1968).
HOBHOUSE, L. T., *The Theory of Knowledge* (London, 1896).
—— *Liberalism* (London, 1911).
—— *Social Evolution and Political Theory* (New York, 1911).
—— *Development and Purpose: An Essay towards a Philosophy of Evolution* (London, 1913).
—— *The Metaphysical Theory of the State* (London, 1918).
HOBSON, J. A. and GINSBERG, M., *L. T. Hobhouse: His Life and Work* (London, 1931).
HOFSTADER, R., *Social Darwinism in American Thought 1860–1915* (Boston, rev. edn., 1955).
HOGG, Q., *New Charter* (London, 1969).
HOLDSWORTH, W. S., *History of English Law* (A. C. Goodhart and H. S. Hanbury (eds.)) (London, 1956), vol. 5.
—— 'The conventions of the eighteenth century constitution' (1932) 17 *Iowa Law Review* 161.

HOLMES, O. W., *The Common Law* (Boston, 1881).
—— *Justice Oliver Wendell Holmes, Vol. 1. The Shaping Years* (Cambridge, Mass., 1957).
—— *Holmes–Laski Letters: the correspondence of Mr. Justice Holmes and Harold J. Laski, 1916–1935* (M. De W. Howe edn.) (London, 1953).
HORWITZ, M.J., 'The Rule of Law: An Unqualified Human Good?' (1977) 86 *Yale L.J.* 561.
HULL, N. E. H., 'Some Realism about the Llewellyn–Pound Exchange over Realism: The Newly Uncovered Private Correspondence, 1927–1931' 1987 *Wisconsin L. Rev.* 921.
—— 'Reconstructing the Origins of Realistic Jurisprudence: A Prequel to the Llewellyn–Pound Exchange over Legal Realism' 1989 *Duke L.J.* 1302.
HUNTINGTON, S. P., 'Conservatism as an Ideology' (1957) 51 *American Political Science Review* 454.
HUTCHINSON, A., *Dwelling on the Threshold. Critical Essays in Modern Legal Thought* (Toronto, 1988).
IGNATIEFF, M., 'John Millar and Individualism' in I. Hont and M. Ignatieff (eds.), *Wealth and Virtue: The Shaping of Political Economy in the Scottish Englightenment* (Cambridge, 1983).
INGLIS, F., *Radical Earnestness: English Social Theory 1880–1980* (Oxford, 1982).
Institute for Public Policy Research, *The Constitution of the United Kingdom* (London, 1991).
JACKSON, R. M., *The Machinery of Justice in England* (Cambridge, 7th edn., 1977).
JAMES, W., *The Principles of Psychology* (New York, 1890).
—— *Pragmatism* (London, 1907).
—— *The Will to Believe. The Works of William James* (F. H. Burkhardt, *et al.* (eds.)) (Cambridge, Mass., 1979).
JENNINGS, W. I., *The Law and the Constitution* (London, 1933).
—— 'The Report on Ministers' Powers' (1932) 10 *Public Admin.* 333.
—— 'In praise of Dicey 1885–1935' (1935) 13 *Public Admin.* 123.
—— 'The courts and administrative law—the experience of English housing legislation' (1936) 49 *Harv. L. Rev.* 426.
JOHNSON, N., *In Search of the Constitution* (London, 1977).
—— 'Constitutional Reform: Some Dilemmas for a Conservative Philosophy' in Z. Layton-Henry (ed.), *Conservative Party Politics* (London, 1980).
JONES, H., *The Principles of Citizenship* (London, 1919).
JOSEPH, K., *Freedom Under Law* (London, 1975).
JOWELL, J., 'The Rule of Law Today' in J. Jowell and D. Oliver (eds.).

JOWELL, J., 'Courts and Administration in Britain: Standards, Principles and Rights' (1988) *Israel L.R.* 409.

—— and LESTER, A., 'Beyond *Wednesbury*: substantive principles of administrative law' 1987 *Pub. Law* 368.

—— —— 'Proportionality: neither novel nor dangerous' in J. Jowell and D. Oliver (eds.), *New Directions in Judicial Review* (London, 1988).

—— and OLIVER, D. (eds.), *The Changing Constitution* (Oxford, 2nd edn., 1989).

KAMENKA, E., 'Demythologizing the law' *Times Lit. Suppt.* 1 May, 1981, p. 475.

KEETON, G. W., *The Passing of Parliament* (London, 1952).

KELMAN, M., 'Trashing' (1984) 36 *Stan. L. Rev.* 283.

KLOPPENBERG, J. T., *Uncertain Victory. Social Democracy and Progressivism in European and American Thought, 1870–1920* (Oxford, 1986).

KRISTOL, I., ' "When virtue loses all her loveliness"—some reflections on capitalism and "the free society" ' in D. Bell and I. Kristol (eds.), *Capitalism Today* (New York, 1970).

—— *Two Cheers for Capitalism* (New York, 1978).

KUHN, T. S., *The Structure of Scientific Revolutions* (Chicago, 2nd edn., 1970).

London School of Economics, *Calendar 1987–88* (London, 1987).

LANDAU, M., *Political Theory and Political Science. Studies in the Methodology of Political Inquiry* (New Jersey, 1972).

LASKI, H. J., *Studies in the Problem of Sovereignty* (London, 1917).

—— *Authority in the Modern State* (New Haven, Conn., 1919).

—— *The Foundations of Sovereignty and Other Essays* (London, 1921).

—— *A Grammar of Politics* (1925: London, 5th edn., 1967).

—— 'The Growth of Administrative Discretion' (1923) 1 *J. of Public Admin.* 92.

—— 'Judicial Review of Social Policy in England' (1926) 39 *Harv. L. Rev.* 839.

—— *Report of the Committee on Ministers' Powers* Cmd. 4060, Annex V. 'Note by Prof. Laski on the judicial interpretation of statutes'.

—— 'M. Duguit's Conception of the State' in A. L. Goodhart *et al.* (eds.), *Modern Theories of Law* (London, 1933).

LASLETT, P. (ed.), *Philosophy, Politics and Society* (Oxford, 1956).

—— and RUNCIMAN, W. G. (eds.), *Philosophy, Politics and Society (Third Series)* (Oxford, 1969).

—— RUNCIMAN, W. G., and SKINNER, Q. (eds.), *Philosophy, Politics and Society (Fourth Series)* (Oxford, 1972).

—— and FISHKIN, J. (eds.), *Philosophy, Politics and Society (Fifth Series)* (Oxford, 1979).

Bibliography 275

LEE, S., 'Understanding Judicial Review as a Game of Chess' (1986) 102 L.Q.R. 493.

LESTER, A., *Democracy and Individual Rights* (London, 1968).

—— 'The Constitution: Decline and Renewal' in J. Jowell and D. Oliver (eds.), *The Changing Constitution* (Oxford, 1985), chap. 12.

—— *et al.*, *A British Bill of Rights* (London, Institute of Public Policy Research, Consultation Paper No. 1, 1990).

LEWIS, J. U., 'Sir Edward Coke (1552–1633): His Theory of "Artificial Reason" as a Context for Modern Basic Legal Theory' (1968) 84 L.Q.R. 330.

Liberty, *A People's Charter: Liberty's Bill of Rights* (London, 1991).

LIEBERMAN, D., *The Province of Legislation Determined* (Cambridge, 1989).

LLEWELLYN, K. N., 'Some Realism about Realism—Responding to Dean Pound' (1931) 44 *Harv. L. Rev.* 1222.

LOCKE, J., *Two Treatises of Government* (1690) (P. Laslett edn., Cambridge, 1960).

LOUGHLIN, M., *Local Government in the Modern State* (London, 1986).

—— 'Law, Ideologies and the Political-Administrative System' (1989) 16 *J. of Law & Soc.* 21.

—— 'Innovative Financing in Local Government: The Limits of Legal Instrumentalism' 1990 *Public Law* 372 (Pt. I); 1991 *Public Law* 568 (Pt. II).

LUHMANN, N., *The Differentiation of Society* (New York, 1982).

—— *A Sociological Theory of Law* (London, 1985).

—— 'The Third Question: The Creative Use of Paradoxes in Law and Legal History' (1988) 15 *J. of Law & Soc.* 153.

LUKES, S., *Essays in Social Theory* (London, 1977).

MACAULAY, *The Works of Lord Macaulay* (London, 1866), vol. VI.

McAUSLAN, P., *The Ideologies of Planning Law* (Oxford, 1980).

—— 'The Plan, the Planners and the Lawyers' 1971 *Public Law* 247.

—— 'Administrative law, collective consumption and judicial policy' (1983) 46 *M.L.R.* 1.

—— 'Dicey and his influence on public law' 1985 *Public Law* 721.

—— 'Public Law and Public Choice' (1988) 51 *M.L.R.* 681.

—— and McELDOWNEY, J. F. (eds.), *Law, Legitimacy and the Constitution* (London, 1985).

—— —— 'Legitimacy and the Constitution: the dissonance between theory and practice' in McAuslan and McEldowney (eds.), *Law, Legitimacy and the Constitution* (London, 1985).

McBRIAR, A. M., *Fabian Socialism and English Politics 1884–1918* (Cambridge, 1966).

McCARTHY, T., 'Complexity and Democracy, or The Seducements of Systems Theory' (1985) 35 *New German Critique* 27.

MacINTYRE, A., *After Virtue. A Study In Moral Theory* (London, 2nd edn., 1985).

—— *Whose Justice? Which Rationality?* (London, 1988).

—— 'The indispensability of political theory' in D. Miller and L. Siedentop (eds.), *The Nature of Political Theory* (Oxford, 1983).

MACKENZIE, W. J. M., 'Political Theory and Political Education' (1955–6) 9 *Universities Quarterly* 351.

MAGID, H., *English Political Pluralism: the Problems of Freedom and Organisation* (New York, 1941).

MAINE, H. S., *Ancient Law* (London, 1861).

—— *Popular Government* (London, 1885).

MAITLAND, F. W., *The Constitutional History of England* (Cambridge, 1908).

—— Introduction to O. von Gierke, *Political Theories of the Middle Ages* (Cambridge, 1900).

—— 'The Body Politic' in H. A. L. Fisher (ed.), *The Collected Papers of Frederic William Maitland* (Cambridge, 1911), vol. III.

MARQUAND, D., *The Unprincipled Society. New Demands and Old Politics* (London, 1988).

MARRIOTT, J., *The Mechanism of the Modern State* (Oxford, 1927).

—— *English Political Institutions* (Oxford, 4th edn., 1948).

MARSHALL, G., *Constitutional Conventions. The Rules and Forms of Political Accountability* (Oxford, 1984).

MARTIN, K., *Harold Laski* (London, 1953).

MARTINEAU, H., *The Positive Philosophy of A. Comte* (London, 1853).

MEEK, R. L., *Social Science and the Ignoble Savage* (Cambridge, 1976).

MERRETT, A., 'The Nature and Function of Law: A Criticism of E. P. Thompson's *Whigs and Hunters*' (1980) 7 *Brit. J. of Law & Soc.* 195.

MILIBAND, R., *Parliamentary Socialism* (London, 1961).

—— *The State in Capitalist Society* (London, 1969).

—— *Marxism and Politics* (Oxford, 1978).

—— *Capitalist Democracy in Britain* (Oxford, 1982).

MILL, J. S., *On Liberty* (1859) (G. Himmelfarb (ed.), Harmondsworth, 1974).

—— *Auguste Comte and Positivism* (1865: Ann Arbor, Mich., 1961).

—— 'Chapters on Socialism' (1879) 25 *Fortnightly Review* 226.

MILLAR, J., *An Historical View of the English Government*, (1787: Glasgow, 1803), 4 vols.

MILLER, D. and SIEDENTOP, L. (eds.), *The Nature of Political Theory* (Oxford, 1983).

MINOGUE, K., 'What is Wrong with Rights' in C. Harlow (ed.), *Public Law and Politics* (London, 1986), chap. 11.

MITCHELL, J. D. B., *Constitutional Law* (Edinburgh, 2nd edn., 1968).

—— 'Reflections on Law and Orders' 1958 *Juridical Review* 19.

—— 'The Flexible Constitution' 1960 *Public Law* 332.

—— 'The Ombudsman Fallacy' 1962 *Public Law* 24.

—— 'The causes and effects of the absence of a system of public law in the United Kingdom' 1965 *Public Law* 95.

—— 'The irrelevance of the Ombudsman proposals' in D. C. Rowat (ed.), *The Ombudsman* (London, 1965).

—— 'The state of public law in the United Kingdom' [1966] 15 *I.C.L.Q.* 133.

—— 'A Paper Mouse' 1966 *SLT(News)* 65.

—— 'The constitutional implications of judicial control of the administration in the United Kingdom' 1967 *Camb. L.J.* 46.

—— 'Why European Institutions?' in L. J. Brinkhorst and J. D. B. Mitchell, *European Law and Institutions* (Edinburgh, 1969) .

—— 'Government and Public Law in Scotland' in J. A. Andrews, *Welsh Studies in Public Law* (Cardiff, 1970).

—— 'The sovereignty of parliament and community law: the stumbling block that isn't there' 1979 *Int. Affairs* 33.

—— 'What happened to the constitution on 1st January 1973?' 1980 *Cambrian Law Rev.* 69.

—— 'Administrative Law and Policy Effectiveness' in J. A. G. Griffith (ed.), *From Policy to Administration. Essays in Honour of William A. Robson* (London, 1976).

—— 'A Testimony' (1969) in Bates *et al.* (eds.), *In Memoriam JDB Mitchell* (1983).

—— KUIPERS, S. A., and GALL, B., 'Constitutional Aspects of the Treaty and Legislation Relating to British Membership' (1972) 9 *Common Market Law Review* 134.

MUIRHEAD, J. H. and HETHERINGTON, H. J. W., *Social Purpose: A Contribution to a Philosophy of Civic Society* (London, 1922).

NAIRN, T., *The Break-Up of Britain: Crisis and Neo-Nationalism* (London, 2nd edn., 1981).

—— *The Enchanted Glass. Britain and its Monarchy* (London, 1988).

NICHOLLS, D., *The Pluralist State* (London, 1975).

NISKANEN, W. A., *Bureaucracy and Representative Government* (Aldine–Atherton, 1971).

—— *Bureaucracy: Servant or Master?* (London, 1973).

NOZICK, R., *Anarchy, State and Utopia* (Oxford, 1974).

OAKESHOTT, M., *Experience and its Modes* (Cambridge, 1933).

—— *Rationalism in Politics* (London, 1962).

OAKESHOTT, M., *On History* (Oxford, 1983) .

—— *On Human Conduct* (Oxford, 1975) .

—— 'The Authority of the State' (1929–30) XIX *The Modern Churchman* 313.

—— 'Introduction' in T. Hobbes, *Leviathan* (Oxford, 1946).

—— 'Scientific Politics' (1947–8) 1 *The Cambridge Journal* 347.

—— 'The Masses in Representative Democracy' in A. Hunold (ed.), *Freedom and Serfdom: An Anthology of Western Thought* (Dordrecht, 1961).

—— 'The Vocabulary of a Modern European State' (1975) XXIII *Political Studies* 319.

OFFE, C., *Contradictions of the Welfare State* (J. Keane (ed.) London, 1984).

OGUS, A. I., 'Law and Spontaneous Order: Hayek's Contribution to Legal Theory' (1989) 16 *J. of Law & Society* 393.

PAREKH, B., 'The Political Philosophy of Michael Oakeshott' (1979) 9 *Br. J. of Pol. Sc.* 481.

PAUL, J. (ed.), *Reading Nozick* (Oxford, 1982).

PIORE, M. J. and SABEL, C. F., *The Second Industrial Divide: Possibilities for Prosperity* (New York, 1984).

POCOCK, J. G. A., *The Ancient Constitution and the Feudal Law* (Cambridge, rev. edn., 1987).

—— 'Burke and the Ancient Constitution—A Problem in the History of Ideas' (1960) 3 *Historical Journal* 125.

POSNER, R., *Economic Analysis of Law* (Boston, 2nd edn., 1977).

POUND, R., 'Liberty of Contract' (1908–9) 18 *Yale L.J.* 454.

—— 'Law in Books and Law in Action' (1910) 44 *American Law Rev.* 12.

—— 'The Scope and Purpose of Sociological Jurisprudence' (1911) 24 *Harv. L. Rev.* 591; (1911) 25 *Harv. L. Rev.* 140; (1912) 25 *Harv. L. Rev.* 489.

—— 'The Call for a Realist Jurisprudence' (1931) 44 *Harv. L. Rev.* 697.

—— 'A Survey of Social Interests' 57 *Harv. L. Rev.* 1 (1943).

PRIEST, G. L., 'The common law process and the selection of efficient rules' (1977) 6 *J. of Legal Studies* 65.

Prime Minister's Efficiency Unit, *Improving Management in Government: the Next Steps* (London, 1988) (Ibbs Report).

PURCELL, E. A., *The Crisis of Democratic Theory* (Lexington, Kentucky, 1973).

RAWLS, J., *A Theory of Justice* (Oxford, 1972).

—— 'Justice as Fairness: Political not Metaphysical' (1985) 14 *Philosophy and Public Affairs* 223.

—— 'The Idea of an Overlapping Consensus' (1987) 7 *Oxford J. of Legal Studies* 1.

REDLICH, J. and HIRST, F., *A History of Local Government in England* (London, 1958).

Report of the Committee on Ministers' Powers Cmd. 4060 (1932) (Donoughmore Report).

Report of the Committee on Tribunals and Enquiries. (1957) (Franks Report).

Report of the Royal Commission on Legal Services (1980) Cmnd. 7448.

Report to the Scottish People by the Scottish Constitutional Convention, *Towards Scotland's Parliament* (Edinburgh, 1990).

RICHTER, M., *The Politics of Conscience: T. H. Green and His Age* (London, 1964).

RISK, R. C. B., 'John Willis—A Tribute' (1985) 9 *Dalhousie L.J.* 521.

ROBSON, W. A., *Justice and Administrative Law* (London, 1928); (2nd edn., 1947); (3rd edn., 1951).

—— *Public Administration Today* (London, 1948).

—— 'The Report of the Committee on Ministers' Powers' (1932) 3 *Political Quarterly* 346.

—— 'Administrative Law in England 1919–1948' in G. Campion (ed.), *British Government Since 1918* (London, 1950).

—— 'Administrative Justice and Injustice: A Commentary on the Franks Report' 1958 *Public Law* 12.

—— 'Administrative Law' in M. Ginsberg (ed.), *Law and Opinion in England in the Twentieth Century* (London, 1959).

—— '*Justice and Administrative Law* reconsidered' (1979) 32 *Current Legal Problems* 107.

ROGERS, J. A., 'Darwinism and Social Darwinism' (1972) 32 *J. of the History of Ideas* 267.

RORTY, R., *Philosophy and the Mirror of Nature* (Oxford, 1980).

—— *Consequences of Pragmatism* (Minneapolis, 1982).

—— 'Postmodernist Bourgeois Liberalism' (1983) 80 *J. of Philosophy* 383.

—— 'Thugs and Theorists. A Reply to Bernstein' (1987) 15 *Political Theory* 564.

—— 'The Priority of Democracy to Philosophy' in A. Malachowski (ed.), *Reading Rorty* (Oxford, 1990).

ROTTLEUTHNER, H., 'The Limits of Law—The Myth of the Regulatory Crisis' (1989) 17 *Int. J. of Soc. of Law* 273.

ROWLAND, B. M., 'Beyond Hayek's Pessimism: Reason, Tradition and Bounded Constructivist Rationalism' (1988) 18 *Brit. J. of Pol. Sc.* 221.

RUMBLE JR., W. E., *American Legal Realism: Skepticism, Reform and the Judicial Process* (Ithaca, 1968).

SAMUEL, H., *Liberalism: an Attempt to State the Principles and Proposals of Contemporary Liberalism in England* (London, 1902).

—— *Memoirs* (London, 1945).

SANDEL, M., *Liberalism and the Limits of Justice* (Cambridge, 1982).

—— 'The procedural republic and the unencumbered self' (1984) 12 *Political Theory* 81.

SAS, B., 'Regulation of the Privatised Electricity Supply Industry' (1990) 53 *M.L.R.* 485.

SCARMAN, L., *English Law—The New Dimension* (London, 1975).

SCHMITTHOFF, C., 'The Growing Ambit of the Common Law' (1951) 29 *Can. Bar Rev.* 469.

SCHON, D., *Beyond the Stable State* (New York, 1971).

SEELEY, J. R., *Introduction to Political Science* (London, 1896).

SHARLIN, H. I., 'Spencer, Scientism and American Constitutional Law' (1976) 33 *Annals of Science* 457.

SHKLAR, J. N., 'Purposes and procedures' *Times Literary Supplement*, 12 Sept. 1975, p. 1018.

—— 'Political Theory and the Rule of Law' in A. C. Hutchinson and P. Monahan (eds.), *The Rule of Law. Ideal or Ideology?* (Toronto, 1987).

SIMMONDS, N., 'Imperial visions and mundane practices' 1987 *Camb. L.J.* 465.

SKIDELSKY, R., *Politicians and the Slump: the Labour Government of 1929–31* (London, 1967).

—— *John Maynard Keynes* (London, 1983).

SKINNER, Q., ' "Social meaning" and the explanation of social action' in P. Gardiner (ed.), *The Philosophy of History* (Oxford, 1974).

SMITH, A., *An Inquiry into the Nature and Causes of the Wealth of Nations* (W. B. Todd (ed.) (Oxford, 1976).

—— *Theory of Moral Sentiments* (1759) (D. D. Raphael and A. L. Macfie (eds.), Oxford, 1976).

—— *Lectures on Jurisprudence* (R. L. Meek, D. D. Raphael and P. G. Stein (eds.)) (Oxford, 1978).

SPENCER, H., *The Proper Sphere of Government* (London, 1843).

—— *First Principles* (London, 1862).

—— *Social Statics: Or The Conditions Essential to Human Happiness Specified, and the First of Them Developed* (1851: Farnborough, Hants, 1970).

—— *Man Versus the State* (1884: Harmondsworth, 1969).

—— *Principles of Ethics* (London, 1892).

STEWART, R., 'The Discontents of Legalism: Interest Group Relations in Administrative Regulation' 1985 *Wisc. L. Rev.* 655.

STICK, J., 'Turning Rawls into Nozick and Back Again' (1987) 81 *Northwestern Univ. L. Rev.* 363.

SUGARMAN, D., 'Legal Theory, the Common Law Mind and the Making of the Textbook Tradition' in W. Twining (ed.), *Legal theory and Common Law* (Oxford, 1986), chap. 3.

SUMMERS, R. S., *Instrumentalism and American Legal Theory* (Ithaca, 1982).

SUNKIN, M., 'What is happening to applications for judicial review?' (1987) 50 *M.L.R.* 432.

SYPNOWITCH, C., *The Concept of Socialist Law* (Oxford, 1990).

TAWNEY, R. H., *The Acquisitive Society* (London, 1921).

TAYLOR, C., *Philosophical Papers Vol 2. Philosophy and the Human Sciences* (Cambridge, 1985).

TEUBNER, G., 'Substantive and Reflexive Elements in Modern Law' (1983) 17 *Law & Soc. Rev.* 239.

—— 'Autopoiesis in Law and Society: A Rejoinder to Blankenburg' (1984) 18 *Law & Soc Rev.* 291.

—— 'Juridification—Concepts, Aspects, Limits, Solutions' in G. Teubner (ed.), *Juridification of Social Spheres* (Berlin, 1987).

—— ' "And God Laughed . . ." Indeterminacy, Self-Reference and Paradox in Law' in C. Joerges and D. M. Trubek (eds.), *Critical Legal Thought: An American–German Debate* (Baden-Baden, 1989).

—— (ed.), *Dilemmas of Law in the Welfare State* (Berlin, 1986).

—— (ed.), *Autopoietic Law: A New Approach to Law and Society* (Berlin, 1988).

THOMPSON, E.P., *Whigs and Hunters* (Harmondsworth, 1975).

—— *Writing By Candlelight* (London, 1980).

Treasury & Civil Service Committee, Eighth Report, Session 1987–88, *Civil Service Management Reform: The Next Steps*, HC 494.

TULLOCK, G., *The Politics of Bureaucracy* (Washington, DC, 1965).

TURPIN, C., *British Government and the Constitution* (London, 1985).

TWINING, W., *Karl Llewellyn and the Realist Movement* (London, 1973).

ULAM, A., *Philosophical Foundations of English Socialism* (Cambridge, Mass., 1951).

VALERY, P., *History and Politics* (New York, 1962) .

VAN DER KERCHOVE, M. and OST, F., *Le système juridique entre ordre et désordre* (Paris, 1988).

VIBERT, F. (ed.), *Britain's Constitutional Future* (London, Institute of Economic Affairs, 1991) .

VILE, M. J. C., *Constitutionalism and the Separation of Powers* (Oxford, 1967).

VINCENT, A. and PLANT, R., *Philosophy, Politics and Citizenship. The Life and Thought of the British Idealists* (Oxford, 1984).

WADE, E. C. S. and PHILLIPS, G. G., *Constitutional and Administrative Law* (London, 1931: 10th edn., 1985 by A. W. Bradley).

WADE, H. W. R., *Administrative Law* (Oxford, 6th edn., 1988).

—— *Constitutional Fundamentals* (London, 1980).

WADE, H. W. R. 'The Concept of Legal Certainty. A Preliminary Sketch' (1940–1) 4 *M.L.R.* 183.
—— ' "Quasi-judicial" and its background' (1949) 10 Camb. L.J. 216.
—— 'The Twilight of Natural Justice' (1951) 67 *L.Q.R.* 103.
—— 'The basis of legal sovereignty' 1955 Camb. L.J. 172.
—— 'Law, Opinion and Administration' (1962) 78 *L.Q.R.* 188.
—— 'Unlawful administrative action—void or voidable' (1967) 83 *L.Q.R.* 499 (Pt. I); (1968) 84 *L.Q.R.* 95 (Pt. II).
—— 'Sovereignty and the European Communities' (1972) 88 *L.Q.R.* 1.
—— 'Procedure and prerogative in public law' (1985) 101 *L.Q.R.* 180.
—— 'What has happened to the Sovereignty of Parliament?' (1991) 107 *L.Q.R.* 1.
WALLAS, G., *Human Nature in Politics* (London, 1908).
—— *The Great Society: A Psychological Analysis* (London, 1914).
WALZER, M., *Spheres of Justice* (New York, 1983) .
WARDE, A., *Consensus and Beyond* (Manchester, 1981).
WEBB, B., *My Apprenticeship* (Harmondsworth, 1938), vol. 1.
—— *Our Partnership* (London, 1948).
WEBB, S., 'Modern Social Movements' in *The Cambridge Modern History of the World*, vol. XII (Cambridge, 1919).
—— 'Introduction' and 'The basis of socialism: historic' in B. Shaw *et al.* (eds.), *Fabian Essays in Socialism* (London, 2nd edn., 1920).
WEBB, S. and B., *A Constitution for the Socialist Commonwealth of Great Britain* (Cambridge, 1920).
WEBER, M., *Economy and Society* (G. Roth and C. Wittich (eds.)) (New York, 1968).
WEILER, P., 'The New Liberalism of L. T. Hobhouse' (1972–3) 16 *Victorian Studies* 143.
WELDON, T. D., *The Vocabulary of Politics* (Harmondsworth, 1953).
WELLS, H. G., *A Modern Utopia* (London, 1905).
WESTBROOK, R., *John Dewey and American Democracy* (Ithaca, NY, 1991).
WHITE, M. J., *The Origin of Dewey's Instrumentalism* (New York, 1943).
—— *Social Thought in America. The Revolt Against Formalism* (London, rev. edn., 1976).
WILLIAMS, D. G. T., 'Public local inquiries—formal administrative adjudication' (1980) 29 *Int. & Comp. L.Q.* 701.
—— 'The Donoughmore Report in Retrospect' (1982) 60 *Public Admin.* 273.
—— 'The Council on Tribunals: the first twenty five years' 1984 *Public Law* 79.
WILLIS, J., *The Parliamentary Powers of English Government Departments* (Cambridge, Mass., 1933).

—— 'Three approaches to administrative law: the judicial, the conceptual and the functional' (1935) 1 *Univ. of Toronto L.J.* 53.

WILTSHIRE, D., *The Social and Political Thought of Herbert Spencer* (Oxford, 1978).

WOOLF, H., 'Public law-private law: why the divide?' 1986 *Public Law* 220.

ZANDER, M., *A Bill of Rights?* (London, 3rd edn., 1985).

Index